BOOK DESIGN:
FROM THE PRINTING BASICS
TO THE MOST IMPRESSIVE DESIGNS

BOOK DESIGN

Edited by WANG SHAOQIANG

HOAKI

HOAKI

Hoaki Books, S.L.
C/ Ausiàs March, 128
08013 Barcelona, Spain
T. 0034 935 952 283
F. 0034 932 654 883
info@hoaki.com
www.hoaki.com

hoaki_books

Book Design:
From the Printing Basics to the Most Impressive Designs

ISBN: 978-84-17656-30-0

Sponsored by Design 360° — Concept & Design Magazine
Edited, produced, book design, concepts & art direction by
Sandu Publishing Co., Ltd.
info@sandupublishing.com
Chief Editor: Wang Shaoqiang
Contributing Author: Chen Meihuan
Executive Editors: Jessie Tan, Liz Yao
Copy Editor: Palmiche Press
Designers: Makkaihang Design, Wu Yanting
Cover Design: Makkaihang Design

D.L.: B 9919-2021
Printed in China

CONTENTS

PREFACE

If Life Gives You Books, Make Sausages

Ever since *The Epic of Gilgamesh* (c. 2100 BC), authors and scholars and subsequently designers, artists and publishers have been exploring the possibilities of the book. Even though early books came in many forms, from scrolls to wax tablets, the book as we know it today early found its archetypical format, which has remained largely unaltered throughout the centuries. As such, the book is one of the most universally known and recognised objects. Most of us are introduced to books as infants and return to them throughout the different stages of our lives as sources of information, entertainment, inspiration and comfort. The book has become an icon or a symbol. One may even call it a pillar of modern civilisation, definite in its form.

Perhaps, the idea of an archetype has primarily been challenged within the expansive field of artists' books, where traditional formats have been systematically deconstructed over the years. The definition of an artist's book is almost as boundless as the definition of artwork, mainly because an artist's book is just that – an object rather than a book in its traditional sense. An interesting example of this is Dieter Roth's *Literaturwurst* (*Literature Sausage*), made between 1961 and 1974. For each book, Roth, who along with Edward Ruscha is generally credited for defining the modern artist's book, replaced the meat in a sausage with a book or a magazine. The book's cover was pasted onto the sausage casing, which was also signed and dated by the artist. 'From time to time I take books I can't stand or from authors I want to annoy and make: sausages...' said Roth.

Artists are of course less bound by common perceptions of what good book design is than us graphic designers, who normally give books their form. Likely, one reason for this is that in many instances, the artist is, at least in part, free from many of the limitations and constraints related to a commercial book project, such as budgets, distribution logistics and the possibilities offered by mass production. Another reason may be that we, as graphic designers, occasionally tend to overly fetishise the book's tactile aspects, leading us to quickly delve into specifics, such as the choice of certain paper stock or a specific type of binding, before defining and developing a more overarching conceptual leitmotif for the design of the publication. Granted, the graphic designer's main objective is usually to present the content of a book optimally while, as the black-clad kōken on the Noh stage, remaining virtually unnoticed.[1]

1. The kōken are supporting staff of a traditional Kabuki or Noh theatre, usually pass out props on the stage. They are dressed in black and are not part of the play, so the audience are expected to ignore them.

2. This report only includes books with ISBNs and the actual number of published books is likely to be much greater.

For an ambitious survey on book design, such as the one currently resting in your hands, one is inclined to contemplate the status of the book in our digital age. Although the physical book's probable and imminent demise has been predicted on many occasions, often concerning the introduction of new technology, the printed book seems to have retained its relevance. The e-book has won considerable ground, especially in popular fiction, yet still, the number of printed books published today is greater than ever.

Besides the established and commercial publishing houses, self-publishing is flourishing. According to the 2019 Bowker Report, more than 1.5 million print books were self-published in 2018, in the U.S. alone.[2] Comparing those numbers to the statistics from 2013, only a fifth as many titles were published. By 2019, the total number of books, both self-published and commercially published in the U.S., exceeded 4 million. However, the same report suggests that sales numbers and edition sizes are decreasing steadily. Forbes contributor Nick Morgan puts it bluntly in the opening line of his text on self-publishing: 'Here's the problem with self-publishing: no one cares about your book.' With such a high number of titles being published each year, even niche genres are becoming saturated.

Simultaneously, we are becoming acutely aware of the effects of our headless use of the planet's resources, and the dire consequences of our emissions. While print-on-demand solutions offer a more sustainable approach to publishing, it significantly limits the designer's production-related possibilities.

With a steadily increasing percentage of book sales being made through online outlets, we are today less likely to buy a book in a brick-and-mortar store. As a result, many traditional bookstores are fighting for their survival, competing against the faceless giants of the digital age.

Whereas graphic designers could earlier employ more subtle means and, at least in part, rely on tactility as a factor driving sales, the design of a book – prior to its purchase – is today often reduced to a thumbnail of its cover. How then, can the design of a book best present the author's intent, while contributing to making sure that it reaches its intended audience? This book provides many ambitious attempts at tackling this challenge. By way of demonstrating the resourcefulness of a number of the field's leading practitioners, it also clearly demonstrates that, even as many of us spend more and more time in front of a screen, books are still as beloved as they were in the days of Gutenberg. Should the tide ever turn, we may always follow Roth's example and make sausages out of the books.

Andreas Friberg Lundgren
Art director and co-founder of Lundgren+Lindqvist
Publisher and co-founder of Il'Editions

PREFACE

Set Free, and Shape

BOOKS AS MEDIA

When I treated books only as media of text, I did not realise that the way of text dissemination had changed profoundly in these few decades. In this era, E-book has become a necessity and I, a graphic designer who mainly does book design, spend time swiping the screen all day long. It was surprising to find that I spent more than 10 hours doing this a day in my quarantine because it is equal to the sum of the working hours during a normal working day of mine.

So I would have to admit, the book has not been the sole carrier of text long ago. Even worse, a book, as an object to deliver information, could have already passed away. While the people who are used to reading books remember because those experiences still linger. David Pearson once said in *Books As History*, 'If books' rationale is solely textual, their obsolescence seems guaranteed.' For me, books have been awaiting their 'obsolescence' in this long journey of more than 2000 years since their first appearance in human's history.

Books, deemed 'dead' for the domination of the new medium, are 'reborn' at the moment of their 'death'. This object in the shape of a rectangle cube is born again because of its 'death'. Designers and book artists perform with abundant text and visual illusions on the books that are tangible but changeable. They are no longer under the restriction of the recognised way of reading, the common logic of narration, and even the text – as they become extinct in books. What is shackling book design is designers' imagination, publishing materials and cost of sales, and this is the last bit of meaning left behind by a book when it is no longer treated as a medium. Books, as media, were dead. Books, as creations of book designers and artists, are still alive.

BOOKS AS OBJECTS

Books, getting rid of the function of delivering text, reveal their physicality to readers through design – a tool of minds and hands.

In a time when books are the only way of expression, to unify the content and the form, designers tried to play with typography. They hope to arouse readers' interests by creating a poetic sensation beyond the text. Now, the physicality of a book is straightforward to readers after it is intervened by design. When we touch and flip the pages of different textures, colours and brightness, and read the text and graphics, our hearts, sensitive and fragile, will be struck by this experience, urging us to have the same copy and not think about the textual content.

In the display of a book's physicality, combined with the text, the unique sensory experience in a book is brought to the readers when they read and touch the book. The integration of fluid and abstract design mindset and a book's physicality makes me wonder if the text can stay without its tailor-made carrier – a book. Free from the constraint of text, books extend their physicality and bring me to an unknown world where I cannot count on my experiences with different subjects to make a judgement on a book I have never read.

Physicality builds up the maze in a book.

BOOKS AS MINDS

The tool of mind to a designer is design.

The world is composed of objects. What is the kind that is tiny yet influential to humans' minds? Books can be one of them. The rationality hidden beneath a book's editorial design methodology might be trivial. However, it can impose lasting and invisible effects on readers as they read one after one, laying a foundation for individuals' logic, rationality and public conduct.

Book designers direct pages of a book with rationality. On pages, they either arrange text following the text's order and levels or sort out a unique visual logic to guide the reading. In addition, book designers direct the relations among margins, fonts and font sizes, offering the readers pleasure of emotion and reason. Readers, in this case, put themselves in the rational framework and apply this rule in their social life spontaneously.

In an era when the function of a book reaches beyond the expression of text, my duty as a book designer is to think about how books work as media, obejcts and minds from the perspective of design. I hope my thoughts and words can be a laying brick in the building of book design. And I am writing this preface to express my gratitude to the publisher of this book – Sandu Publishing.

'The sun also rises, and the sun goes down, and hurries to its place where it rises.' (*World English Bible*, Ecc. 1:5) I think it is the same with books.

Liu Xiaoxiang
Founder of XXL Studio

WHAT MAKES A BOOK

1. The Physical Structure of Books

Narrowly defined, a book refers to a collection of information with words, images and other symbols bound together between a front and a back cover. Broadly speaking, it is a cultural carrier for people to express ideas, convey knowledge and exchange experiences. It is also important to the accumulation and dissemination of human culture. Book design is the overall composition and organisation of written and visual elements, that is, the design of specific components through the integration of format, text, layout, illustration, printing and binding. Book design impacts multiple steps in the publishing project, from ideation and manuscript development to the creation of the cover and interior pages of a printed book.

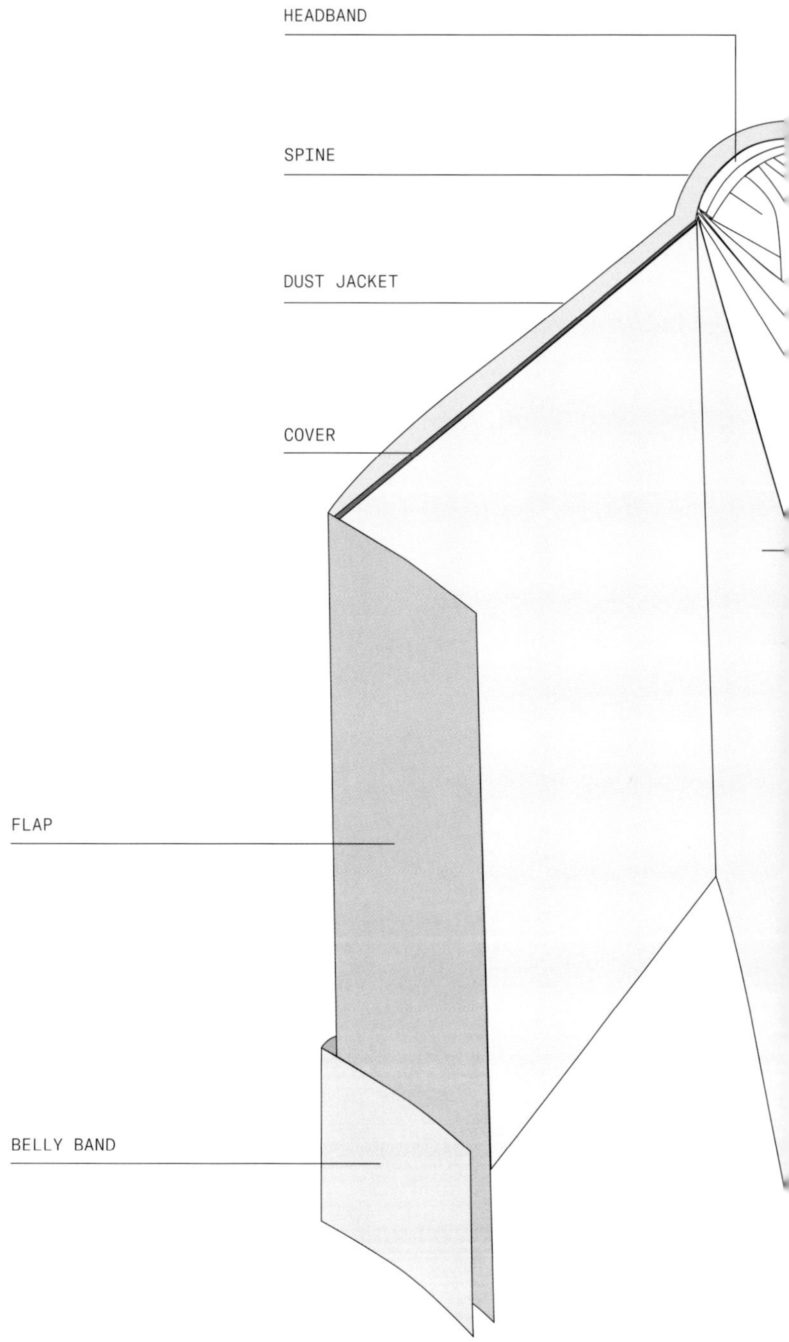

HEADBAND
It is a kind of braid with thick edges, pasted on the top and bottom of the book block. Headbands are used to to align book signatures and to strengthen the ends of a book.

SPINE (ALSO KNOWN AS 'BACK BONE')
It connects the front cover and the back cover and acts as a hinge. It is the place where the pages are bound together.

DUST JACKET (ALSO KNOWN AS 'BOOK JACKET' OR 'DUST COVER')
A piece of material that wraps around the outside of the book cover.

COVER (ALSO KNOWN AS 'FRONT COVER' OR 'PANEL')
It is printed with the title of the book, name(s) of the author(s), the translator and the publisher.

FLAPS
They extend from the outer cutting edges of the front and back cover paper by about 5-10 cm and are folded inward.

BELLY BAND
It generally wraps around the lower part of the dust jacket.

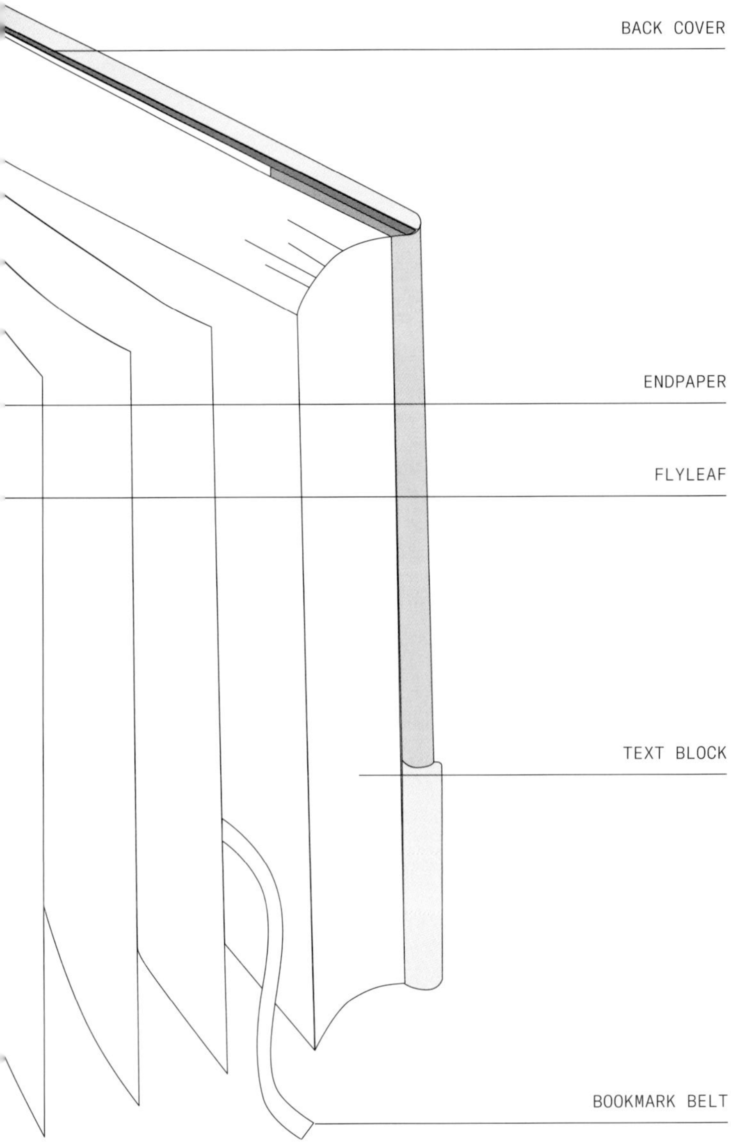

BACK COVER
Oftentimes it is printed with the bar code of the publishing organisation, ISBN and retail price. It also may include a summary of the book.

ENDPAPERS (ALSO KNOWN AS 'ENDSHEETS')
They are the sheets of paper that adhere the front and back covers to the text block.

FLYLEAF
It is the page placed at the front or back of the book, following or preceding the endpapers.

TEXT BLOCK
It is the body text or content of the book.

BOOKMARK BELT
It is a slender label made of silk or other textile.

COLOPHON
It is a page where the edition number and other information is recorded. It usually is located at the bottom of the back of the flyleaf or on the last page of the book.

TABLE OF CONTENTS
It is the outline of the book, extraction of chapters and sections of the book, serving as an index.

FOREWORD AND AFTERWORD
They are short essays by the author or related personnel explaining the reasons for writing the book. The foreword is placed before the body text while the afterword (also known as the 'epilogue') is at the end of the book.

2. Knowing about Types of Paper

Paper, which is the most commonly used material for printing, is a sheet made of fibre that is chemically processed to form pulp. The standard unit 'gram' is used to measure the weight of a square metre of paper. The lighter the weight, the thinner the paper; the heavier the thicker. Paper differs greatly in weight, thickness, colour, texture and other attributes. Designers should be familiar with the material, printing process and texture differences of papers, and choose the appropriate paper to suit the design and printing needs of their projects.

A.

B.

2.1 COMMONLY USED PAPER

Commonly used types of paper in book design include gloss art paper, matt art paper, wood-free uncoated paper, newsprint and paperboard. Among them, gloss art paper and matt art paper are finished with a special coating, and thus are called 'coated papers'. Because of their low price and good colour rendition, gloss and matt art papers are suitable for printing pictures and used extensively in high-end publishing such as glossy magazines and coffee-table books.

Wood-free uncoated paper, as its name implies, is usually uncoated. And papers of different weight are used for different purposes. Thick wood-free uncoated paper is especially appropriate for printing the text block of books. Thin wood-free uncoated paper, on the other hand, is used mostly for printing office documents.

GLOSS ART PAPER
Its surface is shiny due to the coating that the paper manufacturer applies.

MATT ART PAPER
It has a smooth surface that produces little shine.

WOOD-FREE UNCOATED PAPER
It is smooth, tight and light and it absorbs ink evenly, so the printing quality is exquisite.

NEWSPRINT
It is affordable and has very light weight. Ink absorbs fast into the paper, making it ideal for large print runs in little time.

PAPERBOARD
It has low flexibility as well as a certain degree of rigidity, so it is not easy to break when folded.

2.2 SPECIALITY PAPER

Speciality paper is a general category of paper with specific properties or characteristics. Examples of speciality paper include textured paper, metallic paper, tracing paper, plastic-coated paper, non-woven fabric and handmade paper. The different textures and rich artistic effects found in speciality paper can greatly increase the added value of book design.

TEXTURED PAPER
It has a textile-like surface and is often used for printing menus, stationery, etc.

METALLIC PAPER
Its surface has a special effect that can present the printed texts and images with a slight shimmer.

TRACING PAPER
It allows light to go through and has a smooth surface.

PLASTIC-COATED PAPER
It is coated with a plastic layer on the surface to improve water resistance, tear strength and so on.

NON-WOVEN FABRIC
It is a kind of sheet bound together by staple fibres and long fibres.

HANDMADE PAPER
It is manufactured by hand instead of a papermaking machine. This kind of paper usually has deckled edges.

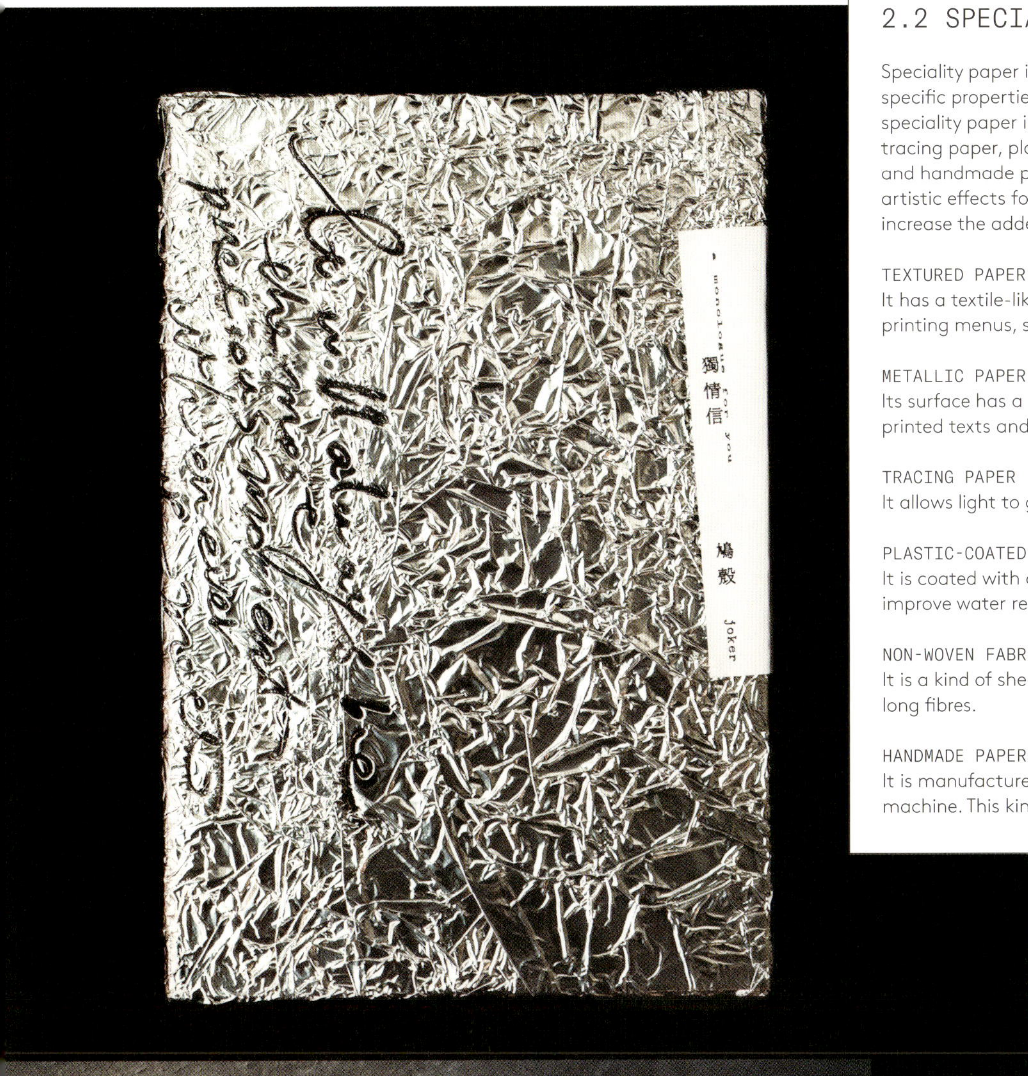

C.

D.

A. TEXTURED PAPER, *WINDY ZONE* DESIGNED BY MISTROOM

B. HANDMADE PAPER, *YU-ICHI INOUE/SHIKO MUNAKATA/KAZUO YAGI* DESIGNED BY QU MINMIN & JIANG QIAN

C. TIN FOIL PAPER, *A MONOLOGUE FOR YOU* DESIGNED BY MISTROOM

D. PAPER MADE FROM RICE STRAW, *MADE IN FUKUSHIMA* DESIGNED BY MOBY DIGG

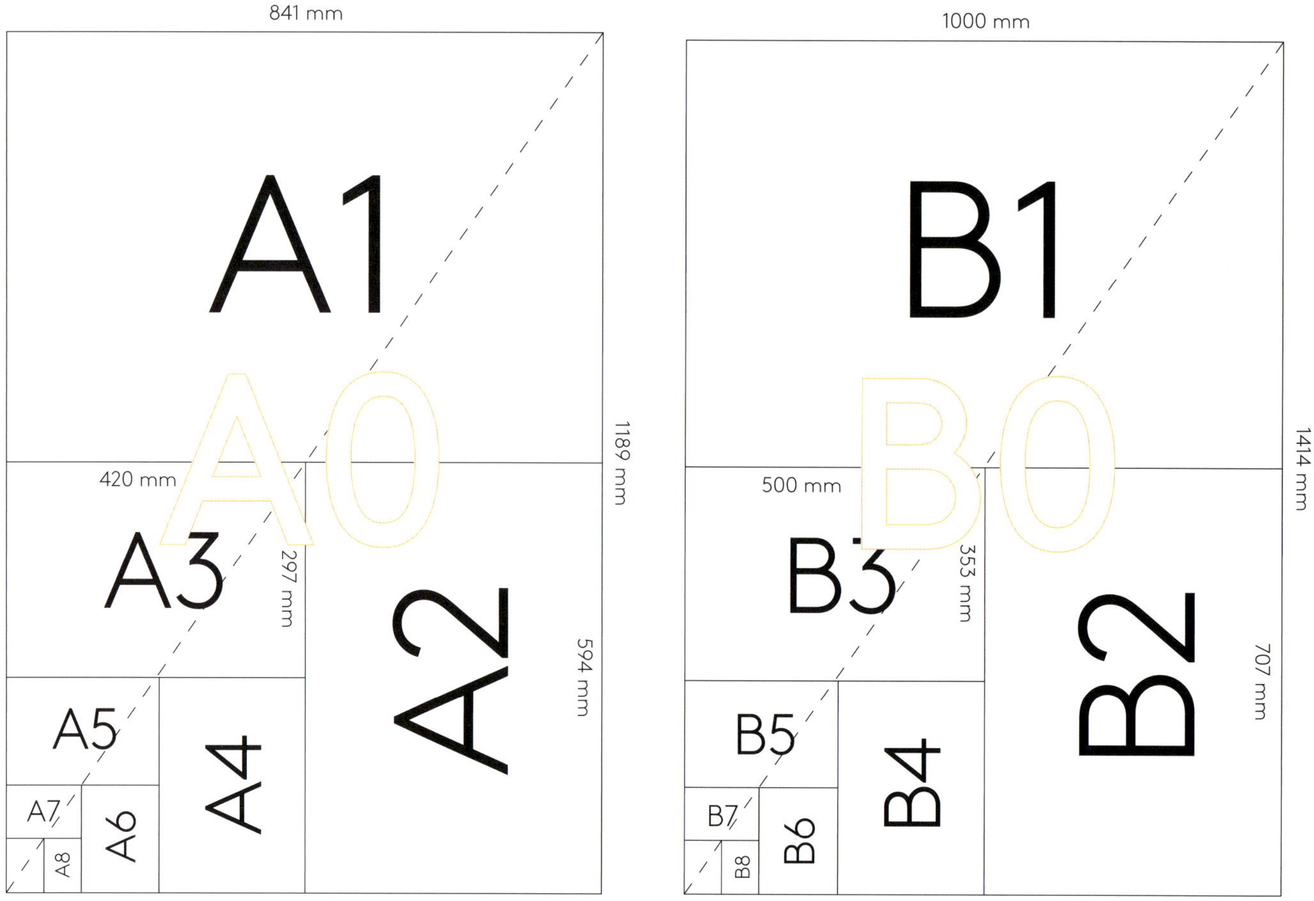

2.3 COMMON SIZES OF PAPER

For Chinese paper size standards, paper specifications are divided into two types: standard and large. The size of a standard sheet of paper is 787 mm × 1092 mm; the size of a large sheet is 889 mm × 1194 mm. The specification of the paper is directly related to the format of the book. 'Format' refers to the size of the book. The format of the book is measured by the book's dimensions, shape and the number of pages which are cut, or slit, from a fully opened sheet of paper. 16K, for example, is the size of the paper that has been equally divided into 16 portions from a fully opened sheet of paper. The alias 'K' is the unit that appears at the end of the name used in the Chinese paper size standard.

PAPER WEIGHT
It is the weight of paper measured in grams per square meter (g/m^2). Generally speaking, paper lighter than $300g/m^2$ is narrowly classified as 'paper'. and paper heavier than $300g/m^2$ is classified as 'paperboard'.

SIGNATURE
In the printing process, it is a group of sheets folded in four or the multiples of four times and works as a unit in bookbinding, also called 'section'. The figure is often seen on the colophon of a book, and it indicates the amount of paper required for printing one copy of this publication.

LEAF
There are two pages on one leaf. The front of the leaf is called 'recto', and the back is 'verso'.

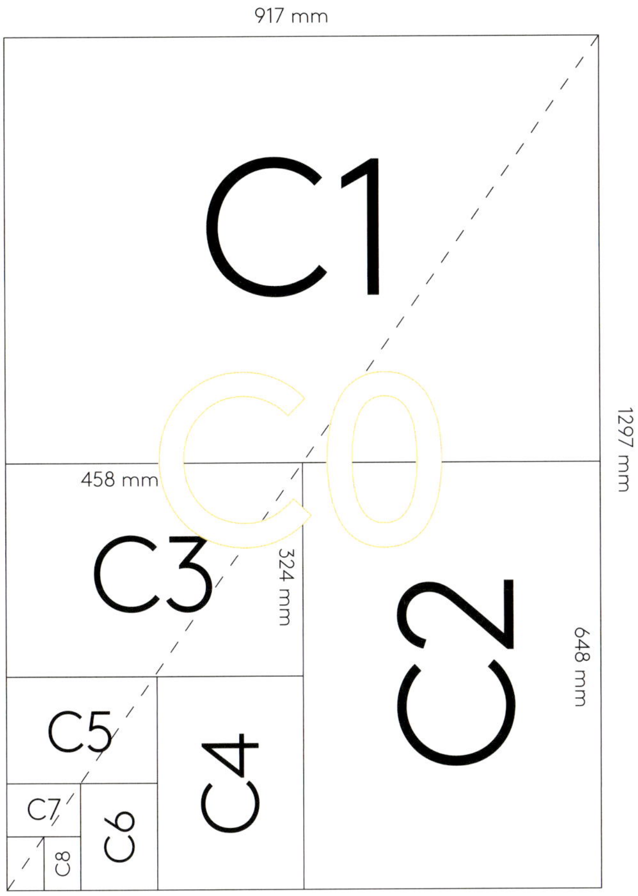

ISO INTERNATIONAL PAPER SIZE

ISO 216 is an international standard for paper sizes, and it specifies the sizes of standard paper used in most countries. This standard originated in Germany and was passed by the German Institute for Standardisation in 1922. It defines the A, B and C series of paper.

ISO INTERNATIONAL PAPER SIZES

ISO 216 A		ISO 216 B		ISO 216 C	
A0	841 × 1189	B0	1000 × 1414	C0	917 × 1297
A1	594 × 841	B1	707 × 1000	C1	648 × 917
A2	420 × 594	B2	500 × 707	C2	458 × 648
A3	297 × 420	B3	353 × 500	C3	324 × 458
A4	210 × 297	B4	250 × 353	C4	229 × 324
A5	148 × 210	B5	176 × 250	C5	162 × 229
A6	105 × 148	B6	125 × 176	C6	114 × 162
A7	74 × 105	B7	88 × 125	C7	81 × 114
A8	52 × 74	B8	62 × 88	C8	57 × 81
A9	37 × 52	B9	44 × 62	C9	40 × 57
A10	26 × 37	B10	31 × 44	C10	28 × 40

Unit of measurement: millimetre

Common Sizes of Paper

Unit of measurement: millimetre

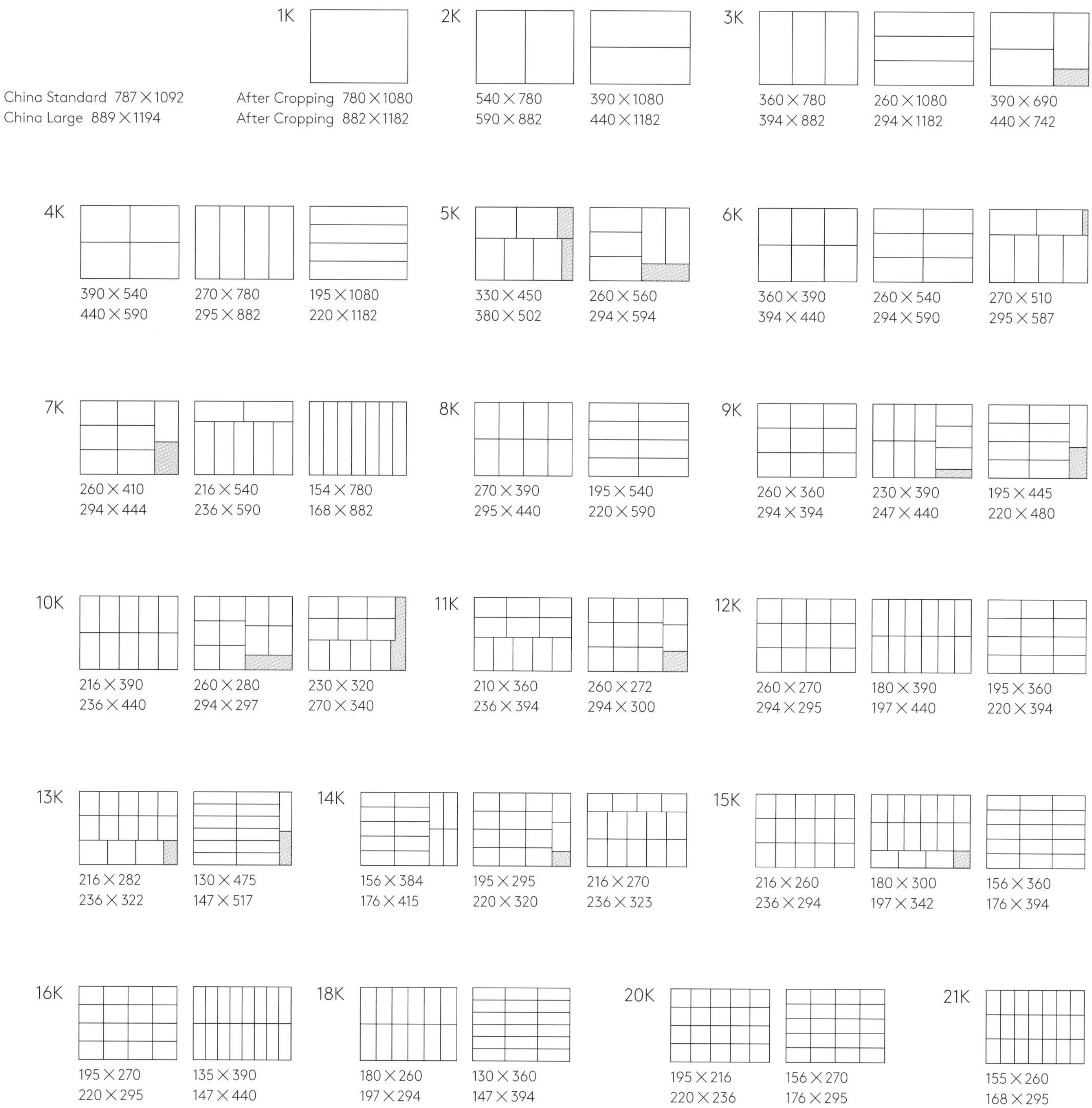

PAPER SLITTING
Paper is usually slit based on geometric progression. For example, if a fully opened sheet of paper is cut at one-half, it turns into two pieces of 2K paper. If the 2K paper is slit several times, it becomes 4K, 8K, 16K, 32K and 64K paper.

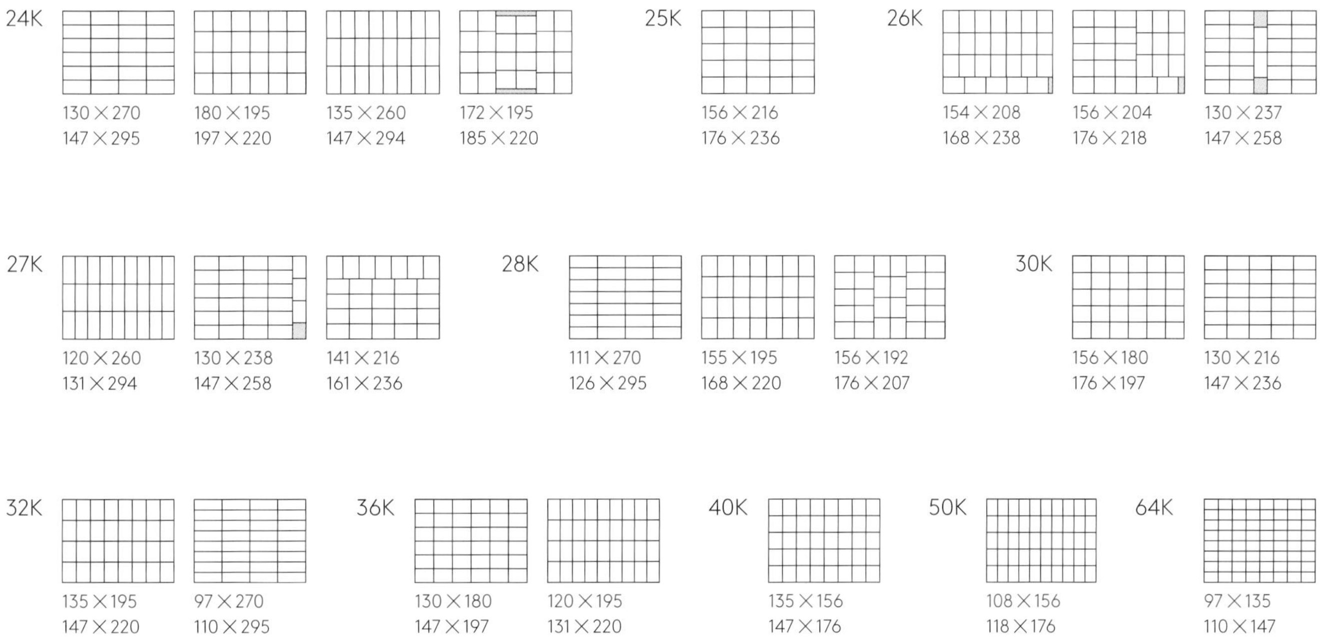

Common Book Format

Standard 2K	520 × 736	Large 2K	570 × 840
Standard 4K	368 × 520	Large 4K	420 × 570
Standard 8K	260 × 368	Large 8K	285 × 420
Standard 16K	185 × 260	Large 16K	210 × 285
Standard 32K	130 × 184	Large 32K	140 × 203
Standard 64K	92 × 126	Large 64K	105 × 148

Unit of measurement: millimetre

3. Page Layout and Grid Systems

3.1 LAYOUT COMPOSITION

Layout composition, also known as 'layout design', refers to the organisation of various visual elements on the page in book design. In short, it is the process of editing and organising text and images to convey specific information. The designer needs to rearrange the title, body text, top margin, bottom margin and other components of the layout, and balance different sections on the page. The layout design serves the content of the book, and its characteristics determine the tone of a book.

LAYOUT
It contains all the elements in the body text of the book, including the fonts and font sizes, the size and orientation of the type area, the number of columns and lines per page, the number of words per line, the line spacing, and the position of tables, pictures, etc.

CUTTING EDGES
Except for the side of a page that is attached to the binding, cutting edges are where the other three sides of the book are cut.

TOP MARGIN
It is the white space, or space without text or images, at the top of each page.

RUNNING HEAD
It is the area at the top of every page on which titles of chapters or page numbers are usually placed and repeated.

TYPE AREA
The printed area on each page where text and graphical elements are placed. Another term for type area is 'print space'.

CROSS COLUMN
It is on a page where columns are divided. Cross column refers to the multiple columns used when text takes up more than one column of space on a page.

GUTTER
It is the white space, or space without text or images, near the bookbinding area.

BOTTOM MARGIN
It is the white space at the bottom of each page.

CUTTING EDGE
TOP MARGIN
RUNNING HEAD
Headline
TYPE AREA
CROSS COLUMN
CUTTING EDGE
GUTTER
BOTTOM MARGIN
CUTTING EDGE

VAN DE GRAAF CANON

3.2 RULES OF COMPOSITION AND PRINCIPLES

RULES OF COMPOSITION

A. VAN DE GRAAF CANON
The Van de Graaf canon is the base for modern book design. Van de Graaf was a 20th-century page designer who analysed the first Gutenberg Bible with this principle. The Van de Graaf canon proposes dividing pages in a pleasing proportion and works well for pages with different ratios of width and height. This can help designers create the margins and the type area. Using the Van de Graaf canon, when the proportion of a page is 2:3, the ratio of the margin remains 2:3:4:6 (inner margin:top margin:outer margin:bottom margin). The ratio can be summarised as 1:R:2:2R when the proportion of a page is 1:R.

B. RAÚL ROSARIVO'S GUTENBERG CANON
In 1947, Argentinian typographer and book designer Raúl Rosarivo published his first booklet, *Divina proporción tipográfica*, after he inspected and analysed the works of Gutenberg and his contemporaries and discovered the rules used in designing these books. This interpretation is named Raúl Rosarivo's Gutenberg canon. It requires designers to divide the height and width of the page into nine equal parts and to use the grid as a reference system with the diagonal rule to position the type area. This rule can be applied to pages of any proportion.

C. TSCHICHOLD'S GOLDEN CANON
Tschichold's golden canon was proposed by Jan Tschichold. He is one of the outstanding typographers and book designers of the 20th century. This rule echoes the Van de Graaf canon, but it is easier to use. Tschichold pointed out that the most pleasing page proportion of width to height should be 2:3. With this rule and proportion applied on a page, the height of the type area is equal to the width of the page, as shown by the circle. Under this rule, the margin's ratio is 2:3:4:6.

D. GOLDEN RATIO
The well-known golden ratio is a rule based on the formula a:b= (a+b):a whereas (a>b>0). The golden ratio is an irrational number with a value of 1.618, and is represented by the Greek letter 'Φ (Phi)'. If a rectangle with a golden ratio – 'a' for the longer side; 'b' for the shorter side – is put next to a square with the same side length as the 'a' of the rectangle, they will form another similar golden rectangle with the longer side 'a + b' and the shorter side 'a'. The relationship between the two rectangles corresponds to the formula a:b=(a+b):a.

RAÚL ROSARIVO'S GUTENBERG CANON

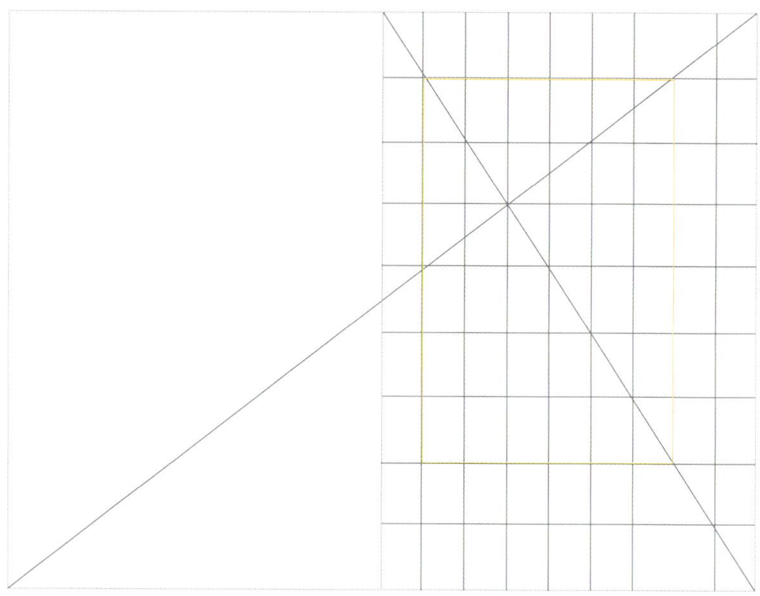

TSCHICHOLD'S GOLDEN CANON

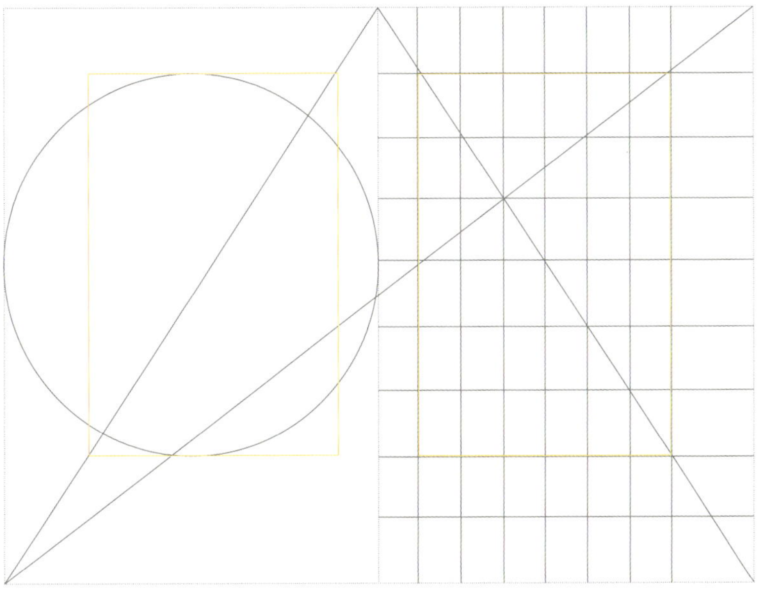

GOLDEN RATION

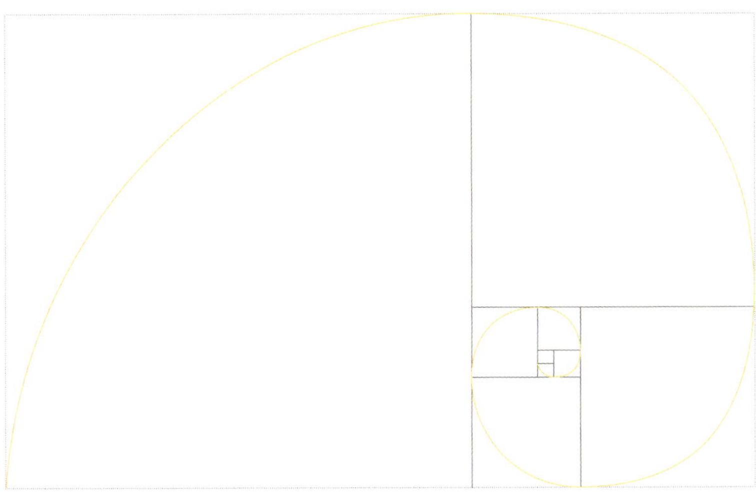

PRINCIPLES OF LAYOUT DESIGN

A. PROMINENT THEME

The purpose of design is to make the layout clear and logical so that information is presented rationally and in a beautifully organised manner. Effective design helps readers understand and to have a better reading experience. One common way designers help convey a topic or theme and to achieve the best visual effect possible is to use the main image as the visual centre and to order topics by levels of importance.

B. UNIFIED FORM AND CONTENT

The premise of layout design is that the layout must be based on the content of the theme, and the theme is expressed through reasonable design forms. Content is expressed through specific design elements such as fonts and graphics, and of course, the text.

C. VISUAL AESTHETICS OF FORM AND OVERALL LAYOUT

The overall layout refers to the design of structure and colours of various layout elements. If the composition is reasonable and orderly, the readers' sight moves smoothly along a certain trajectory with each element in the layout, leading to a rhythmic and effective reading experience.

3.3 GRID SYSTEMS

Grid systems are the foundation of the graphic design field. The 'grid system' refers to a way to position text and pictures with a metric based on sequenced columns and rows. These systems help graphic designers to align text or to know the exact size of text, pictures and other elements.

MANUSCRIPT GRID

COLUMN GRID

MODULAR GRID

BASELINE GRID

COMBINED GRID

HIERARCHICAL GRID

4. Printing and Techniques

FOUR-COLOUR PRINTING

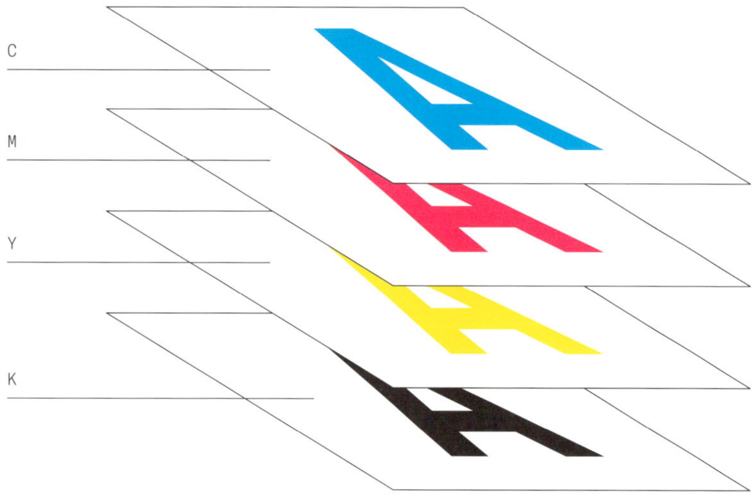

SPOT-COLOUR/SOLID-COLOUR

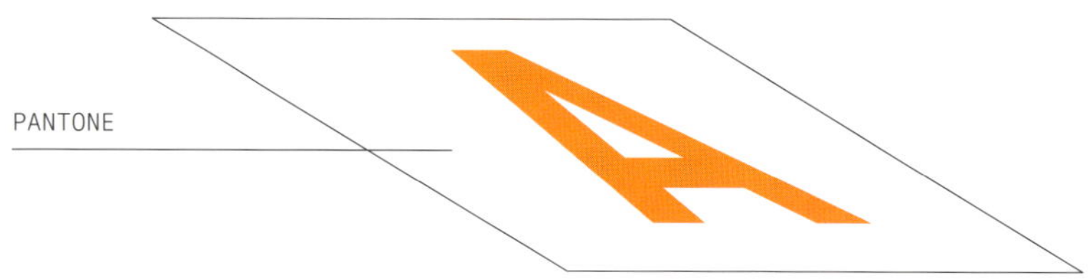

RISO PRINTING

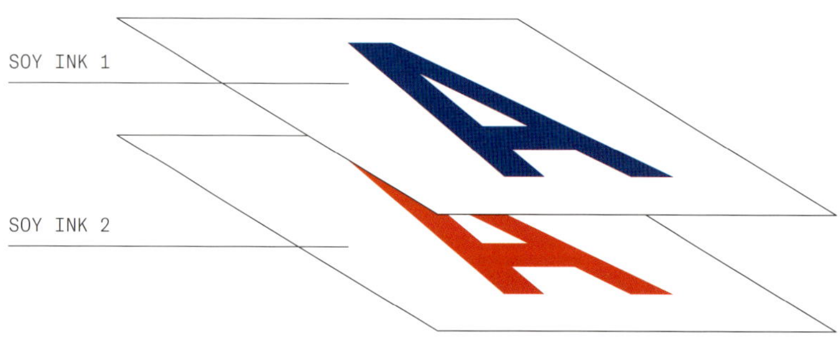

4.1 KNOWING ABOUT PRINTING COLOURS

FOUR-COLOUR PRINTING
Four-colour printing uses four-colour inks corresponding to Cyan, Magenta, Yellow and Key (black) – commonly referred as the 'CMYK colour model' – and reproduces additional colours through overprinting.

SPOT-COLOUR/SOLID-COLOUR PRINTING
With the improvement of book printing processes, spot-colour printing has become more and more common. Spot colours are produced with special inks. This kind of ink is called 'spot-colour ink', which is pre-mixed by a printer or an ink factory, so its printed colours are more precise than those of four-colour printing. It is worth mentioning that the 'Riso digital duplicator', which has become popular in recent years, uses inks extracted from soybeans. Soy ink can be made into high-gloss bright colours, such as fluorescent orange, fluorescent green, fluorescent yellow and fluorescent rose. Because of the inks' high purity, a third colour can be created by overprinting two colours.

A.

B.

C.

A. A FOUR-COLOUR PRINTED BOOK, *WISH/WONEN IN STADSHART* DESIGNED BY STUDIO DE RONNERS

B. A SPOT-COLOUR PRINTED BOOK, *GLOBE IN MOTION 1-2* DESIGNED BY MATÚŠ HNÁT

C. RISO PRINTNG, OLD TEXTBOOKS POSTCARDS BY LAU CHI-CHUNG

4.2 COMMON PRINTING TECHNIQUES

TRADITIONAL PRINTING
Offset Printing, Letterpress Printing, Intaglio Printing, Screen Printing

Traditional printing can produce a large number of copies with a printing plate. Traditional printing techniques are mainly divided into four categories: letterpress printing, intaglio printing, offset printing and screen printing. In modern book printing, offset printing is the most common method due to the lowest cost for a large print run.

LETTERPRESS PRINTING

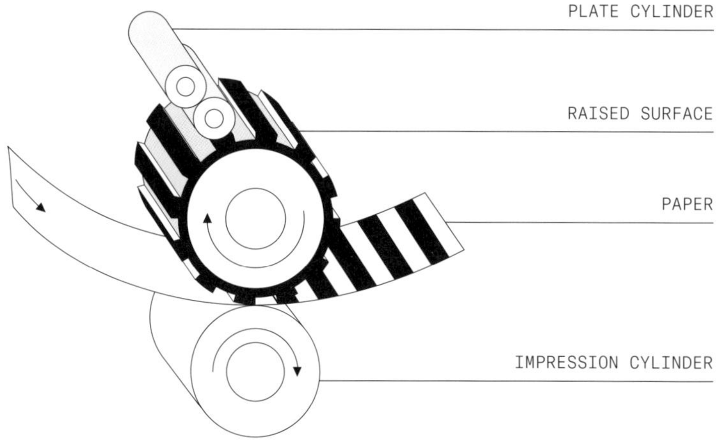

INTAGLIO PRINTING

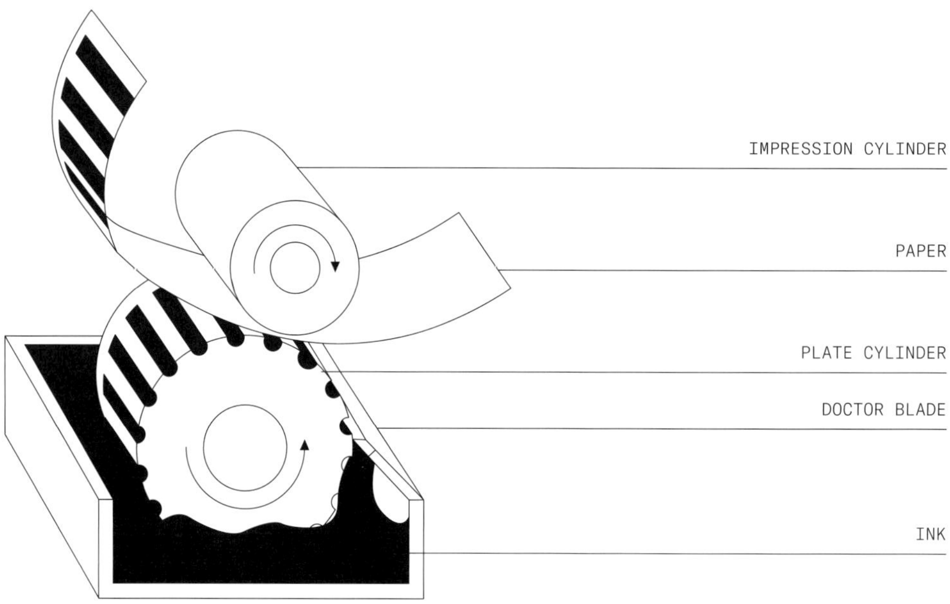

LETTERPRESS PRINTING
It is a printing method where ink is applied to the text area of the printing plate. The inked text area on the plate is significantly raised from the main surface, or blank space, on the plate. Generally, letterpress printing is used for small-sized printed materials including invitation cards, greeting cards, business cards, envelopes, etc.

INTAGLIO PRINTING
It is a printing method where ink is applied to the text area, which is lower than the main surface or blank space of the plate. This technique often is used for the printing of stamps, coins and other artistic works.

A. A LETTERPRESSED COVER, *TEA CANON* DESIGNED BY PAN YANRONG

B. A SCANNED AND PRINTED PICTURE OF A CARVED WOODBLOCK, COVER OF *CRAFTSMAN* DESIGNED BY ZHU YINGCHUN, LUO WEI, YANG XIAOFANG

A.

B.

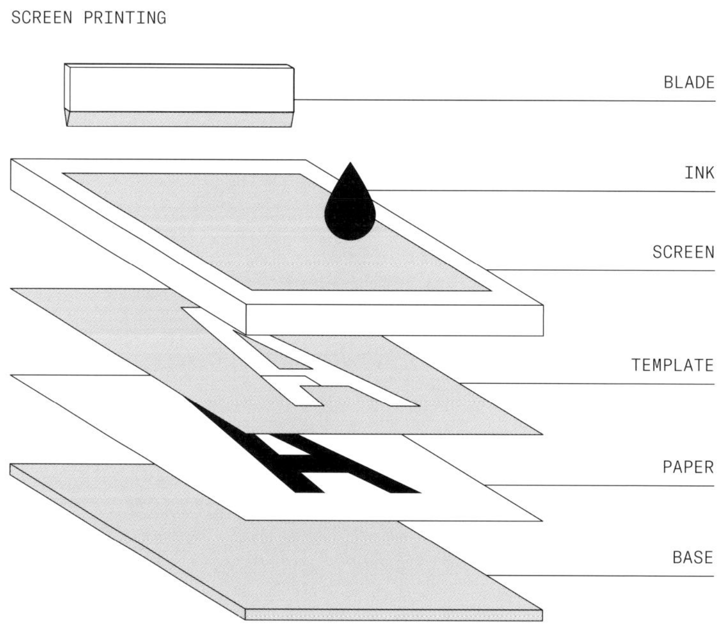

OFFSET PRINTING
It is also known as 'offset lithography'. The inked image on the metal plate is copied onto a cylinder and then transferred to a substrate such as paper. This technique is widely used in colour prints such as books, posters and packages.

SCREEN PRINTING
It refers to the printing method in which the text on the plate can be printed on a substrate after ink goes through a mesh. Silk printing is a kind of screen printing and is used mainly for special materials such as fabrics, metal plates and glass. In recent years, Risograph printing technology has been rediscovered and transformed. Each colour requires a separate roller, and documents of multiple colours need to be printed multiple times. It is often used in the printing of creative works such as books, artist collections and limited edition art posters. Risograph printing is similar to screen printing, but is more creative because it can present a multi-colour effect coming from the transparency of inks. This printing technique is affordable and suitable for independent publishing.

A.

B.

A. AN OFFSET-PRINTED BOOK, *A GARDEN AT NIGHT* DESIGNED BY ATELIER D'ALVES

B. A SCREEN-PRINTED BOOK, *AROMA ISLAND* DESIGNED BY MISTROOM

4.3 COMMONLY USED TECHNIQUES

The book printing process is divided into the pre-printing process, the printing process and the post-printing process. These three stages correspond to the three stages of the printing workflow mentioned before.

The pre-printing process generally includes design, editing and typesetting, which is the core of creative design. The designer needs to anticipate the overall book's form and printing techniques of the book. During the process of printing, the printer and publisher need to select appropriate printing methods and materials to present the design. The post-printing process is the stage where the primary printing product is reprocessed. For books, common finishing techniques are hot stamping, embossing and debossing, UV coating, lamination and die cutting.

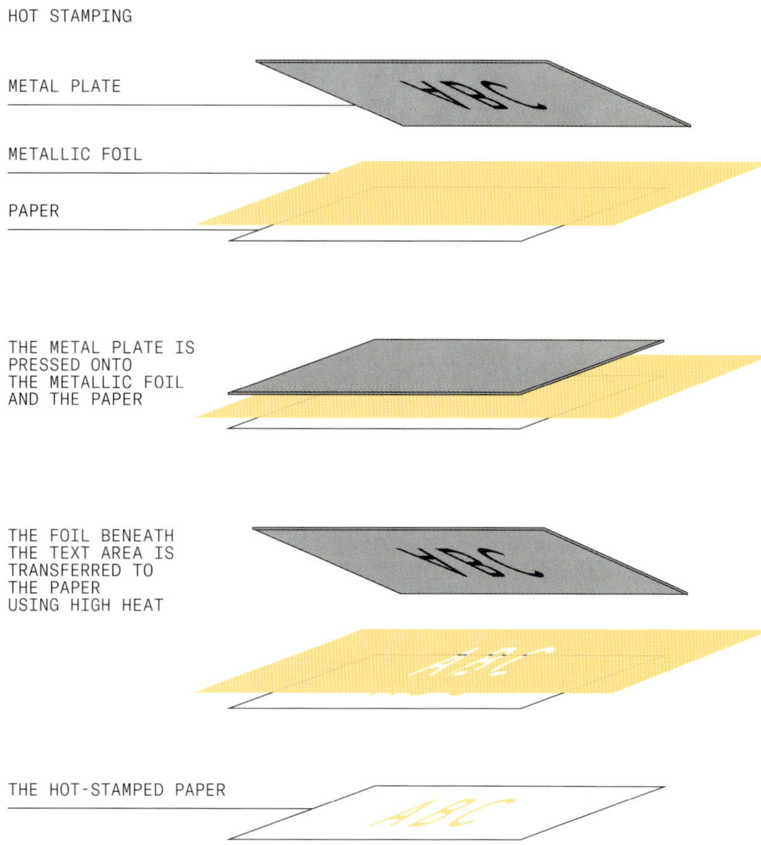

EMBOSSING

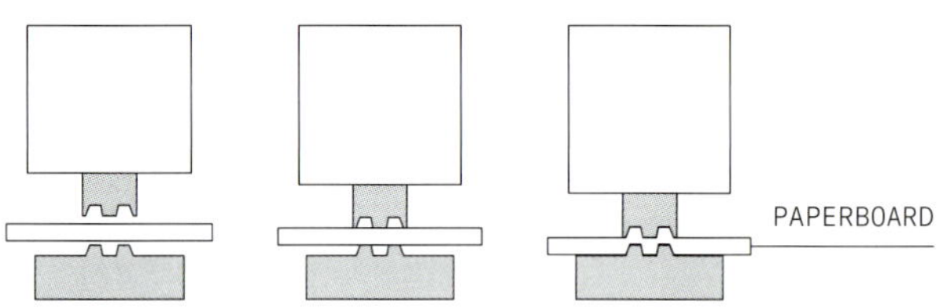

DEBOSSING

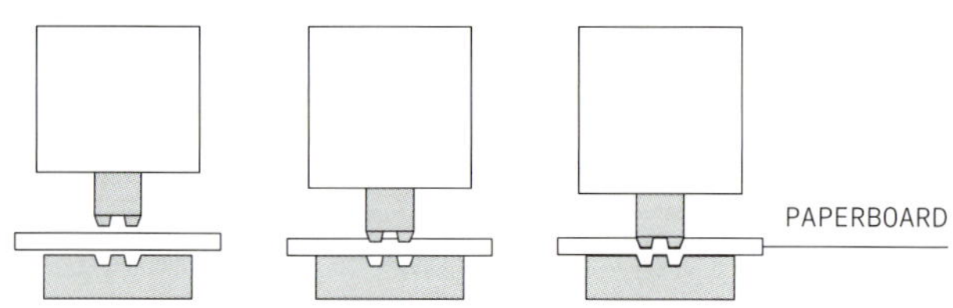

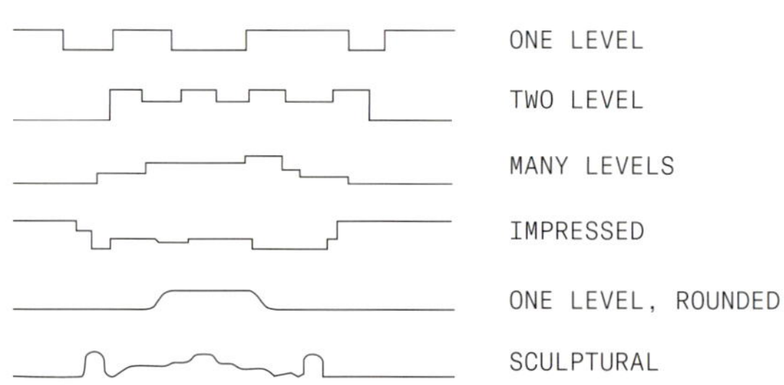

HOT STAMPING

Hot stamping, also known as 'foil stamping', is one of the most common techniques used in the post-printing process. There are gold hot stamping, silver hot stamping, platinum hot stamping, holographic hot stamping and so on. The machine heats the hot stamping plate and transfers the foil to its surface. The foil used for hot stamping is generally made by heating anodised aluminum.

DEBOSSING AND EMBOSSING

Debossing and embossing are post-press processes in which the raised die and the recessed die squeeze printing material to create a three-dimensional effect. Debossing and embossing techniques are a combination of printing and engraving and they can create graphic effects without ink. They are called 'blind embossing' and 'blind debossing'.

A. A HOT-STAMPED COVER, *THE LIVES OF PAINTINGS/ŻYCIE OBRAZÓW* DESIGNED BY RENATA MOTYKA

B. AN EMBOSSED COVER, *BUILDINGS WITH COUR D'HONNEUR IN BUDAPEST* DESIGNED BY ANNA BÁRDY

C. A HOT-STAMPED COVER, *INFINITE BLOOMING* BY HANQINGTANG DESIGN

A.

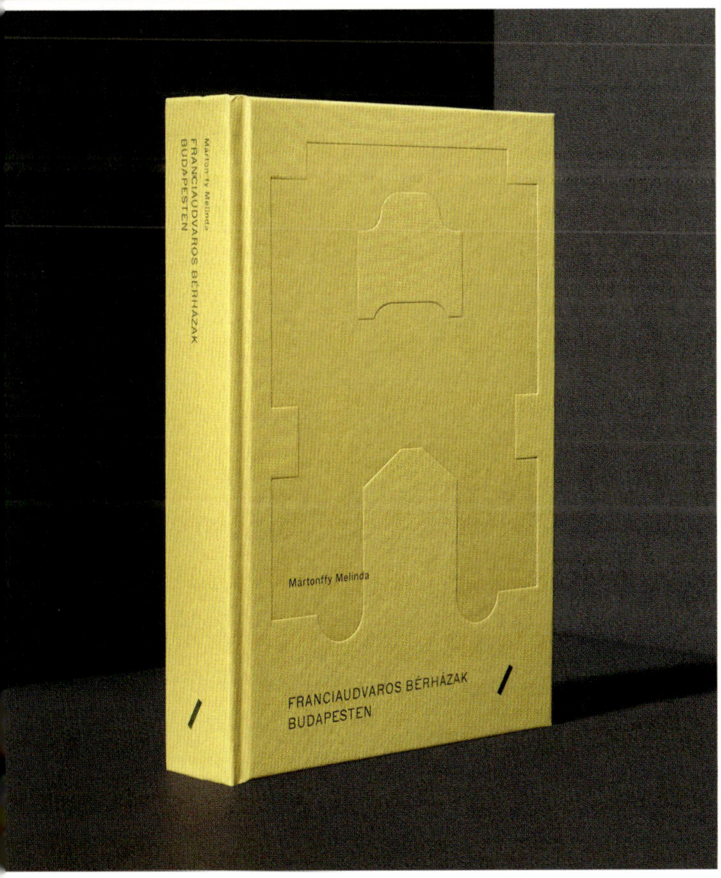

B.

C.

UV COATING
UV coating is to use an ink to cover printed material to produce a glossy effect. UV coating is widely used in book design works such as covers, business cards and brochures.

LAMINATION
Lamination refers to applying a transparent plastic film to the surface of the printed material after hot pressing. Lamination improves the strength, stability, durability and gloss of the product.

DIE CUTTING
Die cutting is an automated operation in which a thin, razor sharp steel blade called a 'die' shears printing material, allowing printers to produce uniquely shaped paper, wood board and other materials.

POLISHING
Polishing is to apply a layer of colourless and transparent coating onto the printed paper by painting, spraying, printing and so on. It is also called 'glazing'.

EDGE PRINTING
Edge printing is to print different colours or graphics on the edges of a book using handcrafted or digital techniques such as gliding, spraying, screen printing and digital printing. Edge printing can enhance the uniqueness of a book.

DIE CUTTING

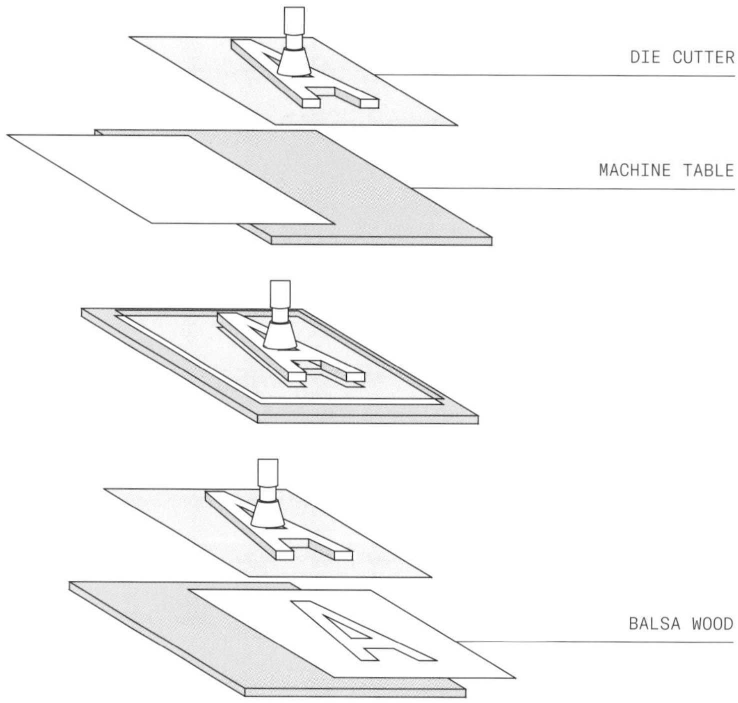

A.

B.

C.

A. A DIE-CUT COVER, *TRAÇOS DE GENTE* DESIGNED BY ATELIER D'ALVES

B. A UV-COATED PAGE, *THE BIRD PROJECT 2006-2017* DESIGNED BY LUNDGREN+LINDQVIST

C. SCREEN PRINTING ON EDGES, *ASIA-PACIFIC DESIGN NO.16* BY MAK KAI-HANG

5. Binding

Binding is the overall process of assembling the printed signatures and attaching a cover to the text block. Modern books and bound periodicals can be divided into two categories: paperback and hardcover. Paperback and hardcover books have different processes, and generally hardcover books go through a more complex process and are more exquisite than paperbacks.

5.1 PAPERBACK

The paperback, also known as the 'softback', is commonly used in modern books. The processing of a paperback is simple, and the cost is low, so it is suitable for books with a small page count and a large print run. Books with a spine width smaller than 20 mm generally use paperbacks. The binding methods of paperback books include saddle stitching, sewn binding, perfect binding, loose-leaf binding, etc.

SADDLE STITCHING
It is a technique that uses wire staples to bind signatures into a block along the fold of the signature. It is the simplest, most convenient and common bookbinding method.

SEWN BINDING
It is a binding technique that uses a special machine to sew the pages with thread through the fold at the spine of each signature. Generally, sewn binding is used for thicker paperback books. This kind of binding allows books to be durable, low-cost and easy-to-read.

PERFECT BINDING
This method does not require stitching. After the book pages are matched with page numbers, the book pages are glued together with a strong adhesive at the spine to make a book block, and then the book block is attached to a cover. Perfect binding is a very widely used method for paperback trade books, text materials and so on.

LOOSE-LEAF BINDING
It is a form of binding in which holes are punched at the hinge of the book, and then the pages are bound together with strips or spirals. It is suitable for publications that require frequent content changes, such as product samples, catalogues and photo albums.

SADDLE STITCHING

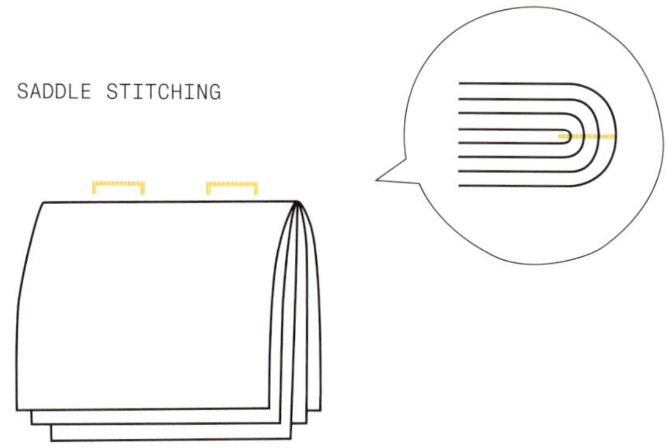

SEWN BINDING

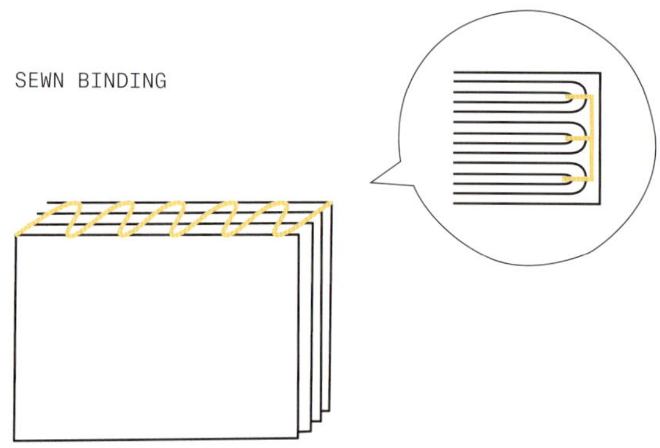

PERFECT BINDING

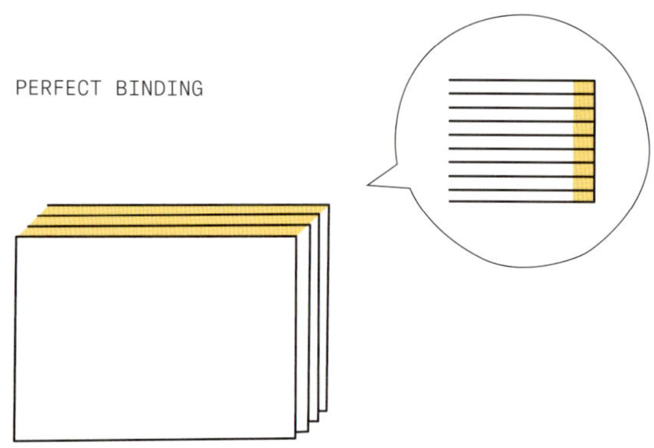

LOOSE-LEAF BINDING

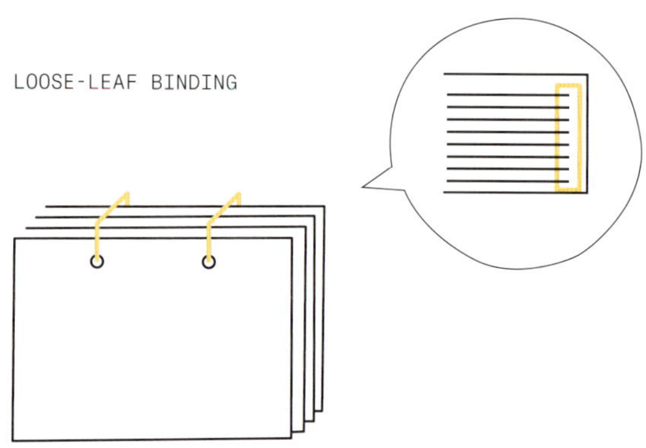

A.

B.

C.

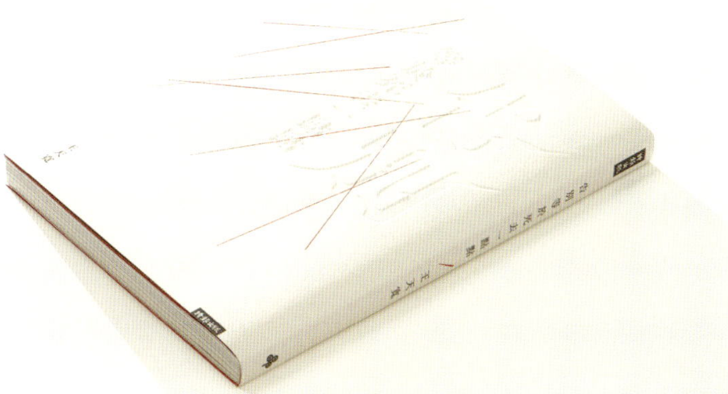

D.

A. A SEWN BOOK, *CARCASSE: THE BUTCHER'S KITCHEN* DESIGNED BY TIM BISSCHOP

B. A SEWN BOOK, *TALK ABOUT KUNQU* BY QU MINMIN & JIANG QIAN

C. A LOOSE-LEAF BOOK, *IDENTITÀ OLTRE IL TEMPO* DESIGNED BY RICCARDO SAVIOLI

D. A PERFECT-BOUND BOOK, *TO SAY GOODBYE IS TO DIE A LITTLE* DESIGNED BY WU CHIA-LIN

5.2 HARDCOVER

Hardcover is a more delicate form of binding in modern book publishing. Hardcover books are bound after the cover, the spine of the book block and the corners of the book go through processing. Hardcover books are used mainly for valuable books such as classic works and fine printed picture albums that need to be preserved for a long time, as well as reference books for frequent consultation.

Round back book is a common form of hardcover book. It is generally suitable for thicker books because it delivers a feeling of fullness and elegance. The round back can increase the thickness of thin books.

Square back book is another common form. Cardboard is mostly used as the lining of the spine. Therefore, the square-back hardcover book is tall, straight and modern.

A shared feature of hardcover books is rigid protective covers. When making a hardcover book, manufacturers use loose-leaf binding, sewn binding and other binding methods.

ROUND BACK BOOK

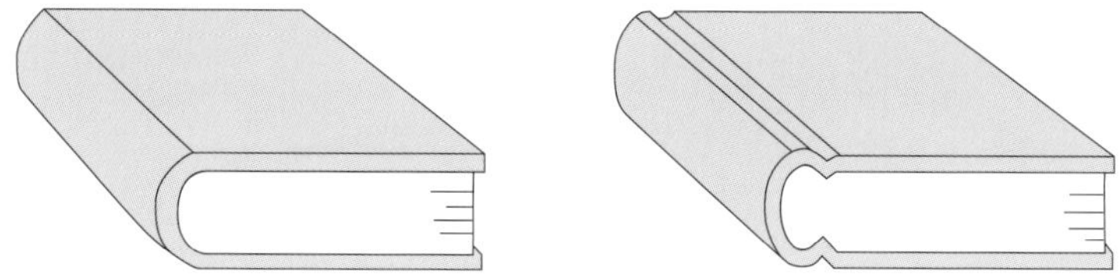

SQUARE BACK BOOK

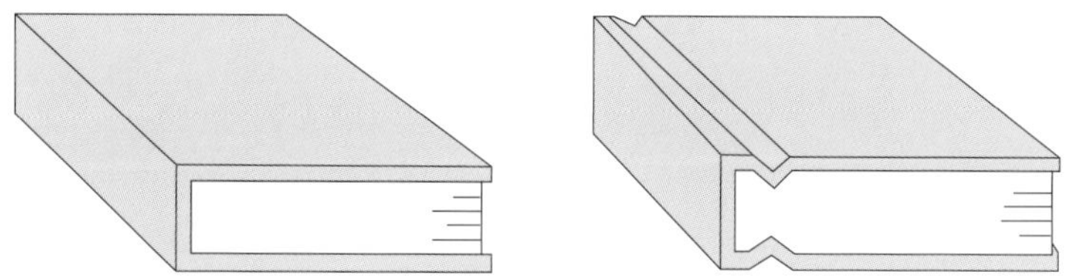

A.

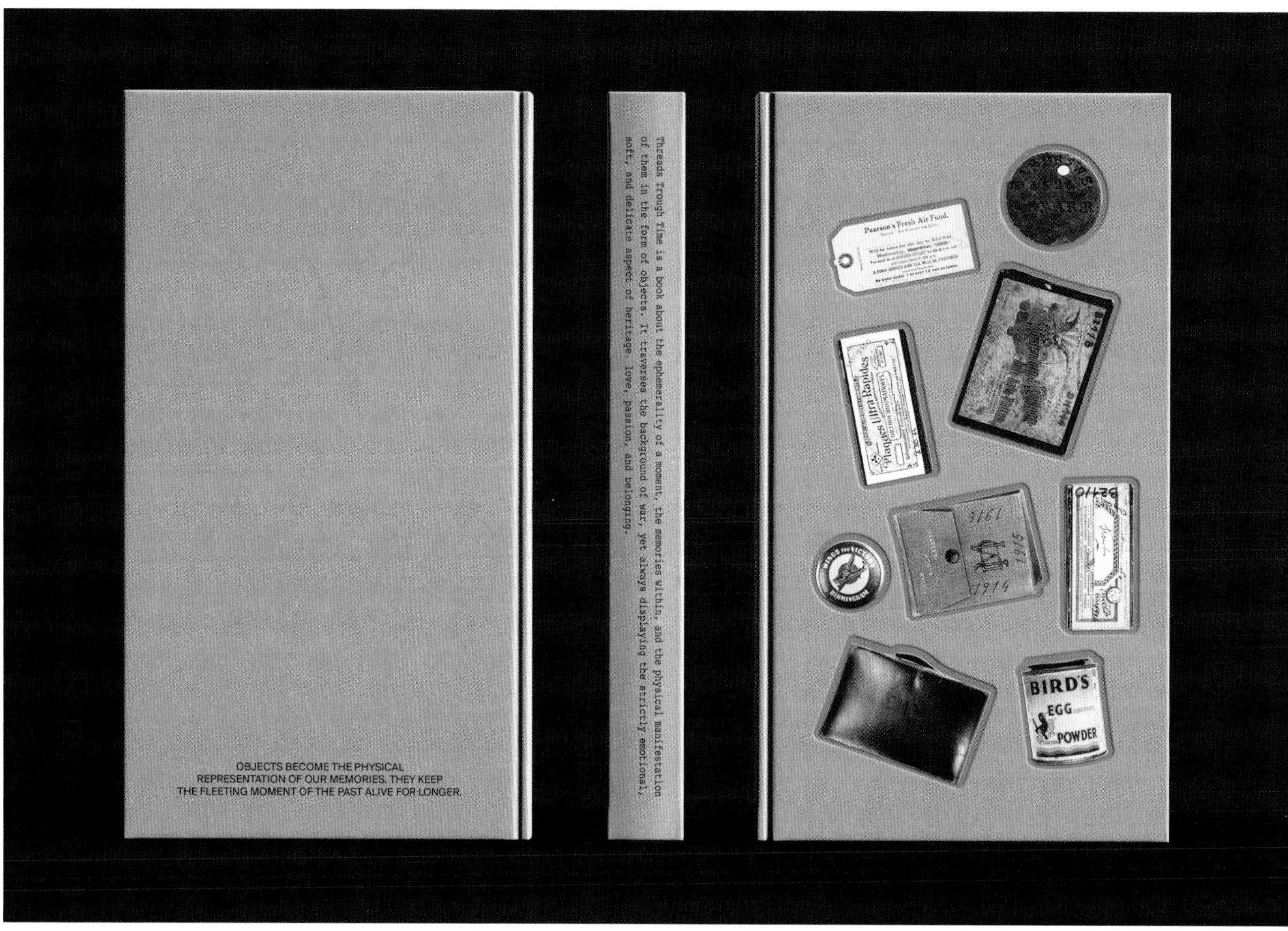

B.

C.

D.

A. A SQUARE BACK BOOK, *THREADS THROUGH TIME - ARCHIVE OF MEMORIES* DESIGNED BY DESISLAVA DANOVA, SUSAN XAVIER

B. A DOS-À-DOS BOUND BOOK, *GOD DOES NOT PLAY DICE* DESIGNED BY KENNETH KUH

C. A SQUARE BACK BOOK, *TYPOGRAPHIC DESIGN IN CHINA* DESIGNED BY PAN YANRONG

D. A SQUARE BACK BOOK, *MAKERS BIBLE - HUMAN SPACE (BLACK EDITION)* DESIGNED BY MELVILLE BRAND DESIGN

MEET THE DESIGNERS

NINETEEN EIGHTY-FOUR

DESIGN
David Pearson

PUBLISHER
Penguin Books

SPECIFICATION
111 mm × 181 mm

BINDING & FINISHING
Paperback

PAPER
–

TYPEFACE
Gill Sans

01

THE MASTERMIND BEHIND COVERS

'It feels important to me to kick back at these expectations though. I can't be satisfied knowing that my next job is going to feel like the last.'

In an era where many people go to e-books for their convenience and high availability, paper books remain attractive because they tell the story not only through text but also through their tactile appeal as an object. As a top creative in his field, David Pearson works as a book designer and never stops craving for the felicitous answer to what works best for a book's cover.

Graduated from Central Saint Martins in 2002, David worked as a text designer and then a cover designer for Penguin Books. His time at Penguin was precious and rewarding, which continues to influence him even long after he left the company. As David said, 'Many "Penguins" remain close friends and as a freelancer the company has handed me some of my most enjoyable projects. And that's in addition to the huge number of Penguin design heroes I have gathered over the years.'

After he left Penguin, David set up his studio Type as Image. The well-received Great Ideas series and other collections David designed or art directed kept him associated with Penguin. The most 'rebellious' one – the cover of George Orwell's *Nineteen Eighty-Four*, on which legibility and confusion blend well enough to encourage readers' interpretation, made a lasting impression. When he designs books, the studio's name 'Type as Image' is exactly what David embraces, giving each book a delicate touch.

Genuine enthusiasm and sheer persistence for cover design drive David to think and try. In addition to working with Penguin, he designed covers for other publishers. The colourful and intriguing collection by the French publisher Éditions Zulma stood out in the market. The result was good though David changed his design approach. Always being passionate and creative – as you will be aware in his talks about his book design career, David claimed, 'I can't be satisfied knowing that my next job is going to feel like the last.'

Great Orwell

DESIGN
David Pearson

PUBLISHER
Penguin Books

KEEP THE ASPIDISTRA FLYING

SPECIFICATION
111 mm × 181 mm

BINDING & FINISHING
Paperback

PAPER
–

TYPEFACE
Akzidenz Grotesk Roman, Bold

DOWN AND OUT IN PARIS AND LONDON

SPECIFICATION
111 mm × 181 mm

BINDING & FINISHING
Paperback

PAPER
–

TYPEFACE
Akzidenz Grotesk Roman, Bold

The Great Orwell series is a reissue of English author George Orwell's classics. David captured the essence of each title and created a distinctive style for each of them. Fonts are the key visual elements in some of the covers while a Picasso-esque drawing was also created for the cover illustration of a title. The most notable one is his design for *Nineteen Eighty-Four*. Despite the iconic Penguin's orange and white colours, the debossed title and the author's name are hidden beneath the bar-shaped matt black foil, which can only be noticed upon a closer look.

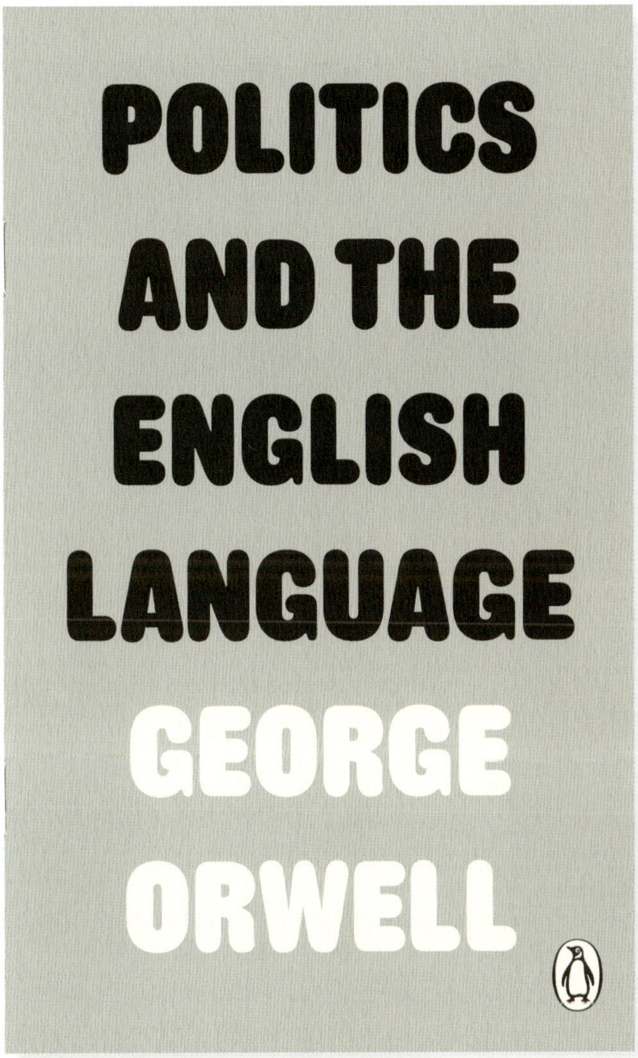

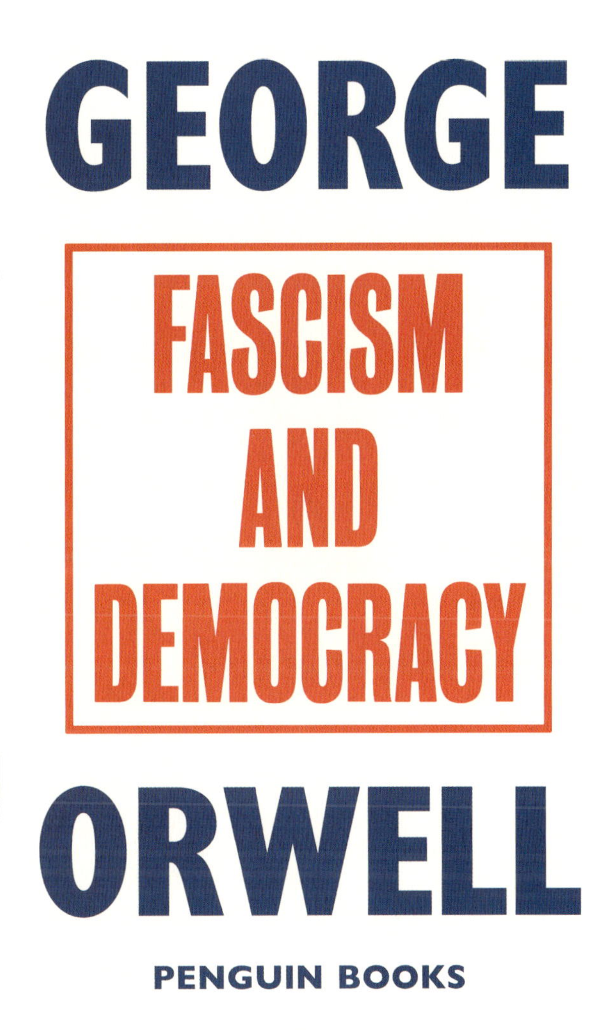

POLITICS AND THE ENGLISH LANGUAGE

SPECIFICATION
111 mm × 181 mm

BINDING & FINISHING
Paperback

PAPER
–

TYPEFACE
Caslon Great Primer Rounded

FASCISM AND DEMOCRACY

SPECIFICATION
111 mm × 181 mm

BINDING & FINISHING
Paperback

PAPER
–

TYPEFACE
Gill Sans Condensed Heavy, Heavy; Stephenson Blake Condensed Sans No.14

Book Design

Great Ideas

DESIGN
David Pearson

PUBLISHER
Penguin Books

SPECIFICATION
111 mm X 181 mm

BINDING & FINISHING
Paperback

PAPER
–

TYPEFACE
Hand lettering (B, D); Jimbo Black (F); Futura Black (G); Fifteen36 (H); Fulgora Negra (I); Antique No.6 Bold Italic, Garamond (J)

A.

B.

C.

D.

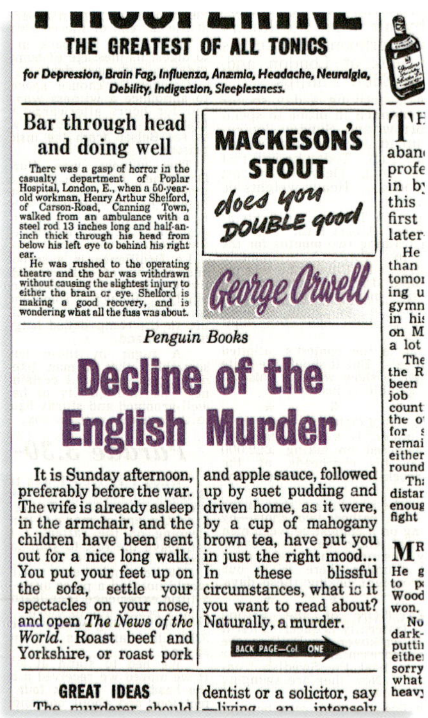

E.

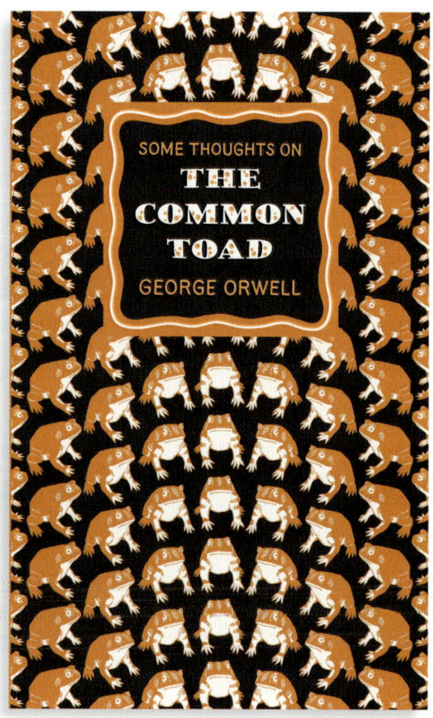

F.

The Great Ideas series included world-changing, influential titles of various topics. David designed or art directed some of the books in this series, which was a process bringing him creativity and solidifying his thinking of workflow. The challenge of designing the series was to develop a unique cover for each title but to keep them aligned with the whole series. It took the designer a lot of effort to discover the hidden information, but it was also fun to experience different topics at the same time.

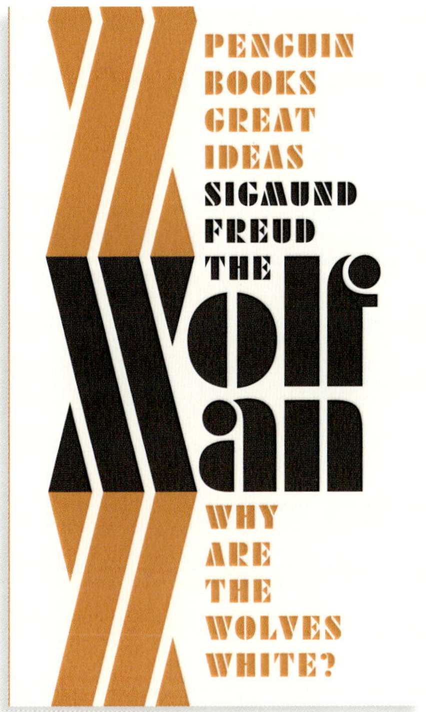

G.

H.

I.

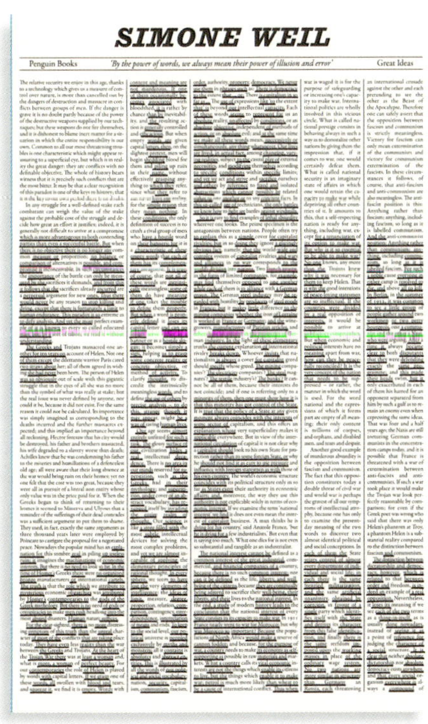

J.

GREAT IDEAS VOLUME III

A. BOOKS V. CIGARETTES

B. DAYS OF READING

C. NATURE

GREAT IDEAS VOLUME IV

D. AN APOLOGY FOR IDLERS

E. DECLINE OF THE ENGLISH MURDER

GREAT IDEAS VOLUME V

F. SOME THOUGHTS ON THE COMMON TOAD

G. THE 'WOLFMAN'

GREAT IDEAS VOLUME VI

H. ONE SWALLOW DOES NOT MAKE A SUMMER

I. THE FREEDOM TO BE FREE

J. THE POWER OF WORDS

Éditions Zulma

DESIGN
David Pearson

PUBLISHER
Éditions Zulma

SPECIFICATION
A-F. 125 mm × 190 mm
G. 115 mm × 175 mm
H. 140 mm × 210 mm

BINDING & FINISHING
Paperback

PAPER
–

TYPEFACE
Futura Meidum, Caslon, Caslon Italic

A.

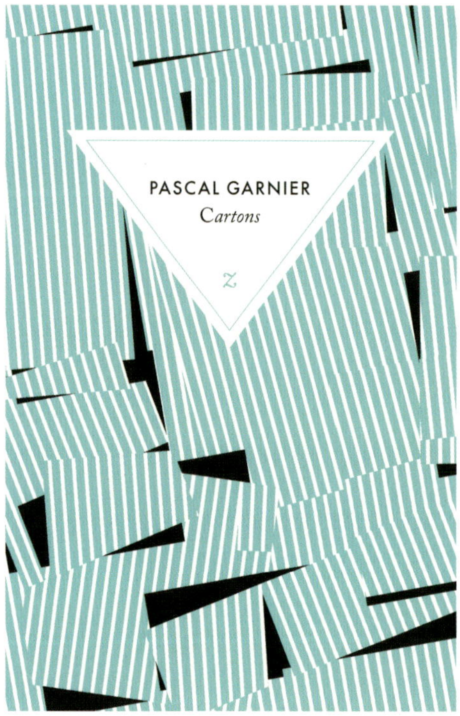

B.

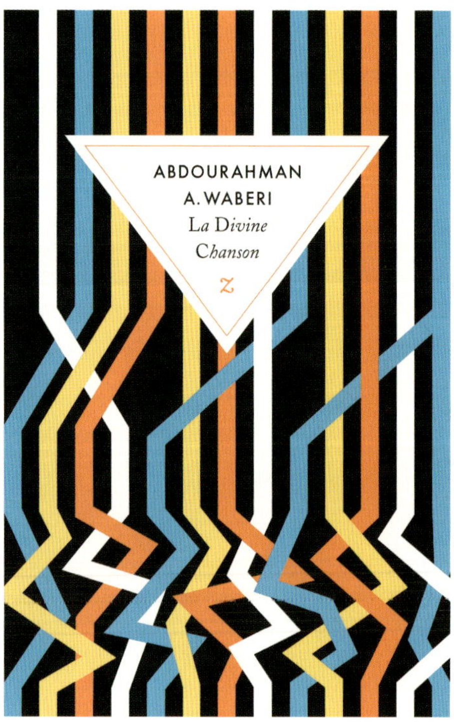

F.

G.

Having used fonts as the key visual element in his previous design, David turned to the power of colours and patterns for this French series. He grouped the author's name and the title neatly in a label-like triangular shape. The author's name is displayed in all-caps Futura and the book's title in Caslon Italic. Specifically, the initials of the book's title are in roman. Though the typefaces are different, they balance well and the title looks unified.

C.

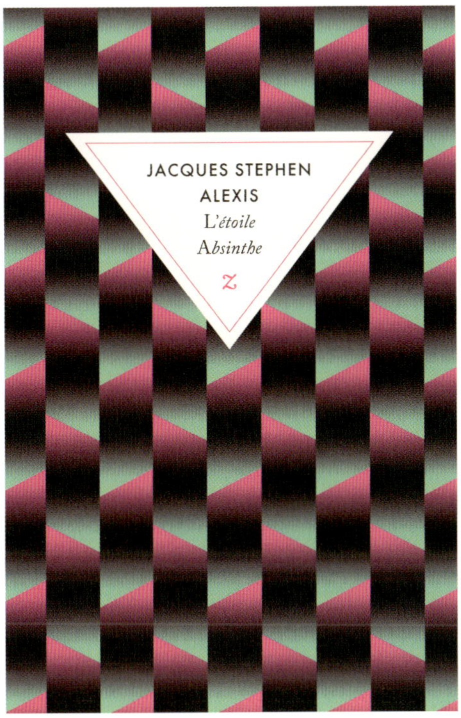

D.

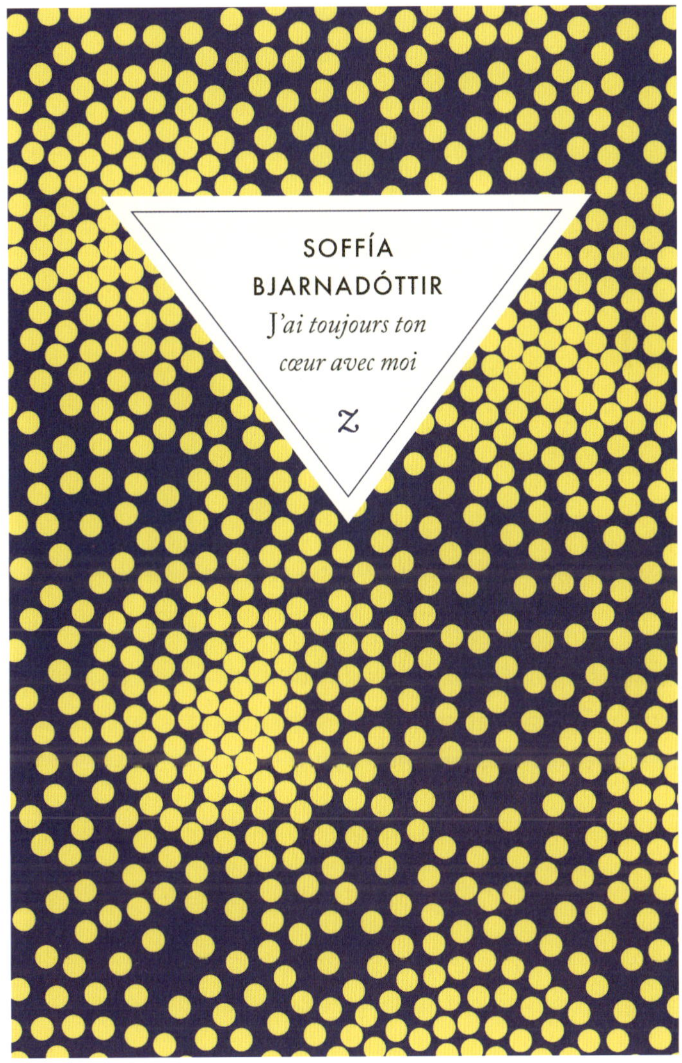

E.

H.

A. BY THE RIVERS OF BABYLON

B. CARTONS

C. FRIDAY ET FRIDAY

D. L'ÉTOILE ABSINTHE

E. J'AI TOUJOURS TON COEUR AVEC MOI

F. LA DIVINE CHANSON

G. LE MAÎTRE DU JUGEMENT DERNIER

H. MISS ISLANDE

Dtv Bibliothek

DESIGN
David Pearson

PUBLISHER
dtv Verlag

A. WENN TOREN AUS DER GESCHICHTE FALSCHE SCHLÜSSE ZIEHEN

B. ES KOMMT DARAUF AN, DIE WELT ZU VERÄNDERN

SPECIFICATION
126 mm × 196 mm

BINDING & FINISHING
Hardcover

PAPER
–

TYPEFACE
Neue Hass Unica Black

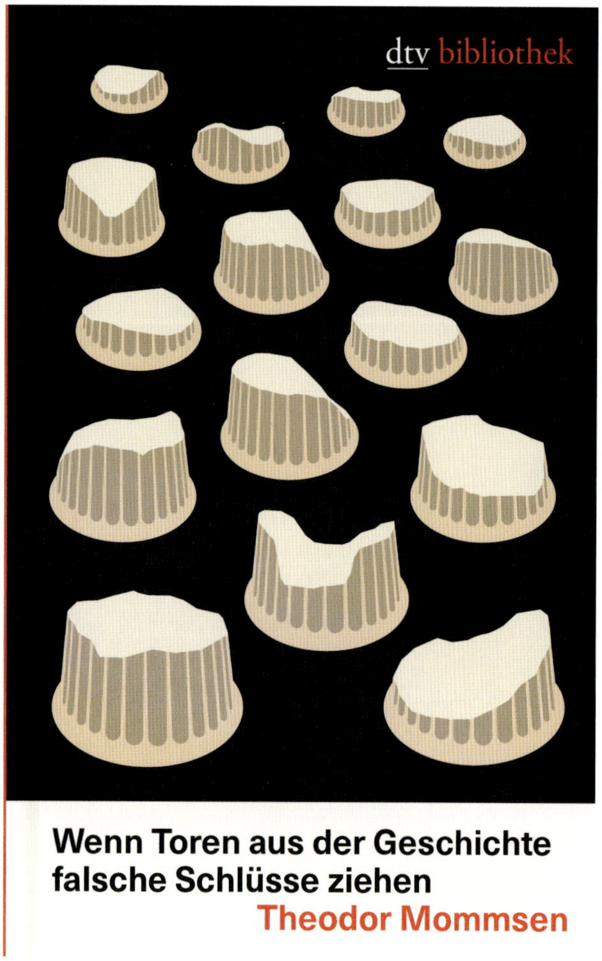

A.

B.

The Dtv Bibliothek series includes works and selections of works by influential authors. Theodor Mommsen was a German classical scholar and received the Nobel Prize in Literature in 1902 for his work *The history of Rome*. *Wenn Toren aus der Geschichte falsche Schlüsse ziehen* describes his life, work and time, and each text is accompanied by an explanatory preface. *Es kommt darauf an, die Welt zu verändern* is written by Karl Marx, chronologically recording his thought about selected text, including *The Communist Manifesto*.

01 ‘Avoiding well-worn tropes is essential if we are going to make books feel relevant today and have a place in our world tomorrow.’

We know that you learned typography from Phil Baines. What kind of influence does he have on you?

Phil has had a huge influence on my life, both personally and professionally, and continues to do so.

He taught me to be to an inquiring and detail-focussed designer but also, crucially, to never forget that this job should be fun.

His work creates such a pleasing effect. You are left with no questions when you see it, only a sense of ‘just so’ satisfaction (and often a wee bit of awe).

What influence does Penguin have on you?

Penguin has influenced me in more ways than I could communicate. I was a fan when I joined the company as an impressionable junior designer and learned from some of the best in the business while I was there. Many ‘Penguins’ remain close friends and as a freelancer the company has handed me some of my most enjoyable projects. And that’s in addition to the huge number of Penguin design heroes I have gathered over the years.

What does it mean to you to leave Penguin and set up your studio?

It can feel incredibly satisfying breaking out on your own but of course terrifying too. The trade-off is well worth it though and I take pride in managing all aspects of my business, even doing my accounts. It’s a level of autonomy that most creative people crave I think, especially as we grow in years. Also, not knowing where the next job is coming from – or what form it will take – keeps things endlessly fresh.

Which project are you most satisfied with and why?

I’m not sure I feel particularly satisfied with anything for long but when I look backwards I do feel good about the amount of work I’ve shared with other designers and illustrators. As a freelancer it can sometimes be hard to ‘share the wealth’ but I never regret doing so and have gotten to work alongside many of my heroes as a result.

I am proud of the fact that my cover for *Nineteen Eighty-Four* effectively made the title harder to read but was still well received. We are constantly told to make type more legible, but legibility is too often confused with communication (as David Carson once said) and this was one occasion where placing barriers in front of the readers actually aided their understanding.

Fonts and graphics, as visual languages, appear very often in your work. The concept is communicated mainly through fonts in the Great Ideas series, while graphics are used in the Éditions Zulma. Why?

It really depends on the stipulations outlined in the brief and on the tone the book sets but also the cultural requirements and tolerances of different markets. The brightly-coloured, abstract patterns of Zulma’s covers stand out in the French market because they are competing mainly with sparse-looking typographic covers and literal imagery. The Great Ideas series, on the other hand, is sparring with dialled-up, full-colour covers in the UK, so they benefit from their spartan appearance. So it’s a horses-for-courses approach that I adopt, or rather I am trying to find a different animal to put into a horse race!

Great Loves

DESIGN
David Pearson

PUBLISHER
Penguin Books

A. THE KREUTZER SONATA

B. THE VIRGIN AND THE GIPSY

C. A RUSSIAN AFFAIR

D. THE SEDUCER'S DIARY

SPECIFICATION
111 mm × 181 mm

BINDING & FINISHING
Paperback

PAPER
–

TYPEFACE
Gill Sans

A.

B.

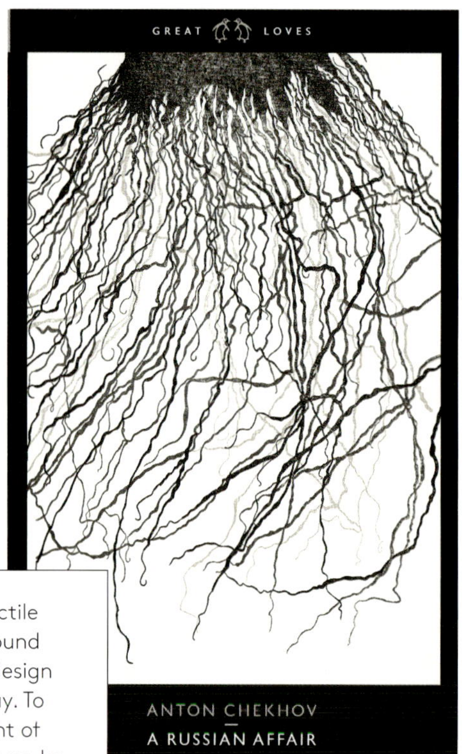

C.

D.

The books in this series have the same tactile appeal as the Great Ideas series. David found his inspiration in botany and decided to design the books in an abstract but symbolic way. To create the reminiscent images, he thought of using traditional printing methods. However, he then had to find a more realistic way to achieve similar effects due to budget limitations.

You have done cover designs for the Great Ideas series a couple of times. Is it challenging to keep each cover unique while maintaining the overall style?

It's the most enjoyable challenge: having to constantly switch gears to prevent people from tiring of the concept. This can sometimes be hard to achieve using such a limited palette, but the 'struggle' is endlessly enjoyable and my brain tends towards working this way: creating within a tight-turning circle.

In the sixth edition of Great Ideas, fonts are still the key visuals on the covers. Are these fonts tailor-made for each book? How do you manage to design a font that links closely to the book's content?

The vast majority use found type. I rarely have the confidence to think that I can do better myself. Generally speaking, I know my limits and understand that by bringing in the professionals, things will end so much better for me!

Speaking about 'reading a book by its cover', what elements are needed to make an outstanding cover?

It should have a thrillingly singular purpose. It can be quiet or loud, mysterious or explicit, but it should go about its business with an unswerving conviction that leaves me feeling both sick with envy and also elated to know that great commercial art can survive the publishing process.

Do you think your design has a specific style?

I try not to be conscious of any personal style, but I also know that I must have one. I attract work of a consistent nature (mainly backlist republishing) so other people must see that I am acclimatised to such work. It feels important to me to kick back at these expectations though. I can't be satisfied knowing that my next job is going to feel like the last.

Today, online publications are much more popular. What can a book designer do to improve print media in order to keep paper books alive and thriving?

We can do a lot worse than aiming for distinct work, fit for a particular purpose. Too much of publishing concerns itself with copying what already works rather than interrogating why it worked. Avoiding well-worn tropes is essential if we are going to make books feel relevant today and have a place in our world tomorrow.

Are there any book designers who you appreciate? Why?

Na Kim is doing really exciting work for FSG in the US. I am constantly amazed by her ability to regenerate as a designer, never leaning on past-proven styles (a more difficult task than you would imagine). Indeed, Na is more like an artist working within the field of design and her output is surprising and challenging in all the best ways.

BREEZE BLOWS TO THE PAGE, YOU READ

SPECIFICATION
218 mm × 353 mm, 472pp

BINDING & FINISHING
Paperback, saddle stitching, hot stamping, die cutting

PAPER
Munken paper

TYPEFACE
Ya Song by FounderType, Athelas

02 THE MASTERMIND BEHIND BOOKS

'I have issued a challenge for myself to design a portfolio different from theirs and from my works in the past. It is more about promising to myself to make the design different.'

Working as a book designer for more than 20 years, Liu Xiaoxiang, the founder of XXL Studio, distinguishes his book designs from other designers' and books in other languages through his pursue of reading experiences of books as well as his apt use of Chinese characters grid systems. He always aspires to create something different both from others and from his previous artwork, as you can see from his intention to deconstruct pages of *Breeze Blows to the Page, You Read* and to create an upside-down reading experience for *Design Changes Our Reading*.

Once a student dedicated to oil paintings, Xiaoxiang did not choose book design until he was inspired by an editorial design exhibition. His years in book design and the exchange with counterparts from all over the world made him aware that grid systems for Chinese characters should be developed because Chinese is unique in its shape and form. The feeling is the muse of designers, but Xiaoxiang owes the understanding of Chinese characters to rationality, which allows him to have an in-depth understanding of Chinese typesetting.

Said Xiaoxiang, 'Sometimes we think we have to be as innovative as possible, but there might be something we can inherit.' Though always striving for breakthroughs, Xiaoxiang pays tribute to the legacy of human achievement, for example, Eulidean geometry. These lasting and charming findings serve as the foundation of Xiaoxiang and his team's works, building up the proportional relationships within parts of the book.

When asked about the understanding of book design, this tradition-embracing but innovative designer is optimistic about the future of paper books, as he sees the book as a medium to offer readers a different experience. Comparing Chinese book design with that of the West, Xiaoxiang believes the Chinese book design field awaits both a change of designers' mindsets as well as that of the publishing industry.

Breeze Blows to the Page, You Read

DESIGN
XXL Studio

PUBLISHER
Hainan Press

This book is the selected works of the first China's Most Beautiful Travel Book Design Competition. The book's form is like a boat or a whale and the ripples they leave, which is inspired by the location of the selection and exhibition – Hainan Island. Photos of the spreads of the winning books build up the book. If the winning entry is awarded level A, it will be labelled 'A' in the book. Moreover, the selected spread number is also the book page number. For example, pages 26 and 27 of the winning books are also on pages 26 and 27 of this book. If these consecutive pages cannot fully show their design characteristics, then the rest of the pages will be distributed randomly throughout the book to deliver the concept of 'pages read by wind'.

SPECIFICATION
218 mm X 353 mm, 472pp

BINDING & FINISHING
Paperback, saddle stitching, hot stamping, die cutting

PAPER
Munken paper

TYPEFACE
Ya Song by FounderType, Athelas

Design Changes Our Reading

DESIGN
XXL Studio

PUBLISHER
Jiangsu Phoenix Fine Arts Publishing House

SPECIFICATION
171 mm X 257 mm, 336pp

BINDING & FINISHING
Bare spine

PAPER
–

TYPEFACE
–

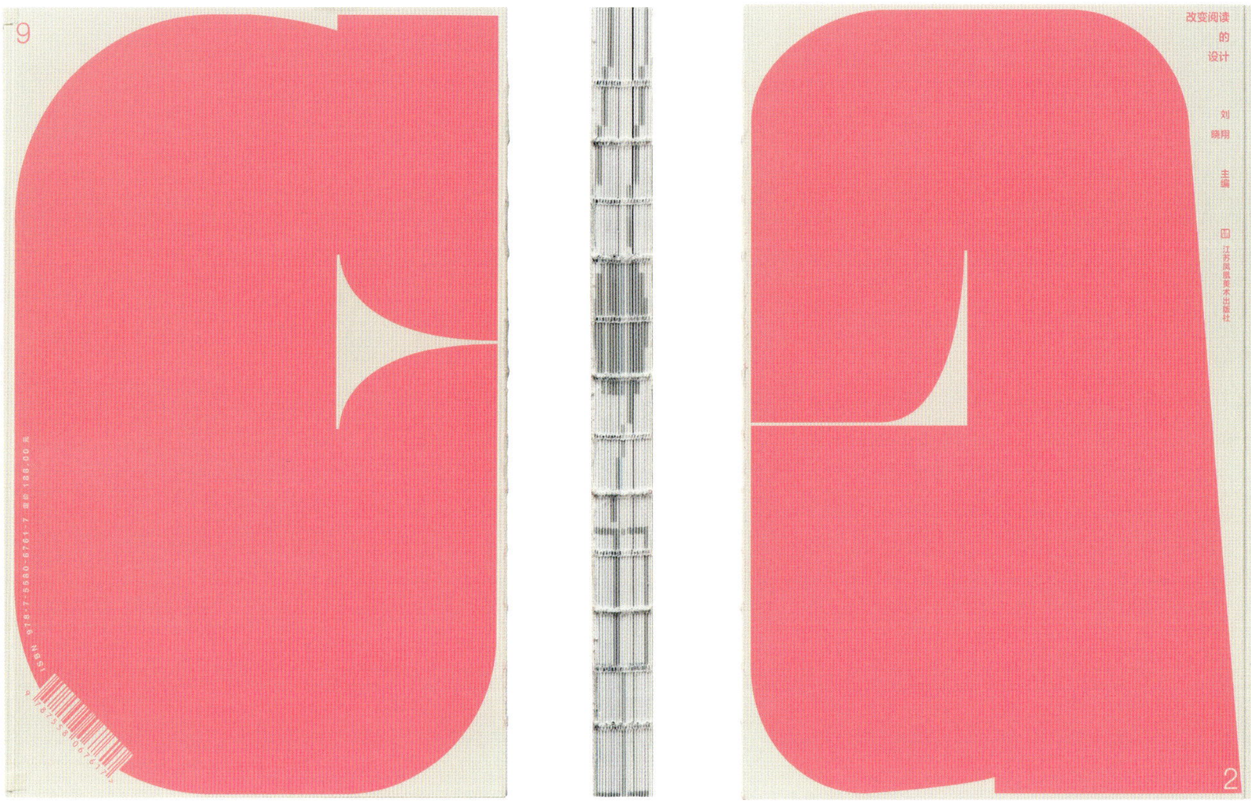

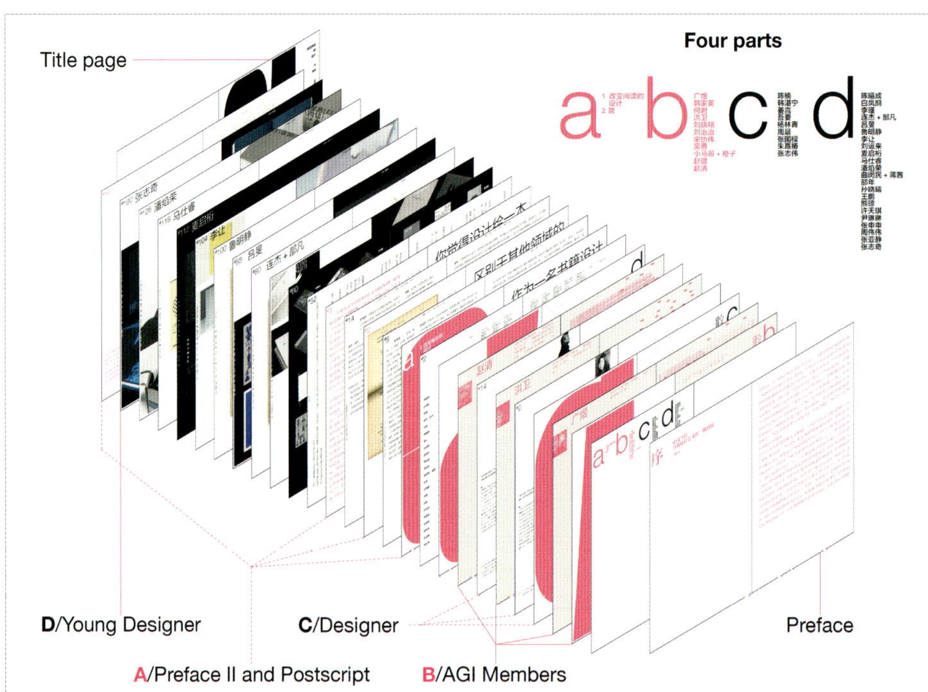

In this book, the designer tried to make the book more interesting to read with a different structure. The design intervenes and changes the linear reading by incidentally bringing some 'troubles' to the readers and asking them to do some finger movements. The book is divided into four sections and does not develop in linear logic. Instead, it is interspersed with flashbacks and fragments that make reading a suspenseful movie experience.

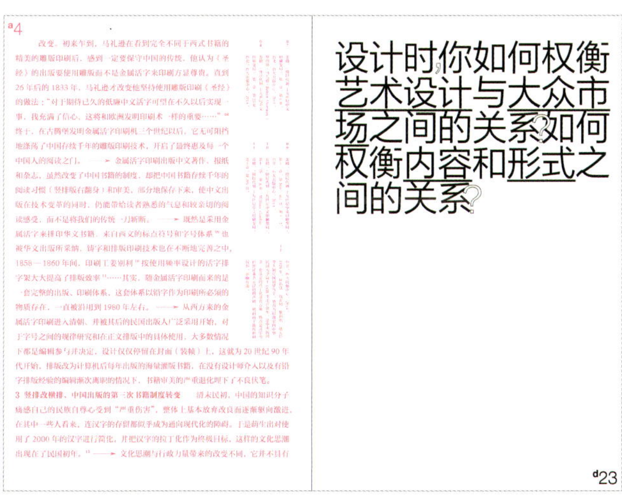

Book Design

Traditional Clothes of Beijing and Western Regions

DESIGN
XXL Studio

PUBLISHER
Beijing Yanshan Press

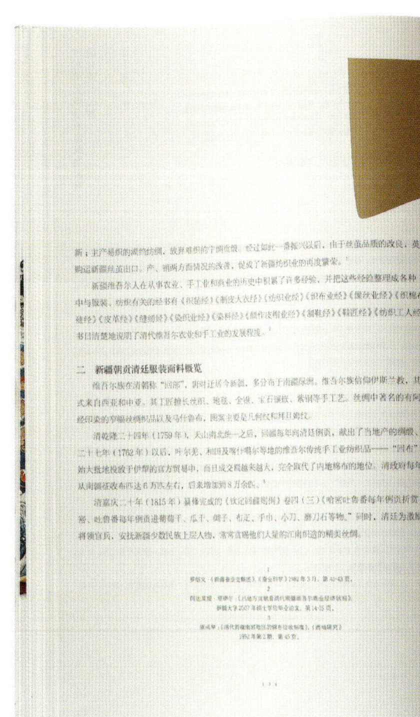

This book is about traditional clothes used in Beijing and in western regions from the time of Qing Dynasty to the Republic of China. The fine, thin paper conveys the elegance of the garments, and the irregular perforations and ribbon-tied binding give the book a soft and airy look. The combination of printing and hot stamping, the pearlescent title and the curves throughout the book bring out the features of 'brocade' and 'robe'. The elegant font and the neat layout of the interior make the book graceful and dynamic.

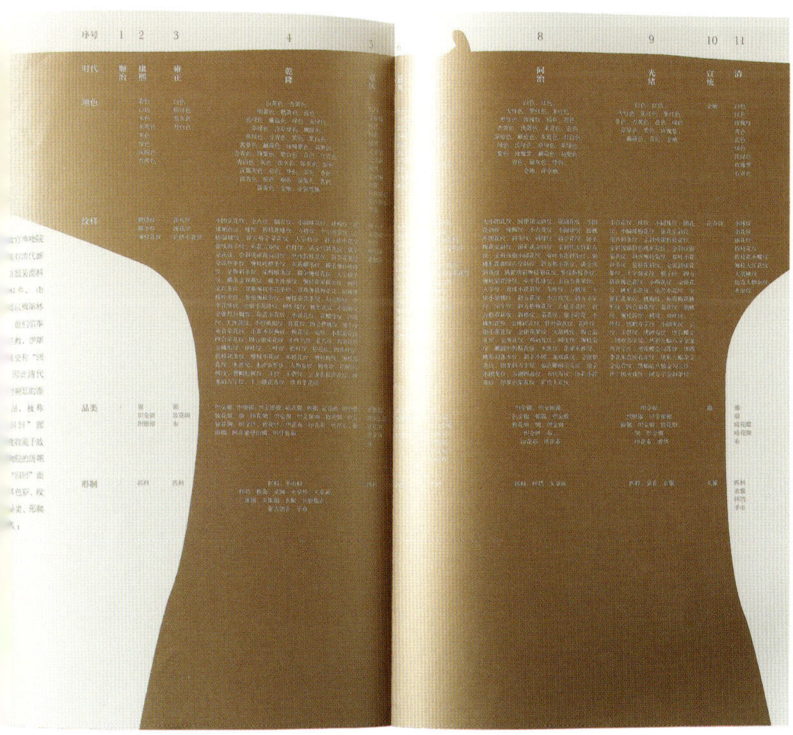

SPECIFICATION
214 mm X 312 mm, 172pp

BINDING & FINISHING
Saddle stitching, hot stamping, perforation, ribbon

PAPER
–

TYPEFACE
Song Yi by FounderType

William Shakespeare

DESIGN
XXL Studio

PUBLISHER
Yilin Press

SPECIFICATION
166.7 mm × 250 mm

BINDING & FINISHING
Round back hardcover, debossing, cobalt black hot stamping, edge printing

PAPER
Corrugated fiberboard, white fine cloth

TYPEFACE
New Shu Song, Song Yi by FounderType

This book is a collection of William Shakespeare's plays. Descriptions of the characters coming on and off the stage and the action stay daintily on the pages, bringing the readers into the reading of Shakespeare's plays and creating a theatre-like textual alignment. The format is set with a golden width-to-height ratio of 2:3 and the golden ratio is also applied throughout the design. The fonts are all from the 'Song' font family, so the text looks crisp and smooth. The poems are in 'Song Yi' by FounderType to bring its literary essence to light, while the librettos are in the contrasting slightly greyer 'New Shu Song'. 1/4 space is inserted after each character to create a drawn-out nature of the librettos.

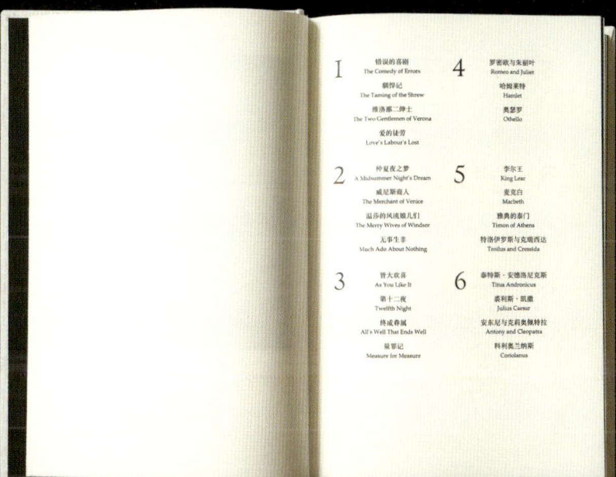

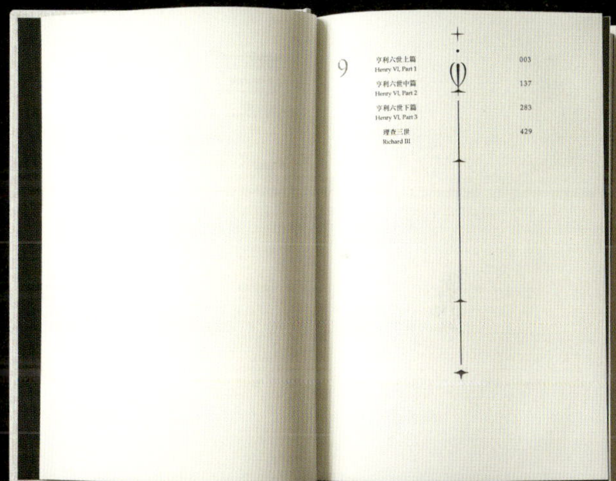

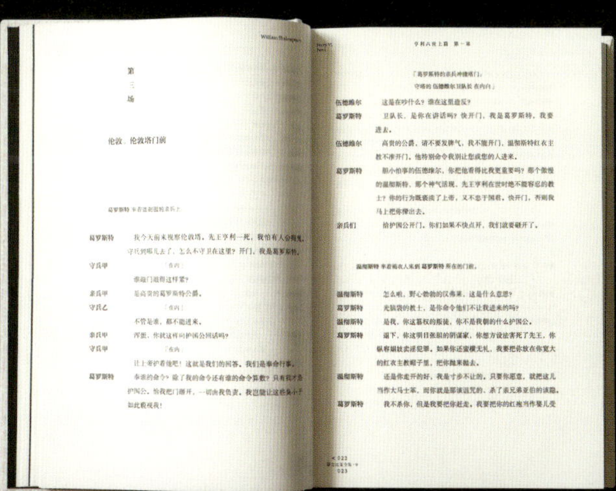

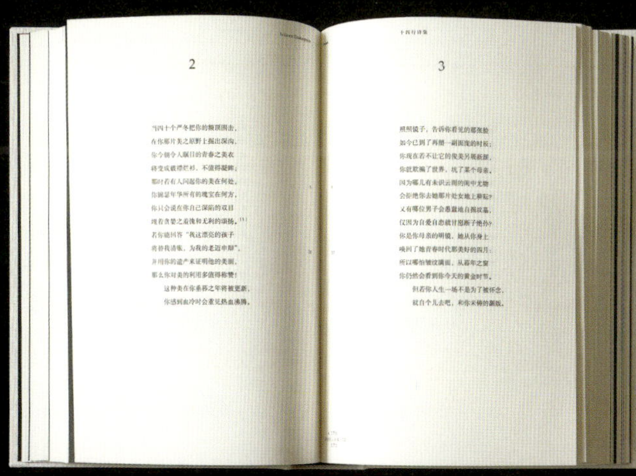

In All the Voices, I Only Listen to You

DESIGN
XXL Studio

PUBLISHER
CITIC Press Group

This book is a bilingual collection of poetry. The book is estimated to sell at an average price in the market. Despite the restriction of cost, the designer negotiated with the publishing house and author about the budget so that better printing techniques and paper were available to bring tactile appeal to the book.

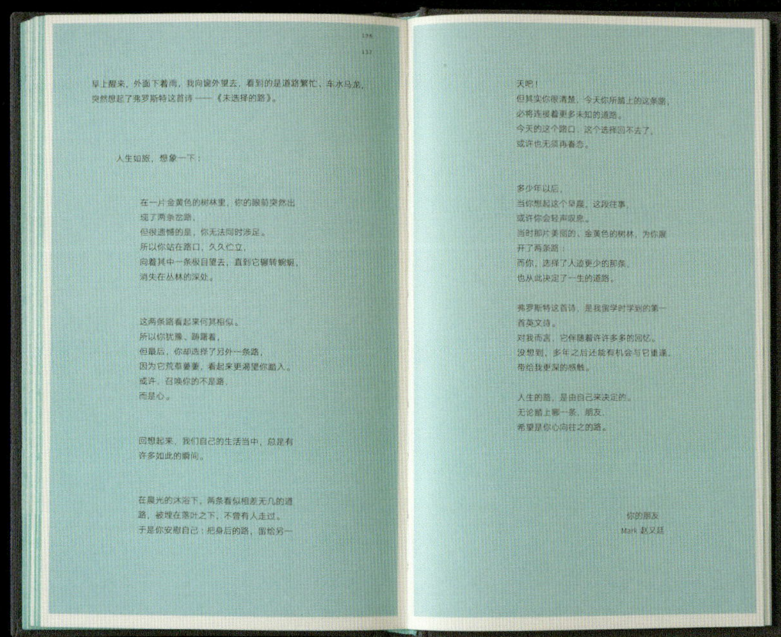

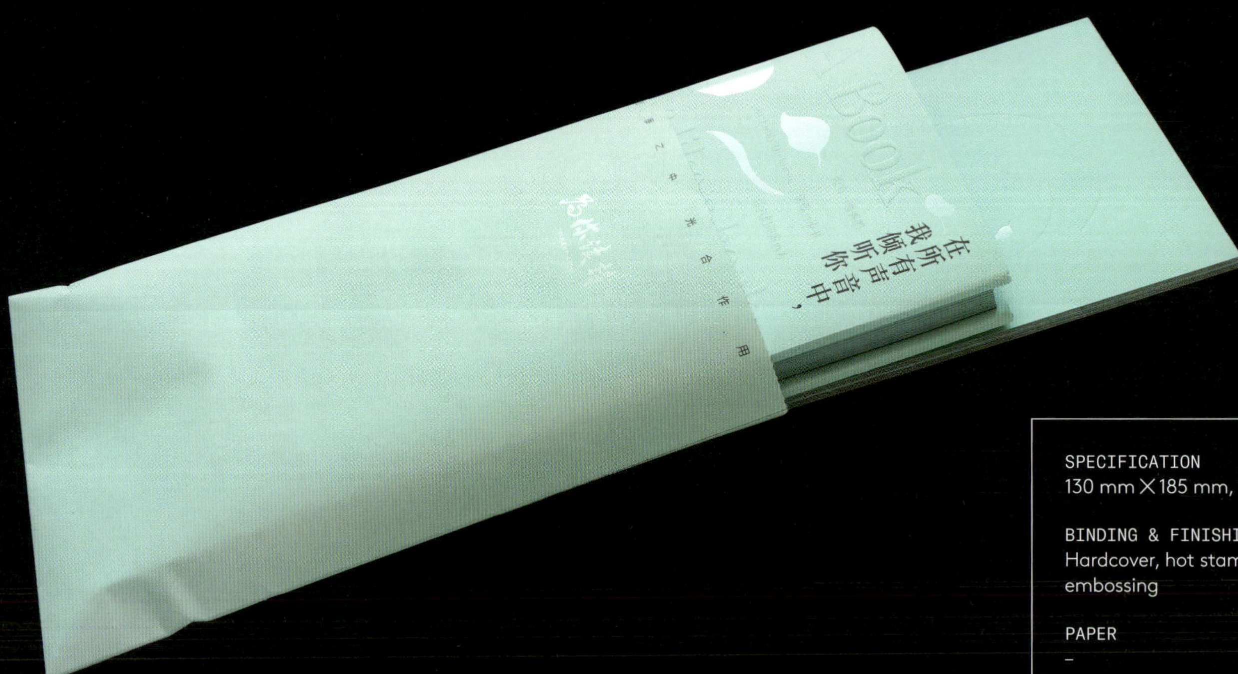

SPECIFICATION
130 mm × 185 mm, 160pp

BINDING & FINISHING
Hardcover, hot stamping, embossing

PAPER
–

TYPEFACE
Shu Song by FounderType

02

'Sometimes we think we have to be as innovative as possible, but there might be something we can inherit.'

Book design in China has gone from cover design to overall book design. What's your understanding of book design?

In an era where different kinds of media co-exist, book design will be more meaningful. We do not rely on the paper book as an exclusive carrier to read; we read on tablets, mobile phones and other new devices. This means paper books offer greater possibilities for designers to create. The core belief of book design in this changing era is to provide readers with different reading experiences which are completely different to those of other media. With this core belief, we make the books easier to read, have tactile appeal and provide features that are unique to a physical object.

Book design is a general concept. For example, to literature books, design is more about the binding, layout, the way we compose the text and images on a double-page spread and the way we arrange different elements. These are all considered book design.

When designing for literary works, how do you deliver the book's theme through the design language?

In addition to the textual language, other forms of languages are also needed in literary books. When designing covers and page margins, it is important to consider the design as a whole so that the literary book is appropriate and comfortable to read. Taking the book *William Shakespeare* as an example, the text area is set with the golden ratio. The text surrounded by wide margins is placed in the middle of the spread, bringing a sublime, dignified and fair visual sensation. Readers' sights will not drop to the ground when they read lines at the edges because the margins are wide and it looks like they are holding up the text.

In terms of fonts, I chose 'Shu Song' because I thought it was suitable for reading. For a book full of text, it is necessary to highlight the contrast between the whiteness of the paper and the blackness of the text and that between the weight of the characters, so that characters are clear to read. If a font is too thin, such as 'Bao Song' or ultra-light 'Song', it will be difficult for readers to read the text. Therefore, the weight of 'Song' makes it a perfect font for reading. I chose a font size of 10.5 points for this book.

Character spacing is also an important factor. It is actually put into consideration in the process of font design. A Chinese-language character does not take up 100% space of the frame, but between 85% and 97%. The remaining space is for spacing between characters. The best line spacing for reading Chinese is when the ratio between the character height and line spacing is 1:1. If we reduce the line spacing, the minimum should not be less than half the character height. Otherwise, a reader cannot read into the next line smoothly.

The principles for typesetting you have just mentioned is closely related to the grid system. Could you give young designers some suggestions about using the grids?

The Chinese characters in ancient books formed a very good layout for printed publications, but at that time the characters were printed with woodblocks. The features of the Chinese characters produce this magnificent layout. It requires rationality to have a thorough study of the features of the Chinese characters. Designing a book often involves rational analyses of the relationship between fonts and font sizes, and the issues of the font, font size, line spacing and character spacing we talked about [in the previous question]. These all are related to rationality.

Therefore, designers should pay attention to rationality in addition to feeling. I think this is a point that young designers should care more about.

How do you usually set the layout grid when you are typesetting Chinese?

Chinese-language books, like the literary works we mentioned, do not need complicated design. What is special about the grid system is that the richer the text style is and the more layers the text has, the better the grid system can handle [visual elements]. When it comes to the setting of the layout grid, one feature distinguishes the Chinese language from western languages is that the ratio of width to height of Chinese characters is 1:1 and that the character is based on the shape of a square.

The font size should not be set with millimetre. In InDesign, there is another unit of measurement called 'point', which is also known as 'pt'. The format can be set using millimetre as the unit of measurement, but the text area and column should be set with point instead of millimetre. If we set the text area with millimetre, it might cause a problem. For example, I need to typeset 30 characters on one line of the text area set with point. An issue arises when I can only arrange 29 characters per line if I change the setting from point to millimetre. This is because 'pt' and 'mm' are not equal measurements. In this case, I have to leave more space between characters, which will lead to the distorted spacing of the text and an impediment to legibility. To avoid this problem, we can set the layout directly with a character grid. It will turn out much better.

For text with complex styles, we have the basic value of minimum font size, and then we expand it into a system for all the font sizes. The relationship between them is important, which is the same as books in western languages. Some designers use the golden ratio 1.618 as a basic reference for setting font sizes. I introduced an architectural concept called 'module', which I incorporated into Chinese characters and call it 'module' too. If [the font size value of] two points is used as the module, I can then use 10 points because it is five times two points. When designing headings at all levels, if the subheading is set in 12 points, then higher-level headings can be set in 16 points, 24 points and 36 points. The characters are closely related to each other with this link.

Let's get back to designing and editing books. Many designers show their editorial mindset in their works. Do you think this is the trend?

I do not think this will be the trend, but I require myself to do so. I edited a few portfolios and I wanted to make each one different. Many foreign designers edit portfolios and they have their characteristics, so I have issued a challenge for myself to design a portfolio different from theirs and from my works in the past. It is more about promising to myself to make the design different.

In *Breeze Blows to the Page, You Read*, I combined the page numbers of the winning entries with the page numbers of this portfolio. If the winning entry is awarded level A, it will be labelled 'A' in the book. Meanwhile, the pages of the winning entries are not consecutive. If the selected spreads are page 10 and 11 and page 40 and 41 in the entry, they will have the same page numbers in the book. This is a way of deconstruction. I also wanted to make a difference in *Design Changes Our Reading*. We wanted to make the book most cost-effectively, so we devoted ourselves to create an entertaining structure. We predetermined the book's structure and wanted readers to read the book upside down. This is a different kind of reading experience.

As a designer, in what aspect of design work do you find the importance of having an editorial mindset?

Editorial thinking is very important for designers because it is about how to deconstruct a book visually. Ups and downs, the transitions and flatness, all these parts have to be presented visually. Without an editorial mindset, a designer will not have overall control of a book. On the one hand, it is also like an editorial idea. Designers are similar to the directors who control the plot, except that designers control the pages. Through the pages and the text, we sort out the logic of the book's visual presentation.

To us, The Beauty of Books in China award focuses more on form, whereas the Best Book Design from All Over the World award is more about the concept and design of the book. What do you think of the difference?

There is a gap between our design at this stage, whether it is book design or others, and countries that have gone through this stage. Including myself, we now focus too much on the form of the book and use too many materials and techniques. Books are commodities so there is pressure on costs. Another thing is the development of books, the attention to reading and the rational control of making a book, that is, how designers can combine their thoughts with that of the whole process of making books. Western designers have done a much better job than we have. That is why their books are basically good to read.

Secondly, they use the simplest techniques, but ours are not. This means that we have not yet entered that stage. However, it won't be too late because most publishers have become very concerned about cost over the last few years. We have to bridge the gap in thinking bit by bit, so being too lenient with designers is not beneficial to their growth. Though there is pressure on costs, we still have to do design. What designers should generally consider is how to do the best job at a low cost.

You have just talked about many aspects of making a book. Could you share your principles of book design? Why are they important?

Generally speaking, when our studio makes books, we pay special attention to the proportion of the format, that is, the proportion between the longer and the shorter sides of the format. We usually adjust the format as long as we get permission from our clients. I think this is the most basic aesthetics of a book. When you look at the book's format, you can see its beautiful proportional relationship. If you trace it back to its origins, you can trace it back to Euclid in Greece and Fibonacci sequence. These are what have influenced our lives to this day. Sometimes we think we have to be as innovative as possible, but there might be something we can inherit.

Generally speaking, I've always been consistent with focusing on the proportions, including those of the format, the text area's position on a page, and the relationship between different text styles. In short, my principle is basically about the format and the text area, and ultimately my principle is to focus on the proportional relationship.

FORMAFANTASMA CAMBIO

SPECIFICATION
210 mm × 280 mm, 192pp

BINDING & FINISHING
Paperback with dust jacket

PAPER
IGEPA Lessebo Design Natural 300gsm, IGEPA EOS 2.0 90gsm

TYPEFACE
–

03 THE MASTERMIND BEHIND BOOKS

'Any book I make is a further exploration of what a book is and can be, and how I see the design field today.'

Being the carrier of information, the book builds the bridge between the reader and the author. The book designer's priority is to disclose the book's information effectively. The Dutch book designer Joost Grootens goes beyond this, playing the role of communicator and further, questioning both the content and form to sustain the value of a physical book.

Trained as an architect, Joost did not choose book design until he had worked in different industries. The emergence of computers made his change of career easier. Because of this, Joost was able to teach himself and became a graphic designer. In book design Joost found his passion and strength, as said in his interview, 'I believe books are powerful information tools to empower readers.'

In book design, Joost benefits from his architectural background and excels at data visualisation. His acute understanding and analysis of a book's content serve to present complex and massive information. He manages to make the information become clear, straightforward yet delicate and informative through typographies, colours, paper, graphics, etc.

Be it an atlas, academic monograph or an artistic compilation, Joost can always find the right layout and format. Believing every type of book has a specific way of presentation, Joost's preference for typology helps him position, deconstruct and combine the book's typologies, which to him is fundamental in designing a book.

Although the heated discussion of e-books and paper books never stops, Joost is not insistent with paper books being the medium of information all the time. But in his mind, a book designer should create a book's long-lasting value and always think about the possible ways to design a book, as he said, 'Any book I make is a further exploration of what a book is and can be, and how I see the design field today.'

Book Design

Formafantasma Cambio

DESIGN
Studio Joost Grootens

PUBLISHER
Koenig Books and
Serpentine Galleries

SPECIFICATION
210 mm × 280 mm, 192pp

BINDING & FINISHING
Paperback with dust jacket

PAPER
IGEPA Lessebo Design Natural
300gsm, IGEPA EOS 2.0 90gsm

TYPEFACE
–

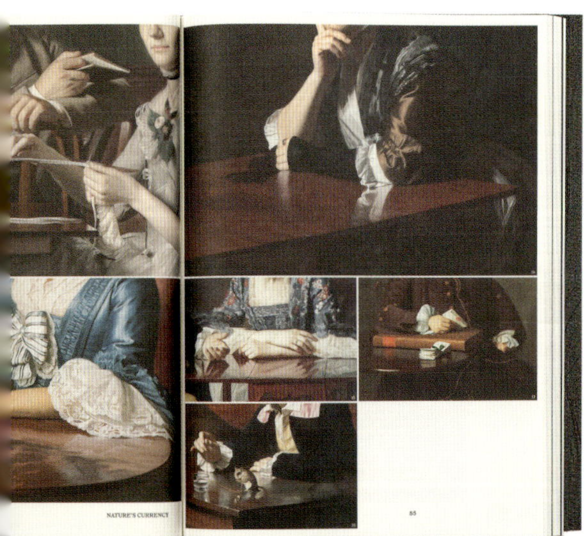

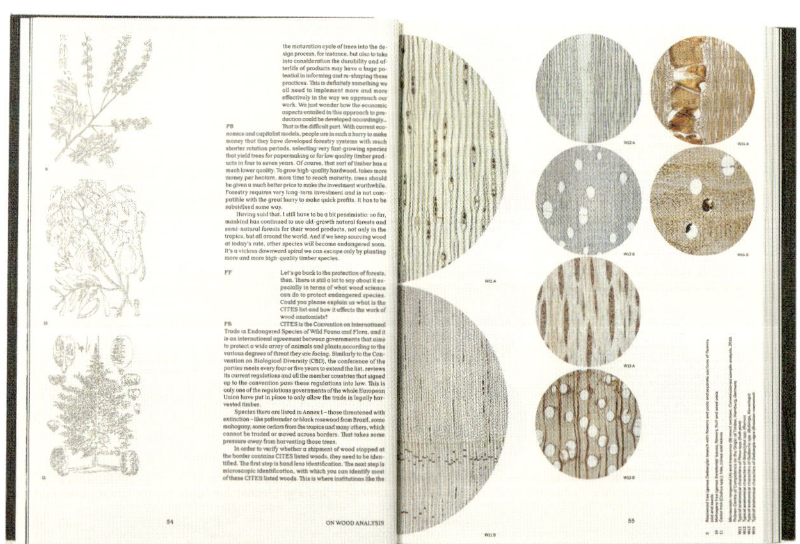

In this project, Formafantasma collected texts, interviews and visual materials from different fields, such as science, engineering, design etc. to trigger the thinking of what role design can play in transforming environmental awareness into actual responses. With this principle applied in the project, the paper used to make this book is not made from endangered species.

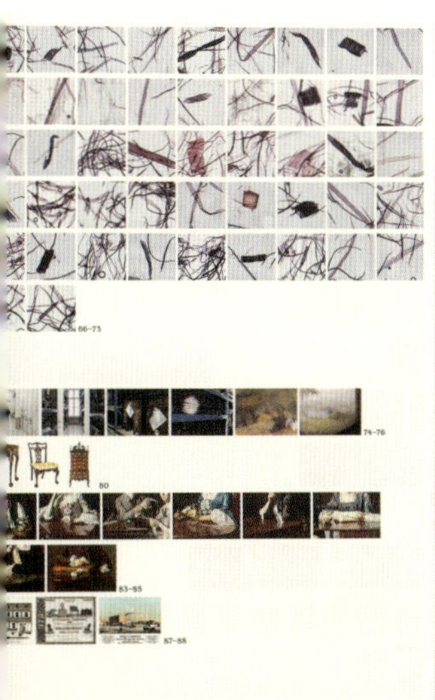

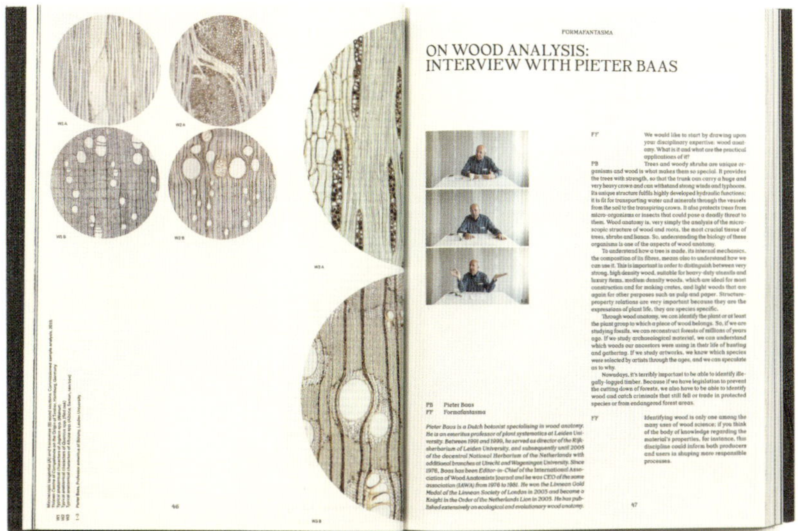

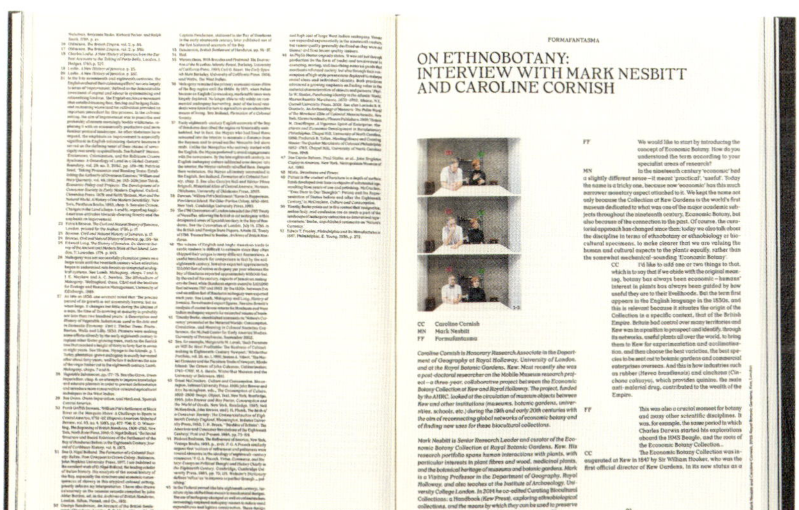

Book Design

The Academy of the Sublime

DESIGN
Studio Joost Grootens

PUBLISHER
Jap Sam Books

SPECIFICATION
215 mm × 280 mm, 192pp

BINDING & FINISHING
Paperback with dust jacket

PAPER
–

TYPEFACE
–

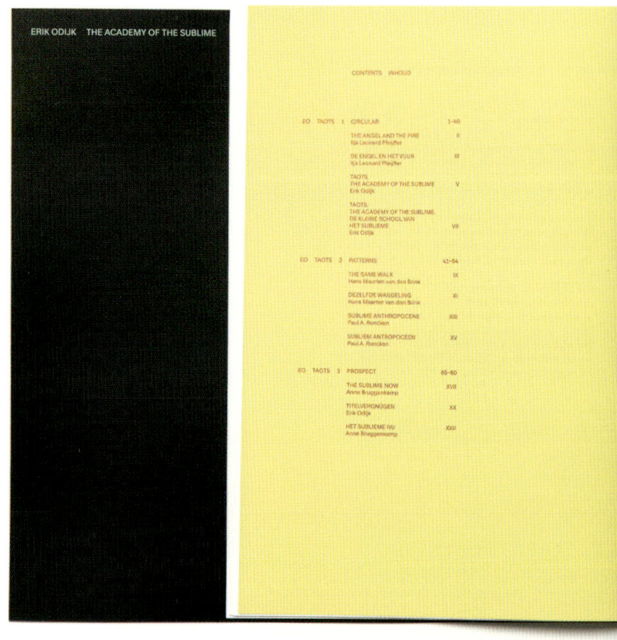

This book collects Erik Odijk's works from 2005 till now, presented in the form of three 'magazines'. This book illustrates the artist's works in three different disciplines. The magazines are in large format and the details of the work are highly visible, allowing readers to immerse into Odijk's works.

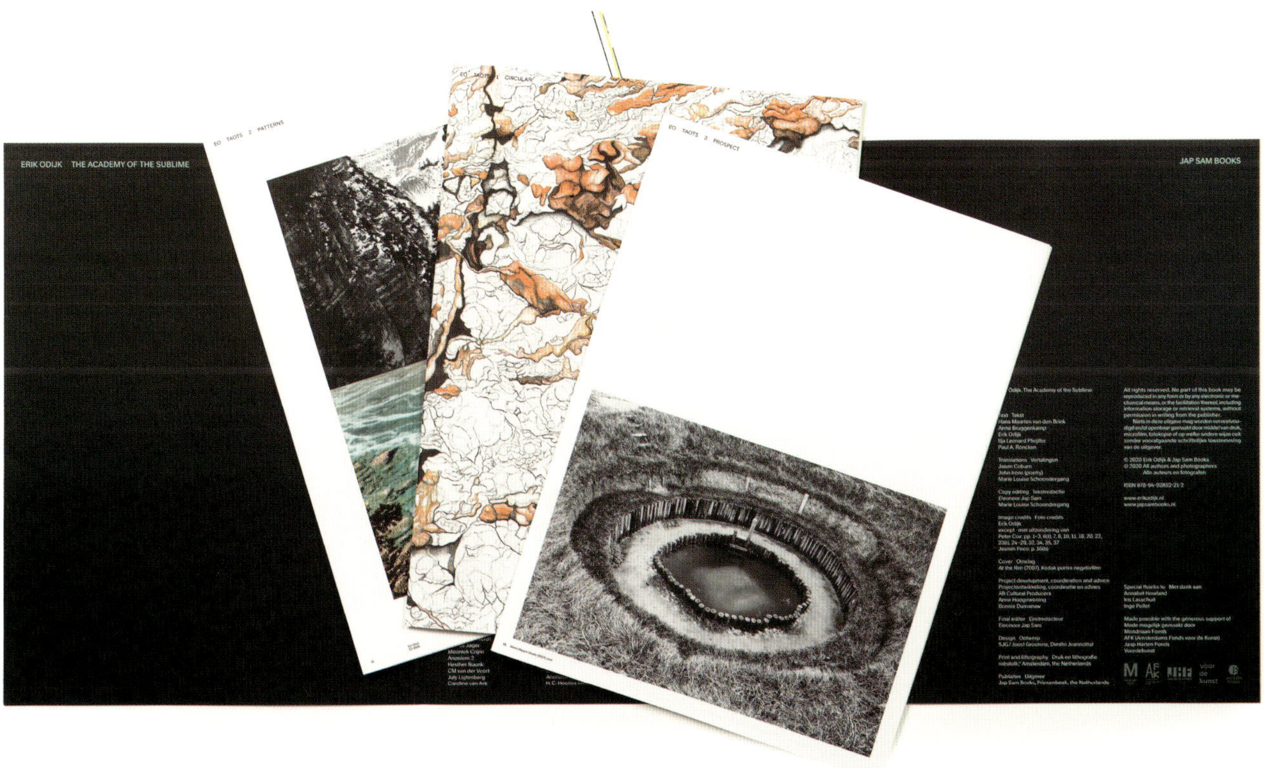

Blind Maps and Blue Dots

DESIGN
Studio Joost Grootens

PUBLISHER
Lars Müller Publishers

SPECIFICATION
300 mm X 320 mm, 192pp

BINDING & FINISHING
Paperback

PAPER
IGEPA Lessebo Design 1.3 300gsm,
IGEPA EOS 2.0 90gsm

TYPEFACE
–

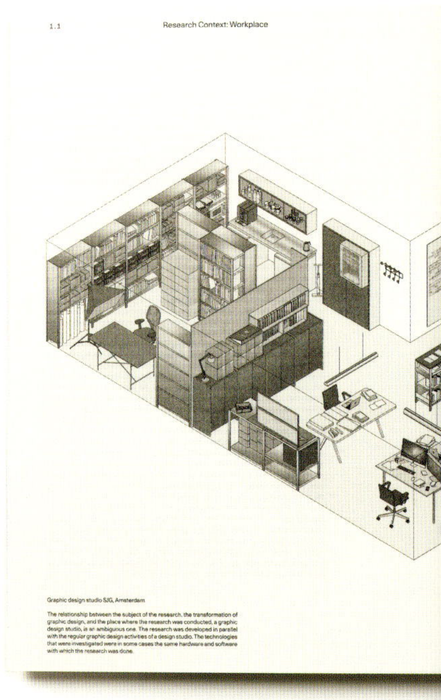

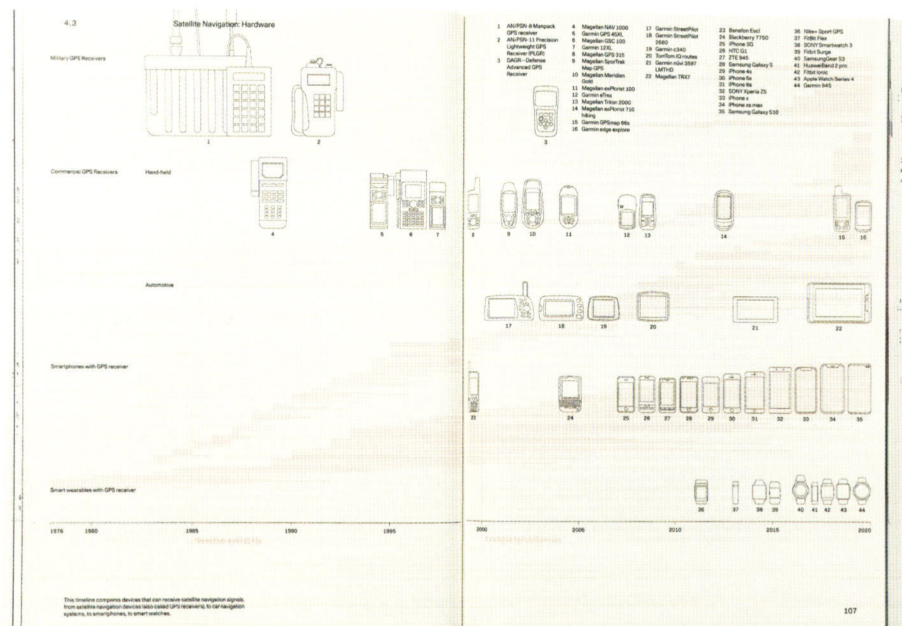

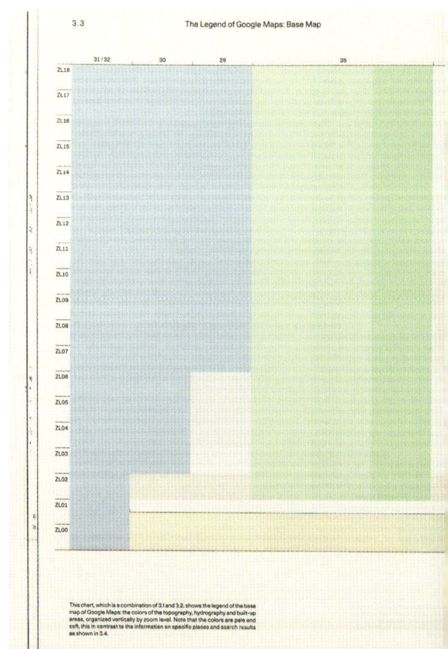

Blind Maps and Blue Dots is a work exploring the disappearing boundaries between producers and users of maps. Three mapmaking practices are used as examples, including the 'Blue Dot', a function in Google Maps; the 'Strava Global Heatmap', a map that records worldwide fitness activities; and the 'Situation in Syria' map, a map of the Syrian conflict. These maps show the blurring distinction between producing and using, and provide a brand-new method to graphic design.

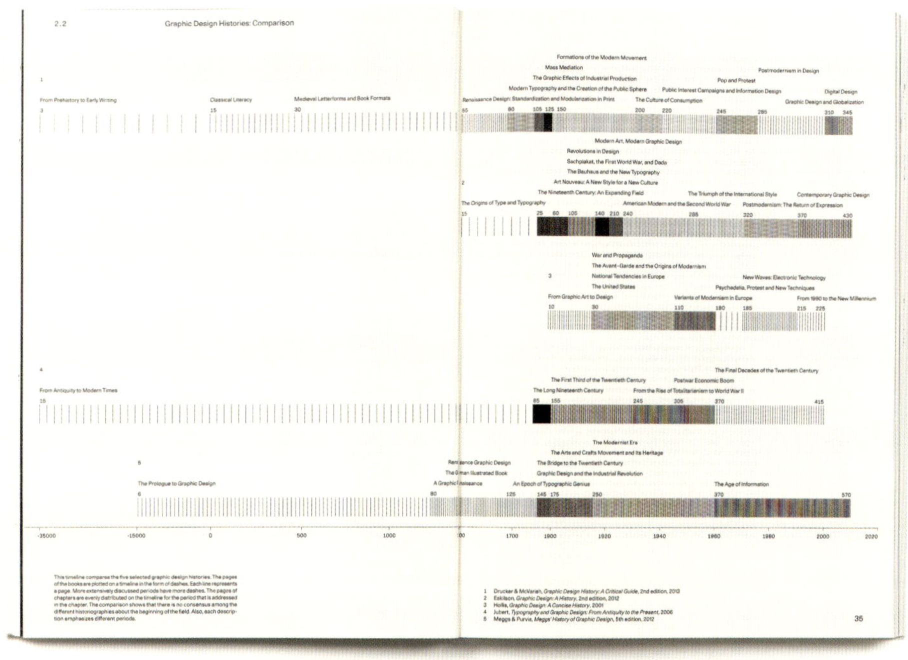

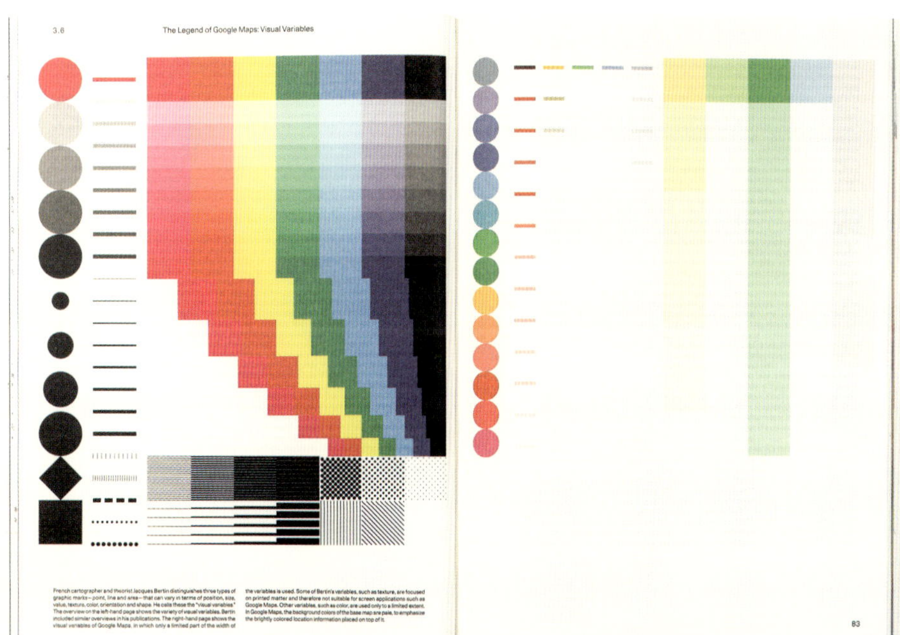

Parliaments of the European Union

DESIGN
Studio Joost Grootens

PUBLISHER
nai010 publishers

SPECIFICATION
300 mm × 375 mm, 272pp

BINDING & FINISHING
Hardcover

PAPER
-

TYPEFACE
-

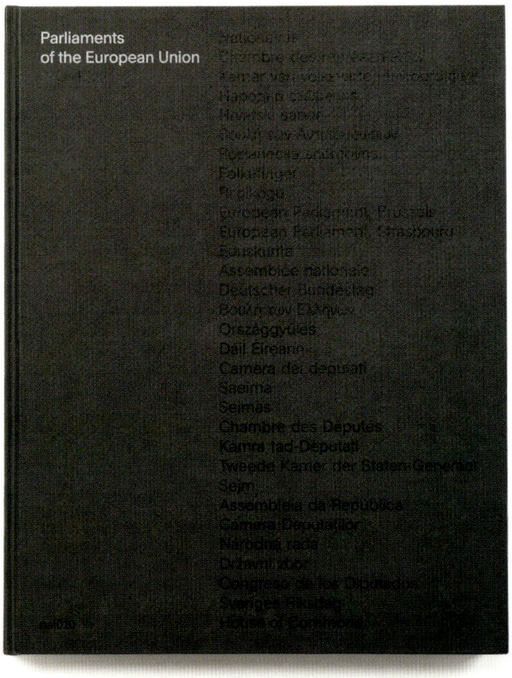

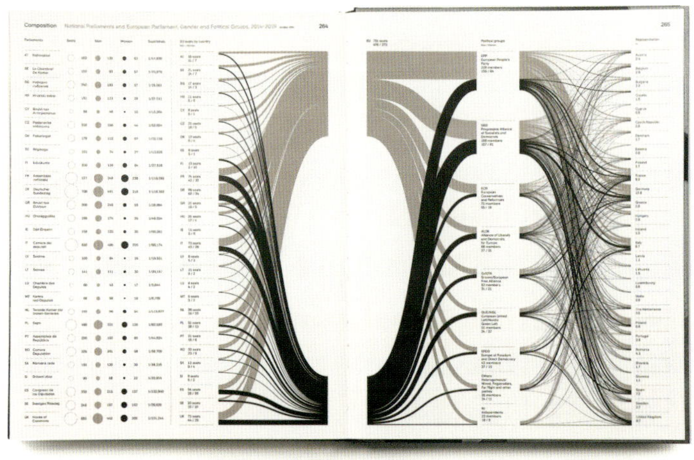

Photographs of the plenary chamber at European Union parliaments are included in the book. This project brings the democratic landscape of Europe and its relevance to light. The architecture, furniture, decoration, colour scheme, and light of parliaments radiate national traits in their way. The project's main goal is to make the readers feel like they are a part of the room.

03

'I believe books are powerful information tools to empower readers. To be such an effective information tool, a book does need to go beyond presenting a single narrative.'

You were trained as an architect first. Why did you choose to develop your career in book design? How does architectural thinking affect your way of doing book design?

From an early stage, I was always more interested in the representation of architecture, from how one presents ideas in the design phase to the representation of a finished building. Moving away from thinking about the building process, the thinking about the representation of ideas about buildings comes naturally.

I started to do graphic design in the mid-90s, a time when the computer had become the universal tool for many design fields. This made it easy for me to transition from architecture to graphic design. Furthermore, from a young age, I have been a lover and collector of books. It is design typology that I understand well, and still am extremely fascinated with. Architectural thinking still influences my work mainly in the process of zooming in and zooming out during my design process. I am constantly switching back and forth within the overall concept, [thinking about] materials, typographical details as well as how these two design scales influence each other.

What is the importance of information design on book design? What should we pay attention to when it comes to visualising data in a book?

I believe books are powerful information tools to empower readers. To be such an effective information tool, a book does need to go beyond presenting a single narrative. It needs to present data and information in a way that readers can discover their narratives. Information visualisations are a really great element for a book's type that leaves room for the reader.

Are there any principles that you have always followed when making a book? Why are they so important to you?

I do not have a fixed method or approach when making a book. First, I listen to the author as well as read and observe the contents to discover what role I need to play. In some books, I need to be a graphic janitor who cleans up the mess and make sure everything works smoothly. In other books, I need to play a more directive role and become an editorial designer first and foremost, someone who shapes the structure and presentation of the content.

From professional academic monographs to an artistic compilation, you have designed books of many different types. How do you decode a book's content and figure out the layout and format that fit the book?

I strongly believe in book typologies. There are certain types of books that have their own rules in size, materialisation, layout, typography, etc. Choosing the right typology and questioning it, or combining two typologies in one, is one of the most important decisions in my design process. Erik Odijk's *The Academy of the Sublime* is a deconstructed book. It questions the bound book and its limits to depict works grandly. And *Blind Maps and Blue Dots* is a combination of an academic dissertation and an atlas. *The Grand Projet* is an academic publication in which the visual argumentation of maps, diagrams and photographs is as important as the discursive text.

The Grand Projet

DESIGN
Studio Joost Grootens

PUBLISHER
nai010 publishers

SPECIFICATION
170 mm X 240 mm, 640pp

BINDING & FINISHING
Hardcover

PAPER
Fly 05 115gsm

TYPEFACE
–

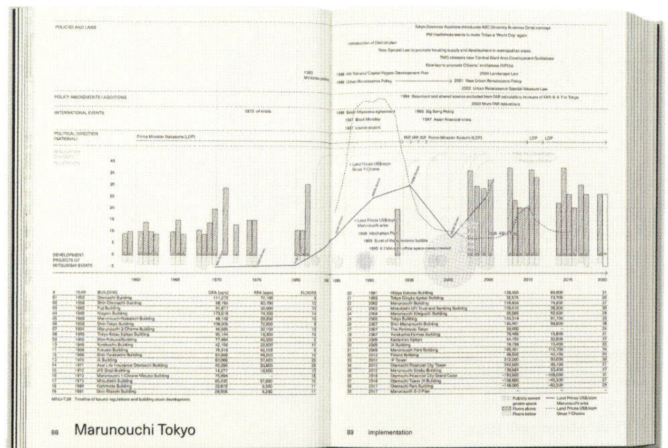

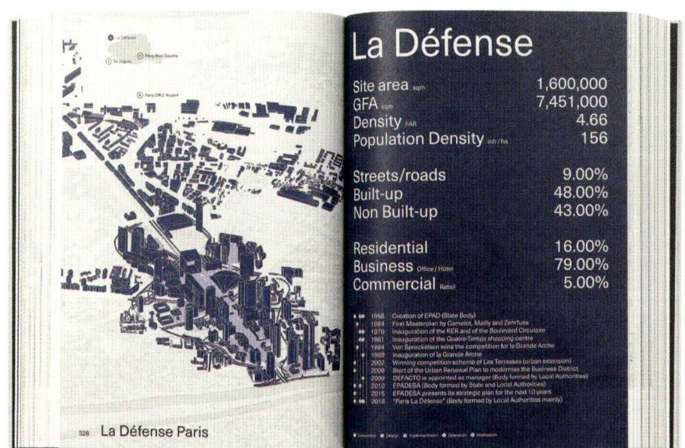

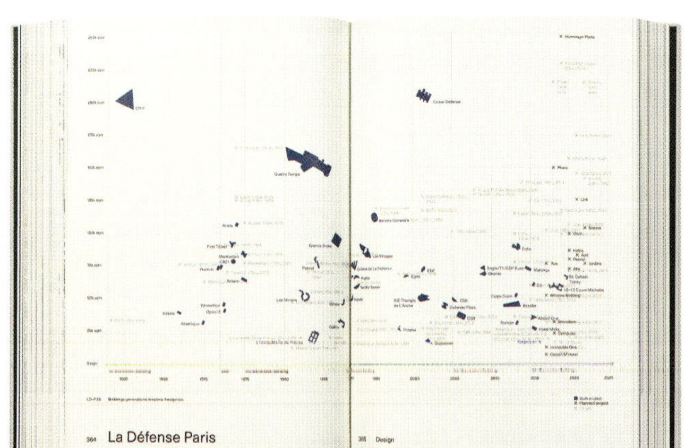

The Grand Projet investigates urban trends in a connected form of concentrated urbanisation all over the world. By featuring eight case studies from different continents, this book focuses on the capacities that urban megaprojects can bring to shape the cities' future.

The layout and finishes of *Formafantasma Cambio* are very attractive. How were the design decisions made? Please share with us the design concept of this book.

For *Formafantasma Cambio*, we wanted to combine the classic 19th-century botanical study book with contemporary design approaches, dealing with qualitative, quantitative and speculative research. This resulted, on the one hand, in typographical, material and visual choices that are rooted in previous book traditions, and on the other, in image indexes, a flexible image-and-text grid, big contrasts in sizes of pictures, and visual cues from the internet and other screen conventions.

Today, online publications are much more popular. What can a book designer do to improve print media and keep paper books alive and thriving?

Not every kind of information needs to be presented through printed matter. Many kinds of information work better on a screen where the information can be updated easily and users can interact with it.

When you choose to make a physical book, you use materials and energy to produce it. As a bookmaker, you should make the book of lasting value and be able to justify the consumption of resources in the production process. This should start with the understanding that a book is a physical object that offers readers time to concentrate. A book also has a physical lifespan often outlasting the subject matter. Therefore, the book needs to address the content on several levels.

On the first and second levels, it should disclose the information functionally and question the content at the same time, so the book remains conceptually valuable beyond the actual data. On a third level, book design is a statement about the book and book design. That is how I see it at least. Any book I make is a further exploration of what a book is and can be, and how I see the design field today.

What are some elements that make an effective book design? Any examples?

Book design is facilitating the communication process between authors and readers. That is the first level. A more critical dimension deals with the responsibility of a book designer, where book design needs to address societal issues like the ecological crisis, cultural prejudice, democracy, etc.

What advice would you give to young book designers?

To design a book well, you have to design it five times.

SPECIFICATION
185 mm × 260 mm, 860pp

BINDING & FINISHING
Section sewing, white and gold hot stamping, embossing

PAPER
Premium light paper (beige)

TYPEFACE
Yan Song, Bao Song by FounderType

04 THE MASTERMIND BEHIND BOOKS

'Over the years, my work has gradually returned to the basics through various design changes and form a more extreme, pure and powerful visual impression than before.'

Having worked in this field for a long time, Zhao Qing started to design books upon graduation and founded his design company Hanqingtang Design in 2000. Over the years, he has been thinking about and putting into practice the mindset of editorial design. To him, in the process of book design, 'designers become creators, for they have made the authors' ideas and their creative expressions come true, creating more value for the books with the authors.'

Born and raised in Nanjing, Zhao Qing traces the essence of his works back to this ancient and elegant city in the Jiangnan region. And yet Zhao Qing's book designs are not constrained to the abstract and loose eastern atmosphere. Instead, he regards design as rational and logical, developing the books with rigorous and modern visual language.

His two books *The Choice of Leipzig 2019–2004* and *Browse Leipzig 1991–2003* record the information of works awarded the Best Book Design from All Over the World with rigour and ingenuity in editorial and design languages. The idea of designing and editing these two books came to him because to him, people should enjoy the beauty of these books and not be hindered by time and space.

While thinking logically and rationally as a designer, Zhao Qing designs books with his sensitivity to art and beauty. His understanding of eastern philosophy and aesthetics help him to feel and deconstruct the books about the East, and design the work with expressive techniques as well as modern design thinking, as in *Infinite Blooming*. In his advice to young designers in the field of book design, he also talked about the understanding of traditional eastern books and the western grid systems. But ultimately, he said, 'Young designers should absorb and digest the essence and then deconstruct these two systems to form their unique styles.'

Infinite Blooming

DESIGN
Hanqingtang Design

PUBLISHER
Phoenix Science Press

SPECIFICATION
185 mm × 260 mm, 860pp

BINDING & FINISHING
Section sewing, white and gold hot stamping, embossing

PAPER
Premium light paper (beige)

TYPEFACE
Yan Song, Bao Song by FounderType

This is a book about botanical art painting. The cover is in green, symbolising the 'heart of grass and wood' simply and naturally. The stamped star-shaped dots and embossed patterns on the cover are like the character ' 卉 (hui)' and the dense plants' veins, showcasing the glamour of Chinese art. To present an abundant and lively manuscript, the seemingly scattered layout is built on a rigorous grid system and helps to present the diverse selected paintings. In the inner pages, the pictures are arranged in the order of the plant system to record the unique plants in China.

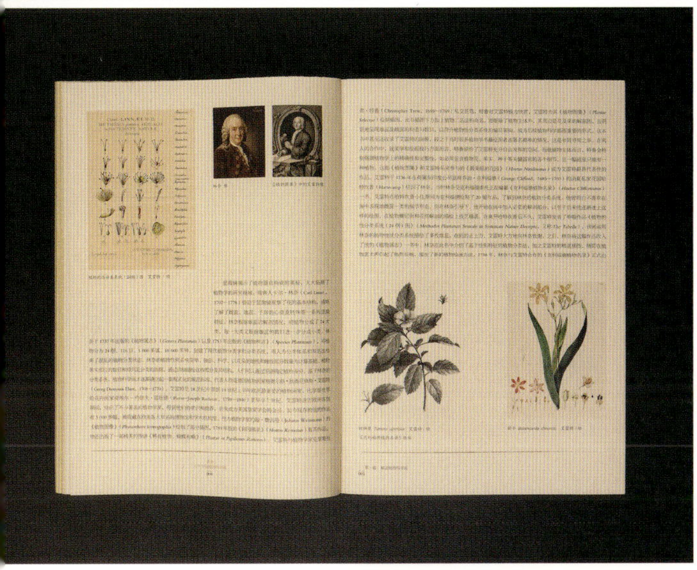

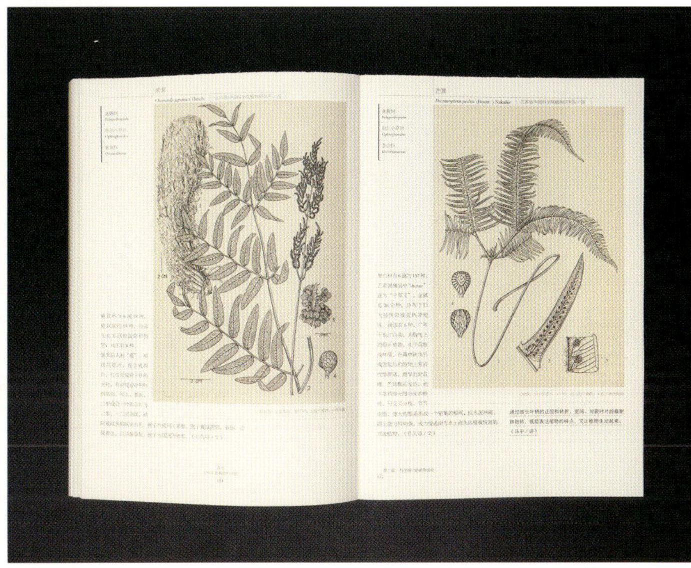

Facing the Sea, Flowers Blossom in Warm Spring

DESIGN
Hanqingtang Design

PUBLISHER
Jiangsu Phoenix Literature
and Art Publishing, Ltd

On one side of the leaf is Hai Zi's poem, and on the other, the illustration of Wei Erqiao. On one hand, it is the eulogy on life, on the other the meditation on death. This book combines the best works of two talented men who died young. The orange colour of sunlight, wheat fields, grains and oranges represents Hai Zi, while the white colour of paleness, hospitals, depression and loneliness speaks for Wei Erqiao. When the two meet, they fall into the buff-coloured land. They ponder life. The design examines them. They love life.

SPECIFICATION
128 mm × 188 mm, 272pp

BINDING & FINISHING
Sewn binding, embossing, white hot stamping

PAPER
Japanese poster paper

TYPEFACE
Fang Song

The Choice of Leipzig 2019-2004

DESIGN
Hanqingtang Design

PUBLISHER
Jiangsu Phoenix Fine Arts Publishing House

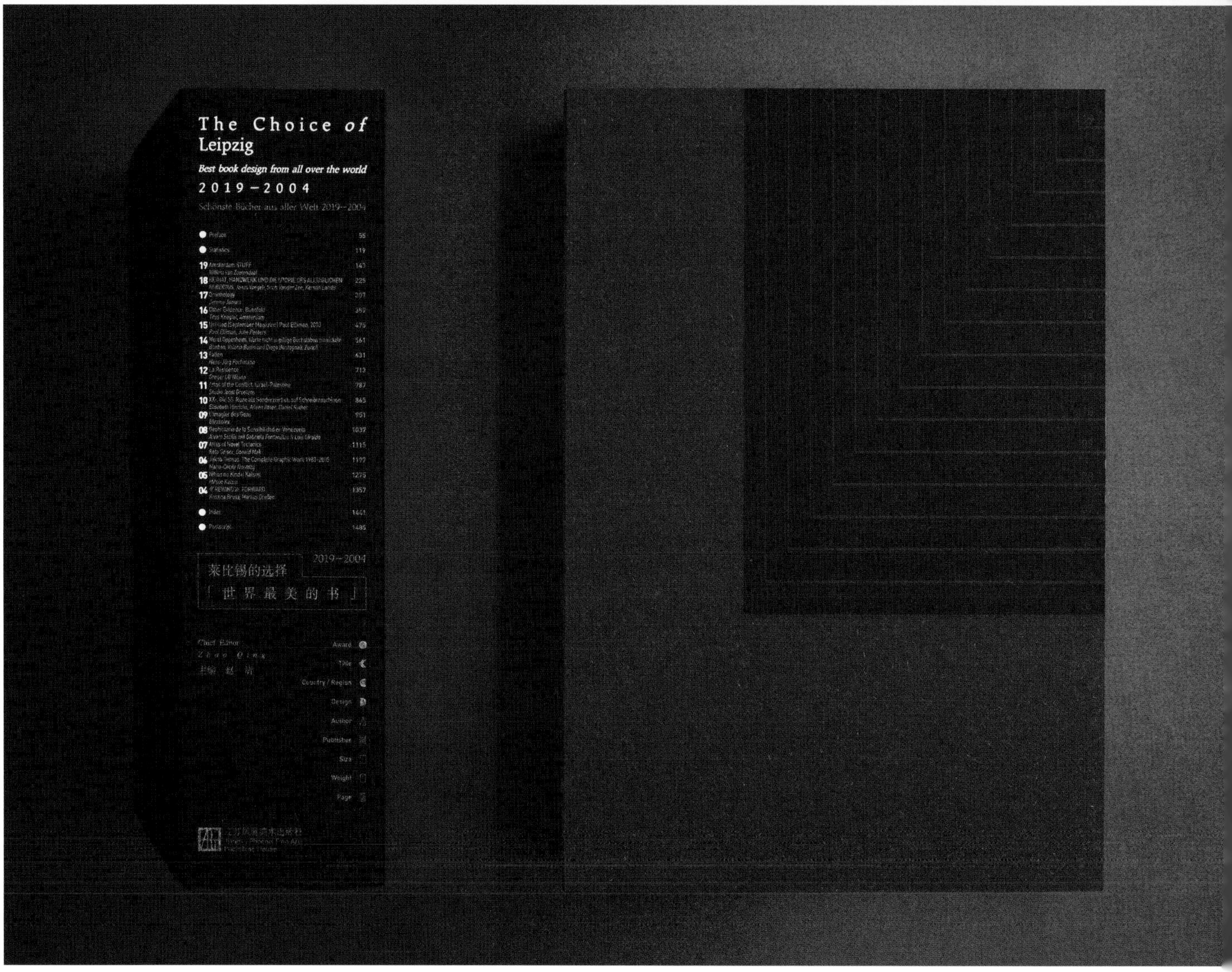

The Choice of Leipzig 2019-2004 collects the 14 books awarded Best Book Design from All Over the World every year from 2004 to 2019. The book contains 1510 pages of detailed information on the winning countries, authors and designers, awards, books' format, weight, commentaries and so on. In addition to the content, the book also analyses and compares the information, data and layout details of all the award-winning books diachronically and synchronically, presenting them through graphics. The horizontal line on the front cover extending to the fore-edge of the book provides a quick search guide. At the back of the book, there is an index organised by award-winning categories. The book is like a statistical dictionary of Best Book Design, with professional data display, prudent and logical layout and concise introduction.

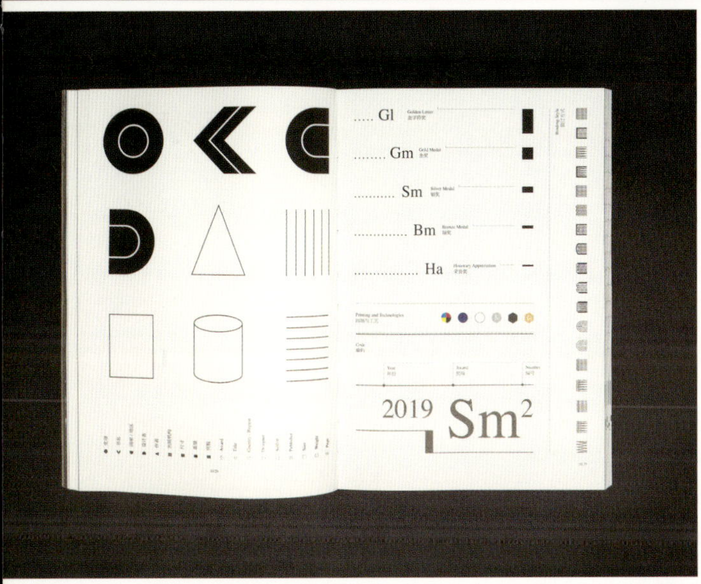

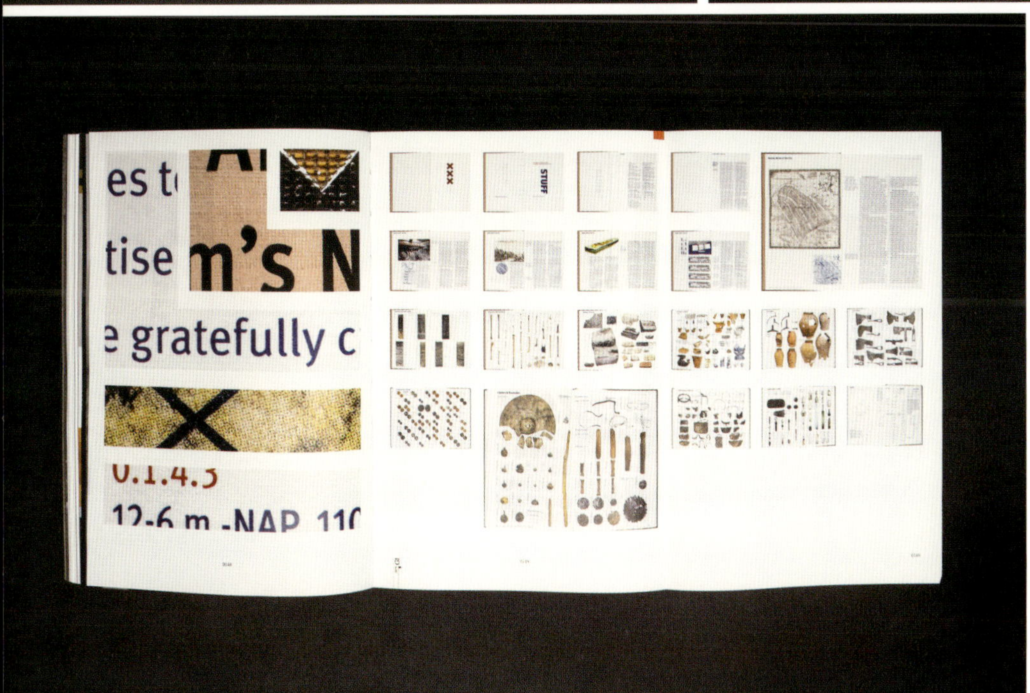

SPECIFICATION
140 mm × 210 mm, 1500pp

BINDING & FINISHING
Section sewing, gold hot stamping, black hot stamping, embossing

PAPER
Nailiang Haoyin

TYPEFACE
Shu Song, Antiqua of Friendship by FounderType

Browse Leipzig 1991-2003

DESIGN
Hanqingtang Design

PUBLISHER
Jiangsu Phoenix Fine Arts Publishing House

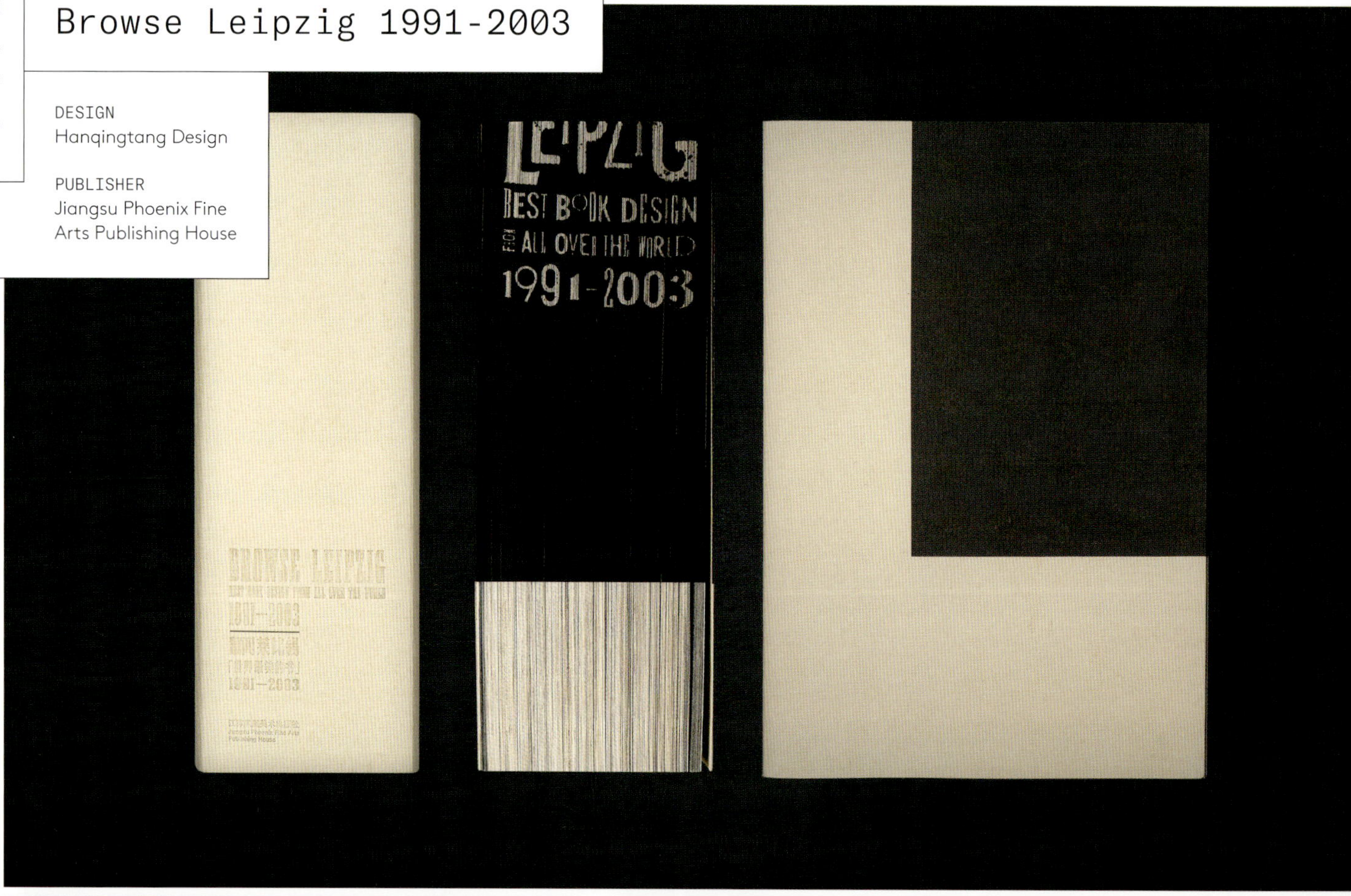

SPECIFICATION
140 mm X 210 mm, 1300pp

BINDING & FINISHING
Section sewing, embossing, black edge printing

PAPER
Munken paper

TYPEFACE
Shu Song, Antiqua of Friendship by FounderType

Browse Leipzig 1991-2003 contains most of the books awarded Best Book Design from All Over the World from 1991 to 2003 in over a thousand red and black pages in both English and Chinese. The book includes the pictures of book packages from around the world, the data for each book as well as extensive details of inner page layouts. It is a prequel to *The Choice of Leipzig 2019-2004*, piecing together the origin of the best book design and commemorating Leipzig's choice systematically.

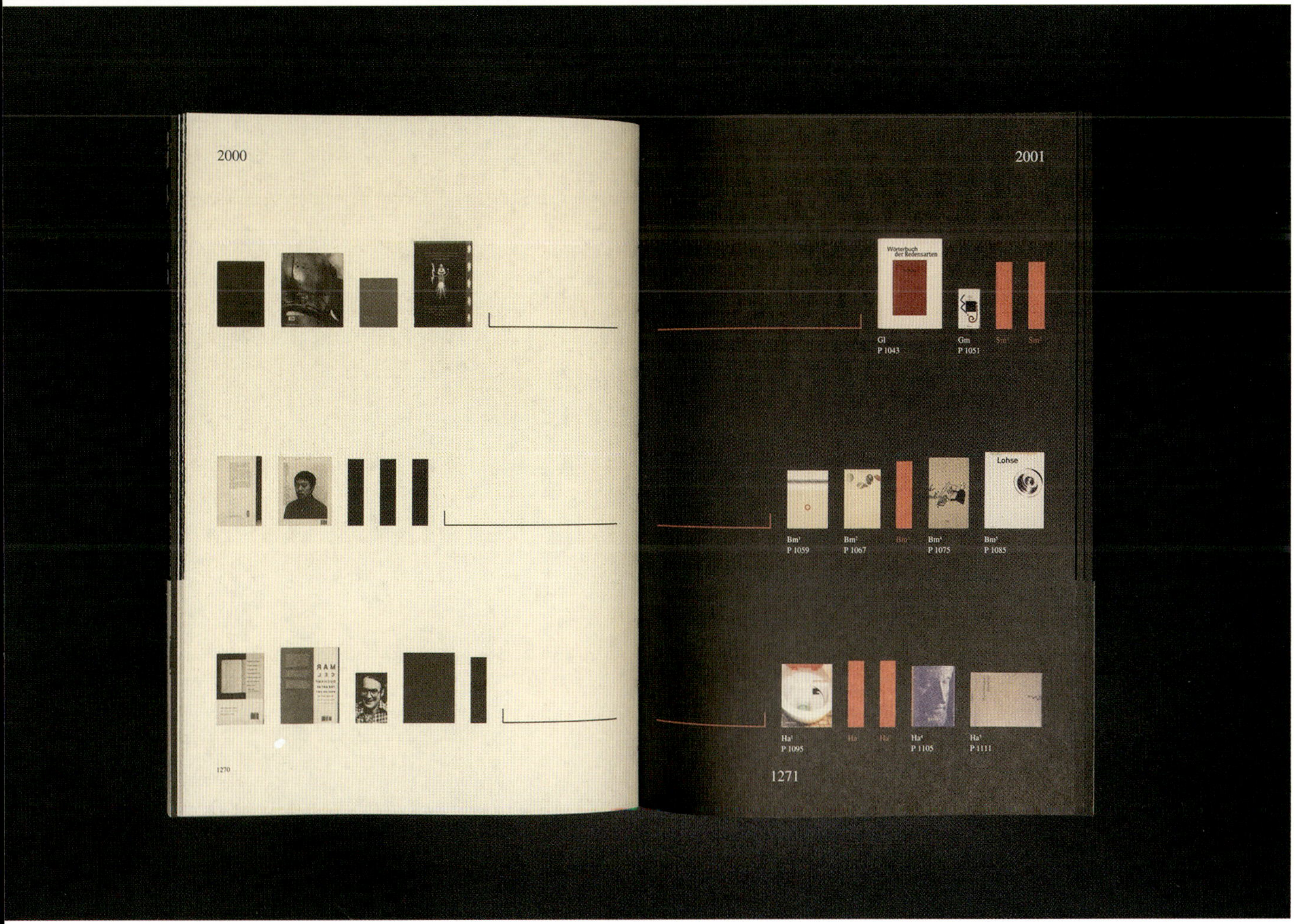

Li·Detach He·Attach

DESIGN
Hanqingtang Design

PUBLISHER
China Architecture Publishing

SPECIFICATION
280 mm × 280 mm, 570pp

BINDING & FINISHING
Section sewing, bare spine, die cutting

PAPER
Newsprint

TYPEFACE
Lantinghei Light by FounderType

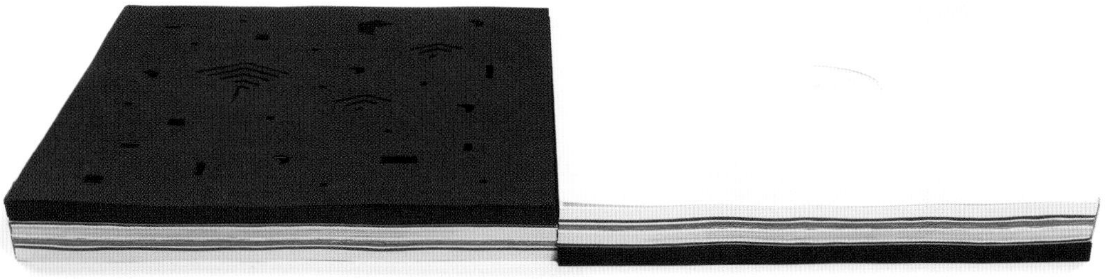

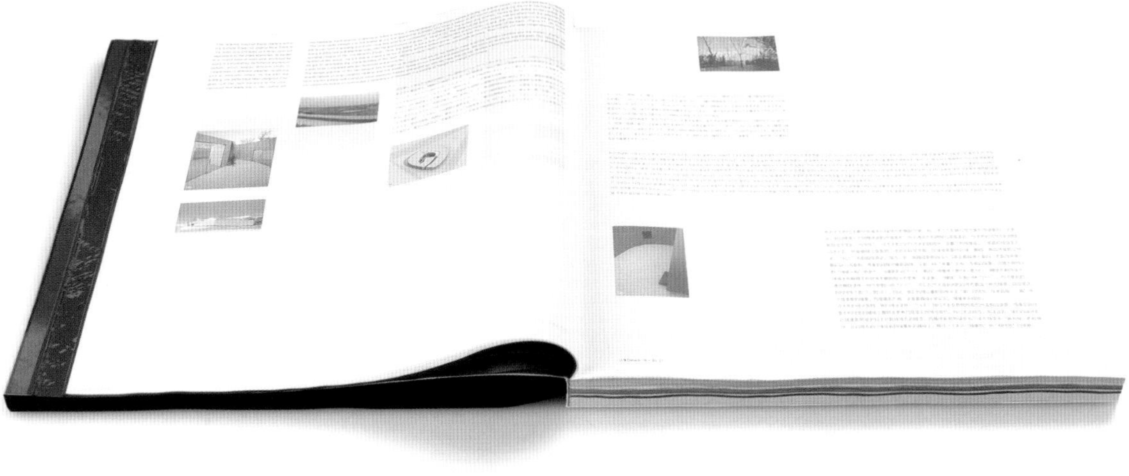

This is a book about Atelier Deshaus from Jiangnan and Zhao Qing, a book designer, exploring the relationship between architecture and books. This book presents architecture in the form of a book to establish a 'paper field' beyond readers' imagination, establishing a complete aesthetic impression with the combination of 'detach' and 'attach'. The work is a 360-degree space formed by the flipping and folding of the paper, and the three-dimensional die-cutting technique is used from the cover to the inner pages. Moreover, readers are immersed in the book's field, surrounded by the fragrance of the book, texture of the paper, characters and the sounds of flipping pages. The readers connect with the book through sight, touch, smell and sound, which illustrates the features of 'detach' and 'attach' and builds an infinite space of architecture in the book.

04

'In this process, designers become creators, for they have made the authors' ideas and their creative expressions come true, creating more value for the books with the authors.'

As a person born and raised in Nanjing, does the city have any influence on your design and working style?

Nanjing has its unique culture and charm. The elegance of Nanjing's landscape and the close relationship between people and the Jiangnan region have affected my design style greatly. Nanjing ranks between China's first-tier and second-tier cities, and the atmosphere of this city is subtle but straightforward, relaxed but intense. These characteristics are not contradictory. Instead, they form a sense of internal order, similar to my rhythm of working. I will push myself to stay in contact with cutting-edge styles while leaving myself with a peaceful mind and time to enjoy my life and to learn about design. Over the years, my work has gradually returned to the basics through various design changes and form a more extreme, pure and powerful visual impression than before. Nanjing has influenced my design, and my design is also leaving its mark on the city.

What is your perspective on designing books? Have you followed a particular set of principles?

Good content determines a book's value, and so does good book design. A book is the carrier of content. Generally, my understanding of editorial design has two aspects. One is to sort out all the pictures and text. After this, a designer should connect the content with visual expression logically and arrange these visual elements on the same plane. The second is that a designer must communicate closely with the author so that they can achieve an agreement.

I am always talking about the mindset of editorial design and I have insisted on this for a long time. Simply put, to give readers a more comfortable and refreshing reading experience, we need to think about book planning, typesetting, paper selection and printing methods carefully and logically. In this process, designers become creators, for they have made the authors' ideas and their creative expressions come true, creating more value for the books with the authors.

In your work *Infinite Blooming*, we can not only feel the charm from ancient China but also see your thinking on modern design. What do you think of rationality and sensibility in design?

Generally speaking, design is rational. It is different from fine art, which merely expresses the artists' opinions. Design serves people, and you need to get a visual solution to the problem by finding out the logic. The work can be more vivid only when you know the logic and add your sensible ideas. The book content of *Infinite Blooming* is massive and complex since it records the works of four generations of Chinese botanist painters over the past century. It is a popular science book and yet reaches a high artistic level.

When I was working on this book, I constantly thought about how to integrate science and artistry, and it took some effort for me to arrange the content. To present an abundant and lively manuscript, the seemingly loose and scattered layout is built on a rigorous grid system. This is the art of negative space, coming from eastern philosophy.

To present the diverse paintings, I put together monochrome spreads and colourful spreads respectively and arranged the characters both horizontally and vertically. This follows how people read nowadays. The way we treated negative space and the arrangement of spreads – contrasting eastern and western styles – do not conflict with each other. On the contrary, they merge and stay together harmoniously, creating a rich and full plant world and building up the flora of *Infinite Blooming* in my mind.

You designed for the collection of poems entitled *Facing the Sea, Flowers Blossom in Warm Spring*. Do literary works require designers to have a complete understanding of the text? How did you integrate your understanding into the design?

Designers must understand and feel the text. In my graphic design career, I seldom design for books spontaneously, and *Facing the Sea, Flowers Blossom in Warm Spring* is one of them. This book is not bound in a complicated way because it is trying to return to the basics. The freshest inspiration is that I created an encounter for Hai Zi and Wei Erqiao in the book, one a genius poet meeting the other, a genius painter. They were born in the same year, and both died young unfortunately, which seems to have some connection.

Therefore, I put the masterpieces of these two talented people into a series by using a warm orange colour to represent Hai Zi and a warm white for Wei Erqiao. Orange is the tribute to life and white is the meditation on death. When readers open the book in the middle, they can find that the whole book centres on the nail. The first and last pages of the book are connected symmetrically. The two middle pages are also symmetrical and connected with the nail. Hai Zi's poems and Wei Erqiao's paintings are presented throughout the book. I recorded their encounter with this binding method, and readers trace back such encounters with their eyes.

The biggest difference between paper books and e-books is the sense of space they bring to readers. You created a sense of space for *Li·Detach He·Attach*. What are the design concepts and strategies?

I completed *Li·Detach He·Attach* with Atelier Deshaus and the book mainly discusses the relationship between books and architecture. Atelier Deshaus wrote about architectural design, while I covered graphic design. These two seemingly irrelevant subjects can merge wonderfully. In this book, I established a concept called the 'paper field'. At the same time, we held an activity called 'Book · Building' to trigger people's thinking of books and introduce the idea about 'field' in design.

A good book design can form a 'paper field' that surpasses readers' imagination, which is also one of the standards to judge a book's design. The content on a piece of paper contains people's feelings during the interactions with the paper. From paper to book, it is about constructing a holographic space – the 'field'. In this 'field', only the combination of 'detach' and 'attach' can establish a complete aesthetic impression.

You edited and designed *The Choice of Leipzig 2019-2004* and *Browse Leipzig 1991-2003*. What is the reason? Are there any similarities and differences between these two books?

Designers tend to follow and collect some international design award-winning works. The intention of publishing these two books is also to share my collection over the years. The German National Library in Leipzig is not open to the public, but I think the artistic beauty of these books should be shown to the public. Therefore, I have opened up a Best Book

Design from All Over the World reading space in the company's office. Due to the constraints of time and distance, it is very difficult for many visitors from other places to come here. That's why the idea of making these two books was born.

The Choice of Leipzig is more lexicographical and popular, and it follows a very rigorous logic. *Browse Leipzig*, on the other hand, is more conceptual, just like the prequel of *The Choice of Leipzig*. The two-book series records the 30-year history of the Best Book Design from All Over the World. Given that the books introduced in *Browse Leipzig* are relatively old, I used a more nostalgic approach to trace the time covered in this book, while *The Choice of Leipzig* is similar to dictionaries and reference books, which conveys the information to readers. As a designer, it was extremely comforting for me to write and edit a book because I could completely deliver my ideas through these two books. Although stages including material organisation, layout design and adjustment are huge challenges, I feel satisfied to have completed the project.

In your mind, what is the difference between China's and the West's selection criteria of the best book designs? What do you think of this difference?

I think the design of award-winning books from the East has two features. One is the sensible reading experience of eastern books, which comes from the use of various traditional paper materials, and their combination with binding and typesetting. The other is that, compared to the West, the cost of paper, printing and binding are relatively low so that designers have more space to deliver their ideas and perform at their best.

As for books from the West, the process of paper cutting is often very simple. Designers will focus on the genre design and editing ideas to make the books unexpected but reasonable. The visual impressions they deliver are not complicated but complement the text perfectly. The difference represents different humanistic cores and individual expressions, so it can broaden and stimulate designers' horizons and creativity, encouraging them to try and create new distinctions, and thus form a virtuous circle.

Some young designers want to develop their career in this field as readers are more aware of book design. What advice do you have for young designers?

I have three pieces of advice for them. First, learn about the fundamental parts of traditional eastern books and invite these feelings into their designs. Second, learn about the rigorous grid system from the West and the methodology for book editing. Third, have an in-depth understanding of these two systems but do not get stuck in them. Young designers should absorb and digest the essence and then deconstruct these two systems to form their unique styles. When they are doing design, they should also try to create with their sensibility and to consider needs based on the real world. When they break through barriers, they will find their true selves.

HISTOLOGY ATLAS

SPECIFICATION
185 mm X 285 mm, 275pp

BINDING & FINISHING
Section sewing

PAPER
White corrugated fiberboard,
Japanese pattern art paper 120gsm,
extra white print paper 115gsm

TYPEFACE
Hei Ti by FounderType, Frugal Sans

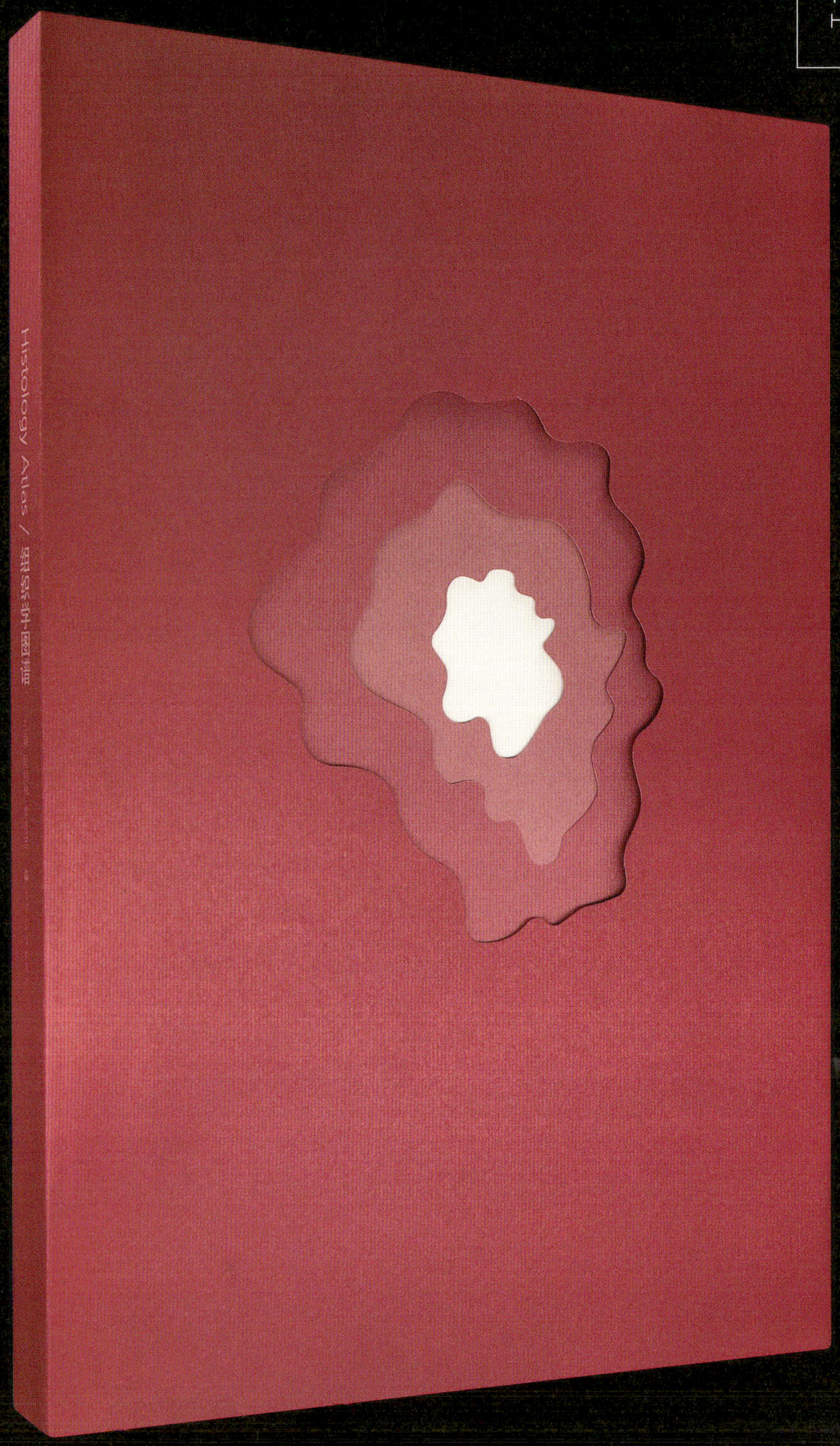

Zhang Zhiqi

Text Design

Cover Design

Print Design

05

THE MASTERMIND BEHIND BOOKS

'I like to experiment with different subjects. The most interesting thing about books is that each one is different and this urges you to design something new.'

Called the 'master of textbook design', Zhang Zhiqi brings a design mindset and aesthetics into the textbook design. His creativity and in-depth analysis of the book's content make an informative but attractive textbook possible.

'I did not choose to do design for these types of books. I was chosen.' said Zhiqi when he was asked about the reasons for designing textbooks. After resigning from an advertising agency, he worked for the Higher Education Press where he was to find a work-life balanced job and treated book design just as his job. It was the time in the Higher Education Press and the tutoring of his senior Liu Xiaoxiang that refreshed his thinking about book design and awakened his passion.

Though lacking the knowledge of design methodologies, Zhiqi was sensitive to the rhythm of reading and designed the *Histology Atlas* in 2012. The design was novel to a textbook then and was awarded The Beauty of Books in China prize. In the following years, his increased knowledge of design methodologies including the application of grid systems, refining design concepts, etc. encouraged him to do well-received designs for textbooks and popular science books, for example, the Ecological Wisdom series. The experience with textbooks became valuable lessons – helping him learn to be practical and patient, which is the virtue of a book designer.

Though renowned for his design of textbooks, Zhiqi also designs books on many topics. He focuses on accurate design and the integration between design language and the content. In his works on cultural books and classics, the layout of text and graphics, the arrangement of content, the use of colours and the selection all serve to present the content and echo with the overall design. The attention to details of a book and reading experiences also comes from Zhiqi's habit of reading. To him as a book designer, 'The passion for book design and reading constantly are very significant.'

Histology Atlas

DESIGN
Zhang Zhiqi

PUBLISHER
Higher Education Press

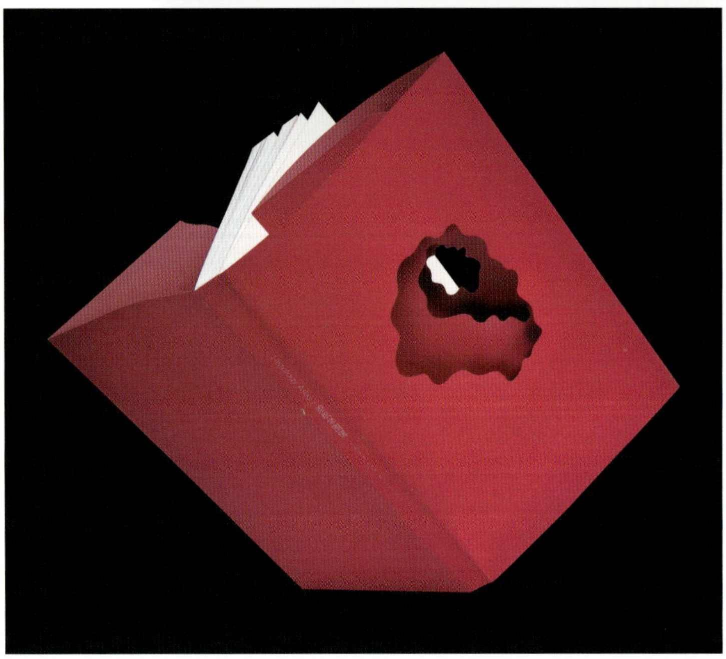

SPECIFICATION
185 mm X 285 mm, 275pp

BINDING & FINISHING
Section sewing

PAPER
White corrugated fiberboard,
Japanese pattern art paper 120gsm,
extra white print paper 115gsm

TYPEFACE
Hei Ti by FounderType, Frugal Sans

Histology Atlas is a medical book that consists of photographs of stained paraffin sections under the microscope. The design is based on the concept of layer-by-layer dissection. The stained images reduce the coldness of the theme. The book box is made through the printing and cutting of the white corrugated fiberboard. The cover is folded and die-cut to complement each other, which is a mind-twisting experiment due to the limitation of cost. The cover delivers the feeling of warmth. And vector icons are used to mark the content and explanation, making it easier for readers to remember and search.

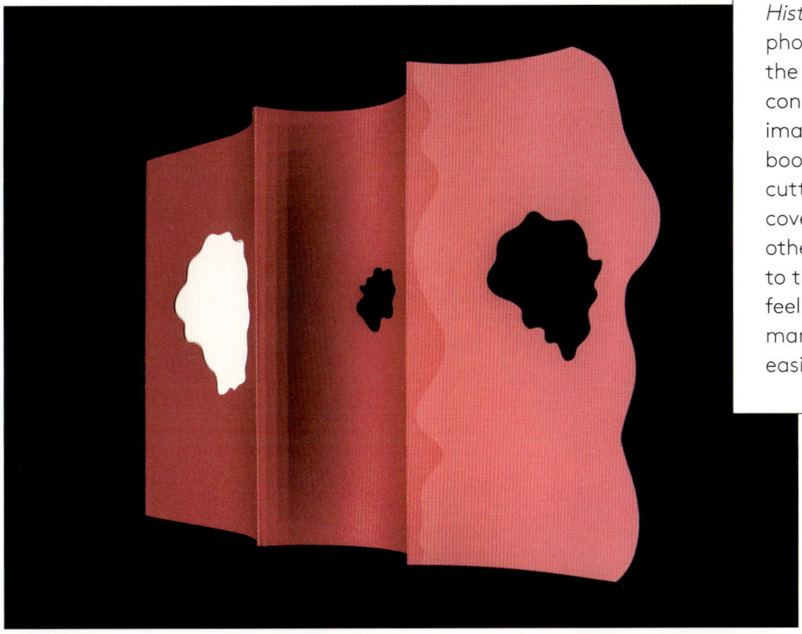

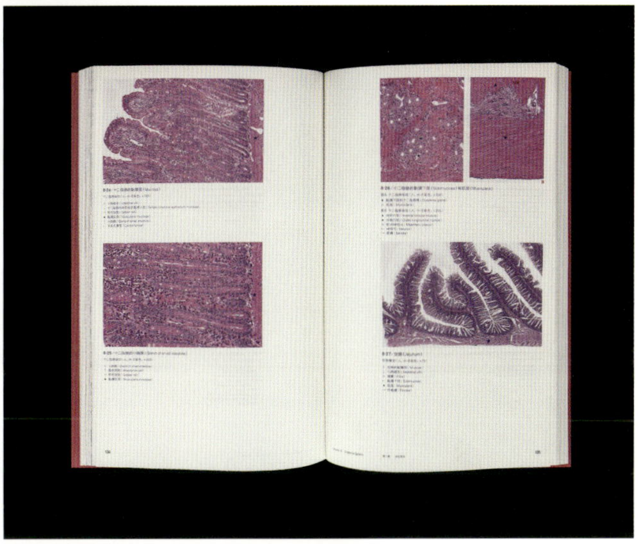

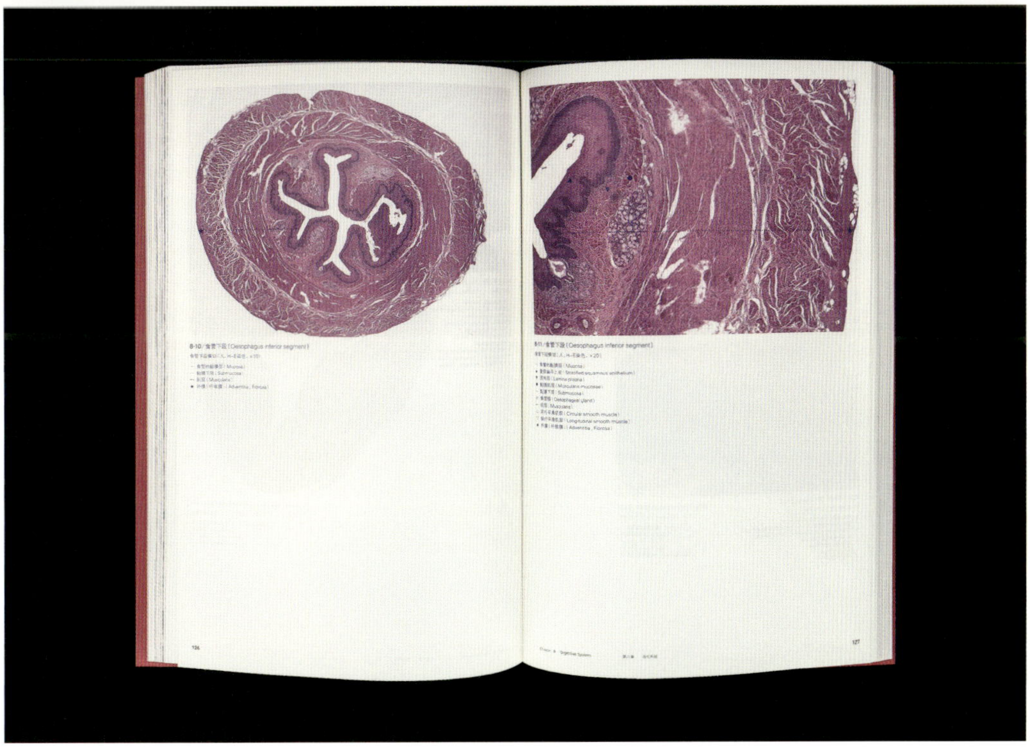

Ecological Wisdom Series

DESIGN
Zhang Zhiqi

PUBLISHER
Higher Education Press

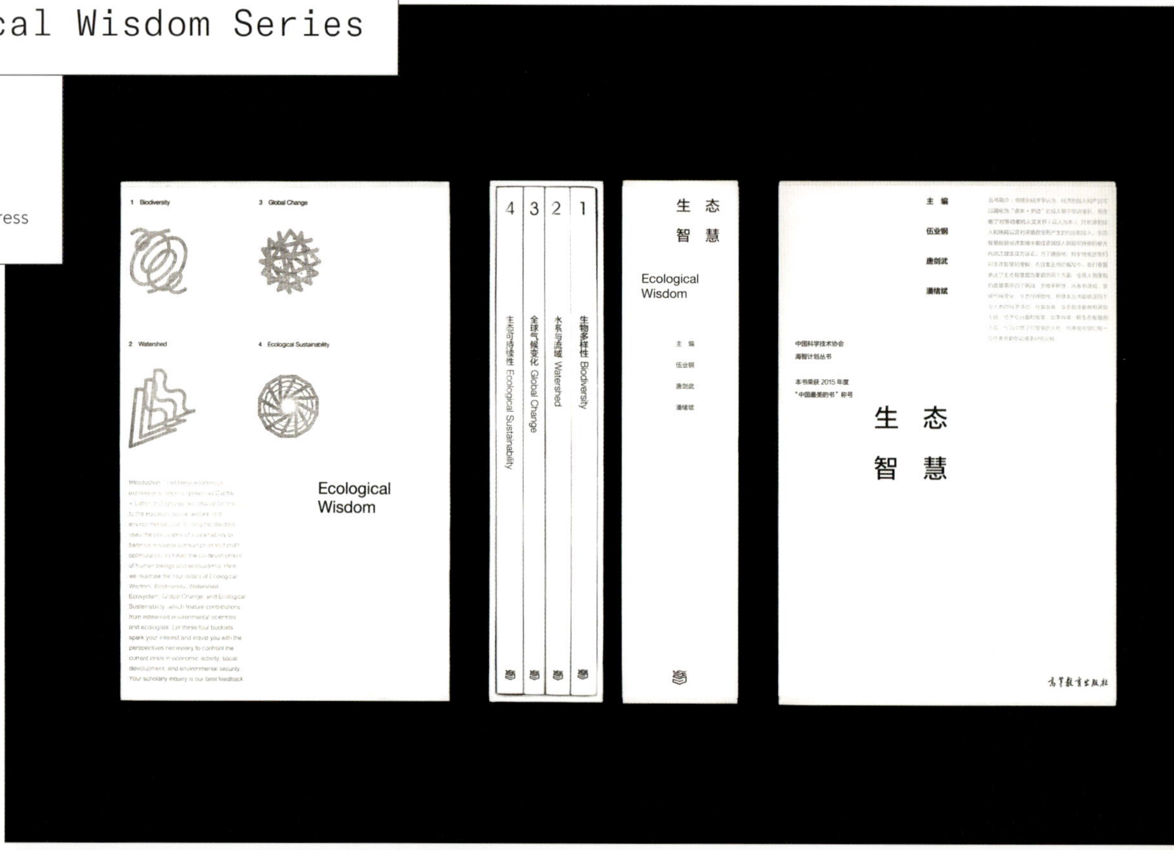

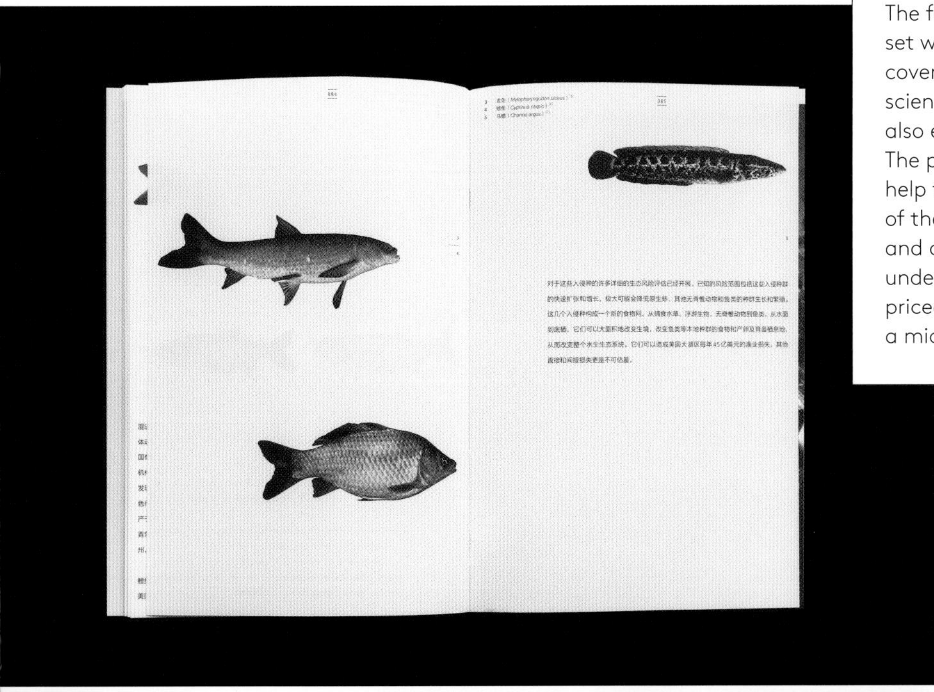

The format of the Ecological Wisdom series is set with the golden ratio. The illustrations on the cover stand for fireworks, showing the light of science and technology. These illustrations are also extended to the flaps to echo the theme. The pictures and text are arranged logically and help to present the rhythm and the development of the narration. The extensive use of silhouette and clear information charts helps readers understand the book's content. Printed on low-priced paper in one colour, the book is similar to a micro museum of science and technology.

SPECIFICATION
170 mm × 255 mm,
140pp/136pp/118pp/168pp

BINDING & FINISHING
Sewn binding, bare spine

PAPER
Cast-coated paper 250gsm, uncoated paper 100gsm

TYPEFACE
Lantinghei by FounderType

Memory Searching of Dances in Talks – the Oral History of Intangible Cultural Heritage Dances in Shandong Province

DESIGN
Zhang Zhiqi

PUBLISHER
Higher Education Press

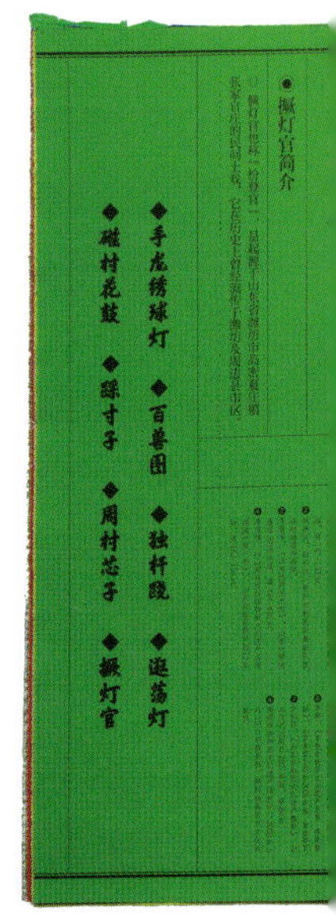

To echo the content, the delightful atmosphere of folk life and folk art pervades the design of the book. Bright-coloured soft tissue paper between each section is just like the colourful ribbon in Yangge Dance, dancing on the pages. The mingling of colour pages printed with text and art paper printed with pictures makes a sharp contrast and creates a perfect rhythm. The middle seam is embellished with multicoloured threads, brimming with folk tinges. Although the book adopts a complicated style of design, it is formatted in a clear way to highlight the 'oral' theme. The roughened edges are natural and colourful, conveying an unspoiled beauty. The book, full of rustic appeal and pleasant folk atmosphere, is a book of warmth and cosiness.

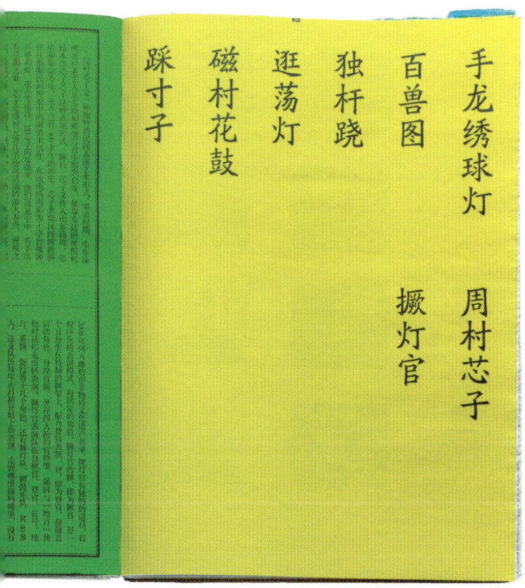

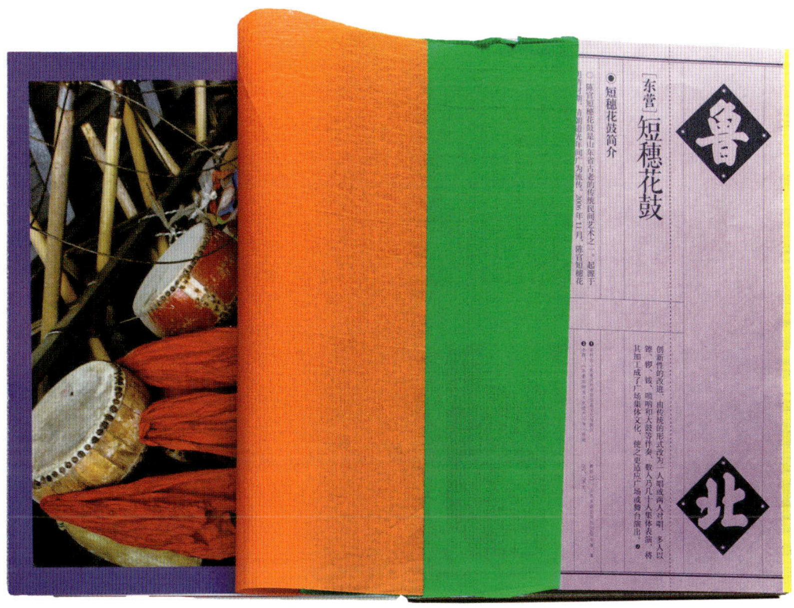

SPECIFICATION
210 mm × 290 mm, 650pp

BINDING & FINISHING
Sewn binding, bare spine, hot stamping, coloured threads

PAPER
Corrugated fiberboard, kraft paper, crepe paper, matt art paper 100gsm, newsprint 50gsm

TYPEFACE
Ya Song, Hei Ti by FounderType

Colourful Childhood

DESIGN
Zhang Zhiqi

PUBLISHER
People's Education Press

SPECIFICATION
210 mm X 300 mm, 427pp

BINDING & FINISHING
Wrapped-ridge binding, hot stamping, debossing

PAPER
Bian Yinghua 60gsm

TYPEFACE
Shu Song by FounderType

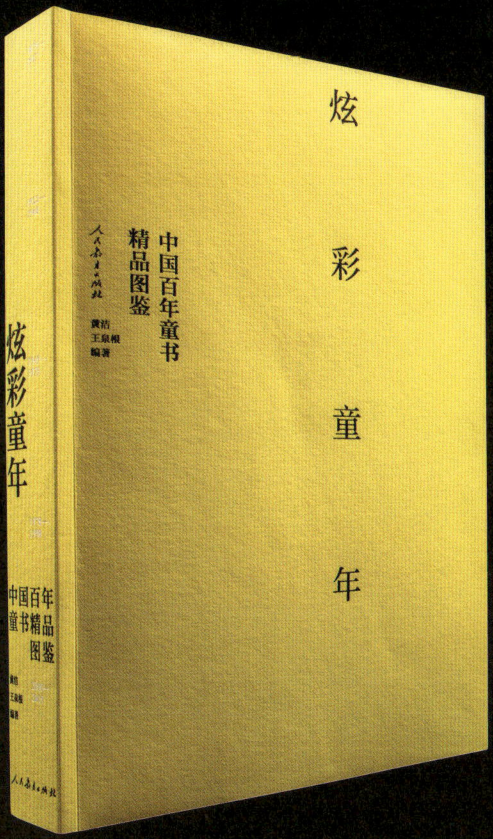

This book demonstrates a modern and contemporary history of China's children's book publishing with photographs. The selected books are categorised into five phases in chronological order. Each book is presented with a summary, book information and photographs. To display the connections among these books from multiple perspectives, the designer used graphic charts to present key information, including the colours of book covers, genres and places of publication. The design of a bookshelf-like index makes this book more fun to read. The illustrations on the dust jacket are printed on holographic paper. They are all from the most representative books in the past, capturing the diversity and characteristics of children's books in China over the last century.

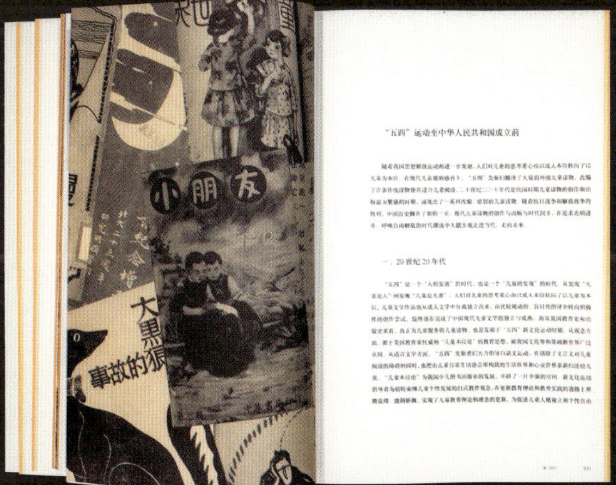

The Old Man and the Sea

DESIGN
Zhang Zhiqi

PUBLISHER
Chongwen
Publishing House

SPECIFICATION
160 mm × 250 mm, 163pp

BINDING & FINISHING
Hardcover, hot stamping

PAPER
Cloth, Munken paper

TYPEFACE
Shu Song by FounderType

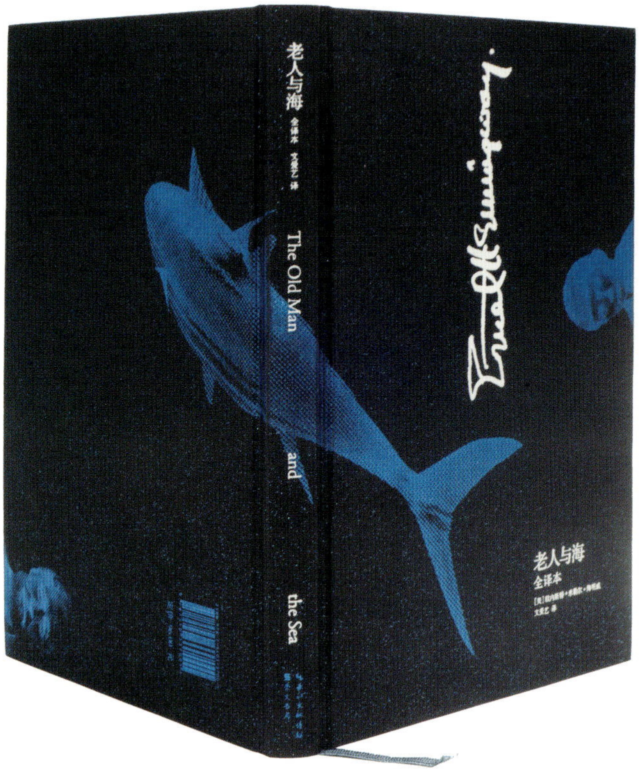

In this book, a large number of blank pages printed in gradient blue precede and follow the text block. It is to express the passing of time and the spatial changes from surface to deep in the sea, centring on the theme: the search for life, the struggle with life and the endless life of all living creatures. Inside the book, there is another book in which some clues are drawn to present the state of existence in different time and space. The reading of the 'book within a book' creates a dual reading experience and brings up complex emotions, and gives the reader blank space to record them. The cover features the reflections of a man and a fish on the sea, alluding to reality and illusion, existence and extinction, and the author's legendary life.

05 'A book designer has to read more often and experience the reading process. Moreover, a designer should find inspiration by observing and recording people's actions in daily life.'

How did you go into the field of book design? Why did you choose to design textbooks and popular science books?

After I resigned from the advertising agency, I took a break for almost three months. A university friend then introduced me to the Higher Education Press. At that time, I thought this job would be easier and did not think much about book design. I had taken a course in book design at university and thought it would not be too difficult. Back then, I was young and felt that I needed only confidence, but it turned out that book design was really difficult.

The books published by the Higher Education Press are mainly university textbooks, academic monographs and so on. My daily work is also about the design of textbooks, but the content covers many subjects, such as literature and history, economics and management, science and technology, social sciences, foreign languages, learning instruction, examination and so on, and there are dozens of different subjects. In this case, I did not choose to do design for these types of books. I was chosen.

You are called the 'master of textbook design'. How do you bring design thinking and aesthetics into textbook design and popular science book design?

I dare not claim the title of 'master of textbook design'. Many designers have done a better job than I have. Designing textbooks can increase a designer's patience and his or her ability to refine and summarise design concept.

I designed the *Histology Atlas* in 2012. I had done similar designs before, except that the images in this book are in four colours. Most textbooks were printed in single or two colours, and not many were in four colours at the time. The cost of the textbooks was tightly controlled because of the cost and pricing, as well as the intention to reduce students' burden on the cost of the textbooks. When I got this project to design a full-colour book, I was very excited and only thought about how to do a good design, not knowing what the book would look like in the end. It is a medical book, but I wanted to make it gentle, less distant and less cold.

At the time, I did not have the knowledge of design methodologies, such as refining design concepts and grid systems, so I just designed and arranged page layouts with feelings. I arranged images of similar colours on the same spread and was aware of the rhythm to arrange images. Moreover, the images were labelled with numbers at that time. The font size of the numbers was so big that many details of the images were hidden, so I needed to relabel the images.

Later, I found out that the images and symbols provided by the author were all combined layers, so I had to photoshop them one by one. Many of the images provided by the authors had to be retouched or replaced, so I appeal to all editors to keep a good eye on the images when receiving manuscripts. The dust jacket and the cover were done through folding and die cutting to reduce the cost and to simplify the process as much as possible. The book box was produced only through printing, die cutting and folding. In total, it took six months to make the book. I was inspired that book design requires designers' dedication and ingenuity and that textbooks can be impressive too.

I designed the Ecological Wisdom series in 2015. In this period, I still focused more on arranging the content and presenting design concepts, but I started to have some insights into the use of grid systems. I designed this book after re-editing and rearranging the content, trying new things in design language. The Ecological Wisdom series is a small collection of four volumes of popular science essays on natural biology and environmental protection. The editor gave me a lot of freedom to design, but I needed to keep the cost within a reasonable range.

To attract young people to read the book, I used some simple graphics to illustrate the abstract title and colours similar to the primary colours to bring the book closer to the readers. In the inner page layout, I focused more on the rhythm of the picture and text arrangement. I also redesigned a large number of infographics based on the images provided by the author. The new graphics are flat and single-colour, which enhances reading efficiency while maintaining a uniform layout design style. The overall design of a book should not only focus on the form and cover of the book, but also the presentation of content. Sometimes design does not have to be made straightforward to people.

Apart from textbooks, you have also designed books of many topics. Do you favour a certain subject? What are the differences between these subjects and the textbook? Do your experiences with textbooks help?

Yes, I like to experiment with different subjects. The most interesting thing about books is that each one is different and this urges you to design something new. My favourites are art, history, literature and so on.

These subjects are quite different from textbooks in terms of design language, such as the reading experience and the form, materials and manufacturing techniques of the book. The cost of textbooks should be reasonable, so designers focus on the editing and layout of the content, emphasising the functionality of reading. Books on culture and arts need designers to pay more attention to the presentation of the content in both the reading process and the book's form.

The design experiences with textbooks helped me a lot. They helped me learn to be down-to-earth and to improve my patience. If you can do well with the boring ones, you should have no problem with the rest. They are all enjoyable.

Memory Searching of Dances in Talks - the Oral History of Intangible Cultural Heritage Dances in Shandong Province is about dance, and its design showcases its individuality. What are the design considerations and strategies of this book?

I started designing *Memory Searching of Dances in Talks* in 2019 and worked on it for half a year, but the printing and binding were delayed for more than half a year because of the COVID-19 pandemic. It took some time to finish the design of this book, because the author cut down the content, and after the book was finished, the layout was adjusted twice. The illustrations and text were so closely related, so I would need to rearrange the layout if any images were added or deleted. When working on this book, I was keen to design it with a combination of papers, as few subjects are suitable for using so many different papers in one book. The book is a collection of interviews with dozens of Yangge dance inheritors and artists and is divided into two chapters.

I used newsprint for the text and photographs that record the movement of the dances. The text is arranged to display the 'oral' nature of the interviews. I used gloss art paper for the documentary colour photographs. The ribbon-like crinkled paper is used as a decoration to echo the dancers' gestures and poses with a strong sense of colour. The book does not have a page for the table of contents because it is on the same page with the chapter pages. Readers can tear this page out along the dotted line and use it as a bookmark. The book's middle seam is stitched with multi-coloured threads, giving a rich feeling of folklore.

The first part of the book, which is about interviews with folk enthusiasts, is more flexible in its design, layout and use of high purity colours. The chapter pages in each section are designed as promotional tabloids for village fairs with large headings. And the twisting dancing gestures on the same page with headings indicate an infectious folklore character. The second part includes interviews with Yangge artists. It is designed to be more rustic and retain a documentary-like reading experience, presented in the form of data collection. The body text of the interviews and the narration is printed in black and white ink, and the ink on yellow-brown kraft paper reminds people of the past. I used a more dense grid because of the complex text style throughout the book. The book is quite challenging in terms of text layout.

Your work has been awarded The Beauty of Books in China several times. What do you think are the standards of a good book design?

Firstly, the design concept of the book and the book's form. Secondly, whether the paper material and page layout are consistent with the expression of the concept. And then, the accuracy of the design and if the design language and content go along with each other. Any mismatch will leave an impression that the design does not fit the content.

When designing classics, such as Hemmingway's *The Old Man and the Sea*, how is it possible to be innovative in design while still conveying content rooted in readers' minds?

Designing for a classic is very challenging, as its content is familiar to readers and the cost is relatively low, and most of the classics are for massive sale. I thought a lot about how to design a book that can stand out from its cluttered and repetitive counterparts and how to present it through a different arrangement of content and a unique reading perspective.

Take *The Old Man and the Sea* as an example. The book is bound in a western-style cloth hardcover. The text area is positioned using the golden ratio. The text is arranged in the same way as the text in a western-style hardcover book so that the Chinese edition can provide a western reading experience as much as possible. The illustrations in the book are fish showing up continuously and representative fish in the content. And the beginning, development, climax and end of the story are all paved and transitioned through analysing the fish. Whereas many books on sale are usually presented from the first-person narrative, this one is from a third-person narrative. The change of the perspective makes a big difference to the reading experience. The time and space in this book are presented through the depth of colours, bringing readers a different visual experience.

Are there any principles you always follow when designing books? Why are these principles important?

The passion for book design and reading constantly are very significant. A book designer has to read more often and experience the reading process. Moreover, a designer should find inspiration by observing and recording people's actions in daily life. Finally, before designing a book, designers need to be familiar with the content, refine the design concept and compose a suitable layout. Effective methods and working habits can help a designer evaluate the design and catch the point of work.

L'ABÉCÉDAIRE DE LA LITTÉRATURE: ULTIME

SPECIFICATION
150 mm X 210 mm

BINDING & FINISHING
Paperback with dust jacket

PAPER
Brisk paper

TYPEFACE
Yu Mincho, Serlio LT Std

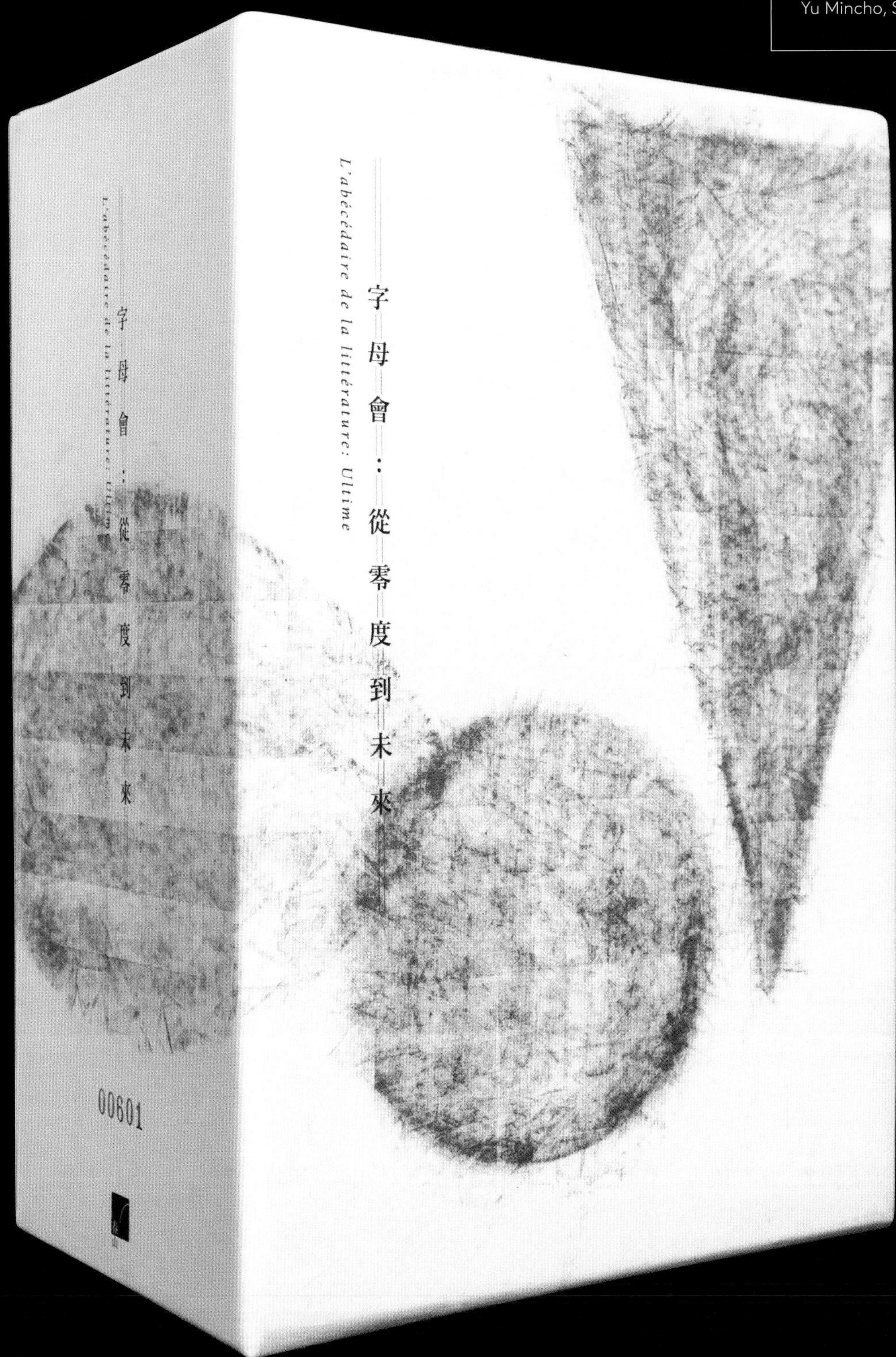

06 THE MASTERMIND BEHIND BOOKS

'It is difficult to separate life from work clearly and to simply calculate our wages by the hour because the nutrients we get in this process are invaluable.'

In addition to delivering information, a book is a container of emotions and thoughts, tracing readers' sensory experiences. Fascinated by the books' tactile appeal and its lasting value as an information carrier, the duo Peng Yu-jui and Huang Jui-i dedicate themselves to book design and founded Mistroom in 2010.

Yu-jui and Jui-i find design inspiration from life and value the bonding with the author, as they said, 'The most essential part is not about the design, but the content of the book.' Being the creative director, Jui-i immerses herself in the text and resonates with the author by living at a similar pace before she comes up with a design concept. And Yu-jui finds out the solution and brings the concept into reality. Working along with their shared philosophy, they can always complete designs echoing with both the readers and the author.

Meanwhile, their works do not stay the same and give readers a fresh feeling. The different papers, binding methods and finishing techniques they choose in response to the theme distinguishes a book. And by bringing in the author to complete the book, as they did in the design for *Aroma Island*, they build up the work's characteristics. At first sight, you will be aware of the subtlety and creativity in their works and later, become amazed by the evocation of sensory memories when reading the books.

To think about and complete the design, oftentimes it takes the designers a lot of time and patience, which is contradictory to the commercial publishing industry that pursues efficiency. But Mistroom accepts and sees the design process as a part of their life, like they said, 'It is difficult to separate life from work clearly and to simply calculate our wages by the hour because the nutrients we get in this process are invaluable.'

L'abécédaire de la littérature: Ultime

DESIGN
Mistroom

PUBLISHER
SpringHill
Publishing

SPECIFICATION
150 mm × 210 mm

BINDING & FINISHING
Paperback with dust jacket

PAPER
Brisk Paper

TYPEFACE
Yu Mincho, Serlio LT Std

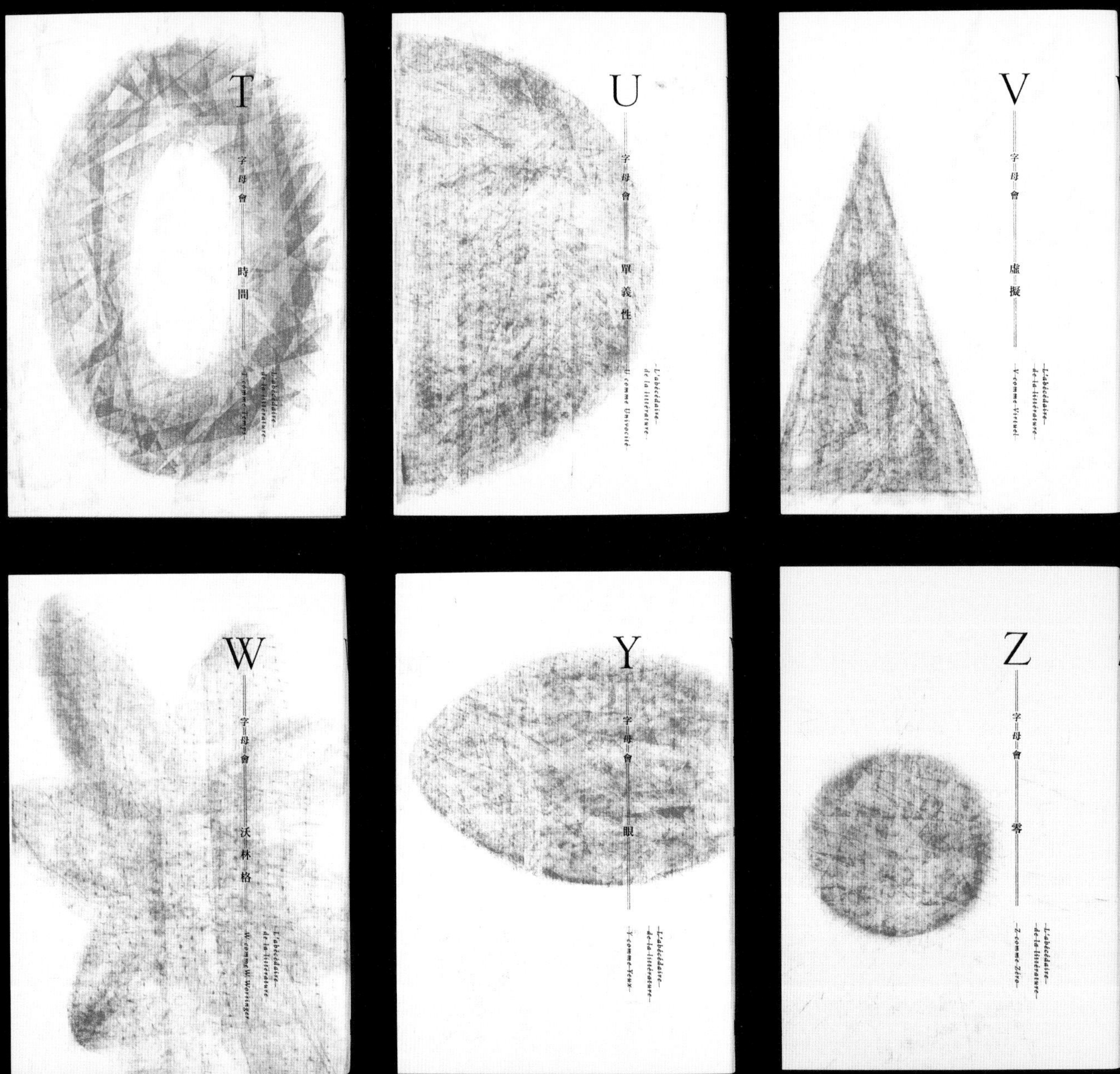

Yang Kai-lin put forward 26 philosophical entries pointing to the core of creation. Seven creators' thinking and their ideas in the literary works are collected in the books and form a new literary landscape. From the perspective of the eighth creator, Mistroom interpreted the concept of the Letter Society Experimental Writing Project through body writing and copying.

As Free As the Ocean

DESIGN
Mistroom

PUBLISHER
Vima House Co., Ltd.

Comparing life to the ocean, the overall design uses the concept of 'free ocean' to respond to the freedom in the author's mind. The designers hope that when the readers see this book, they can feel the light of the ocean shining in their eyes and their heart calm down when they flip through it. They hope readers can feel the wind of freedom, feel the waves and this book can light up readers' heart in the sea and accompany them to find the light of life. When in doubt, they can call the truth in their hearts, because they are not the wave, but the ocean.

SPECIFICATION
128 mm X 188 mm, 272pp

BINDING & FINISHING
Paperback, fore-edge oblique cutting

PAPER
PVC

TYPEFACE
MS Mincho, Garth Graphic Std

A Monologue for You

DESIGN
Mistroom

PUBLISHER
Mistroom International Co.

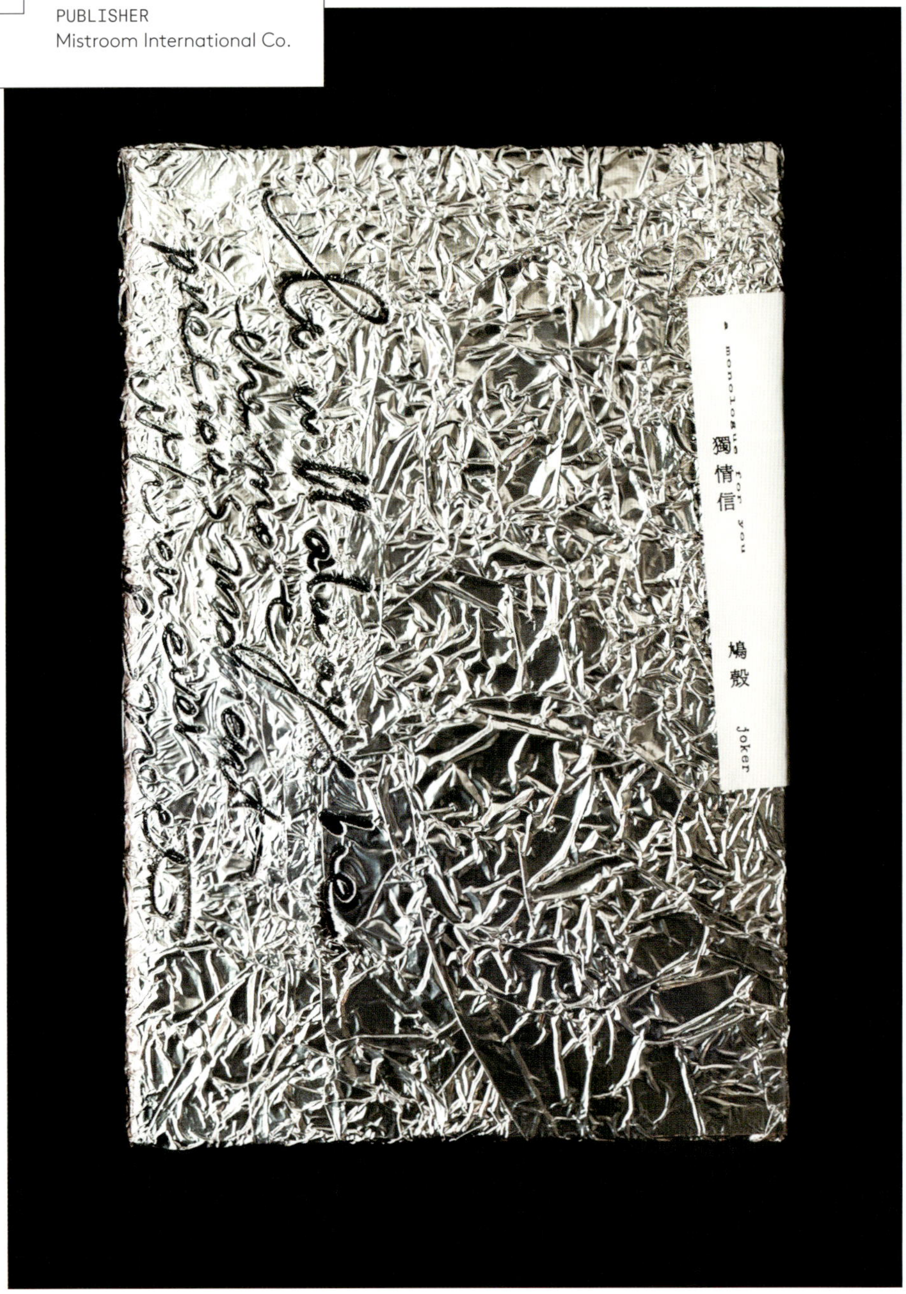

SPECIFICATION
135 mm ╳ 195 mm, 430pp

BINDING & FINISHING
Square back hardcover,
matt black hot stamping

PAPER
Tin foil paper

TYPEFACE
FOT-TsukuMin Pro, Underwood Champion

This poetry includes 212 poems and has only 212 prints. All of them were published on a specific date: 12, February for the only reader of this book, the girl born on 12, February. To stress the special meaning of the book as a birthday present, this book is designed based on the calendar format. The first poem starts on 16, July and there is a poem for each day. After reading one poem, readers can tear the page out to use as a love letter. A portrait of the girl will surprisingly appear if readers assemble the clues on the back of the pages, which expresses the endless feeling of missing the girl.

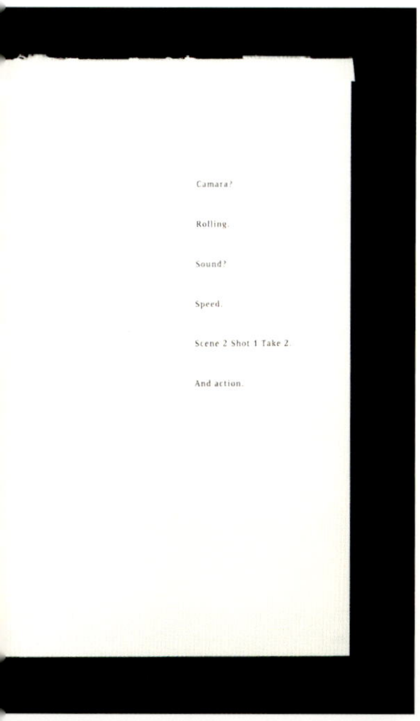

Aroma Island

DESIGN
Mistroom

PUBLISHER
Yiri Co., Ltd.

SPECIFICATION
150 mm X 210 mm, 179pp

BINDING & FINISHING
Hardcover

PAPER
Keaykolour

TYPEFACE
FOT-TsukuMin Pro, Minion Pro

To recall people's memory of the island, the designers interpreted the smell on the idea of the land's fragrance after the rain. The texture of the grass is presented with the paper and the print on the book's cover. The paper box under the book represents the soil. Readers can feel and associate the moisture of the island with the packaging made by tracing paper. Moreover, an essential oil producer is invited to make an essential oil for this book, using the design of top note, middle note and base note to elaborate the three chapters of this book.

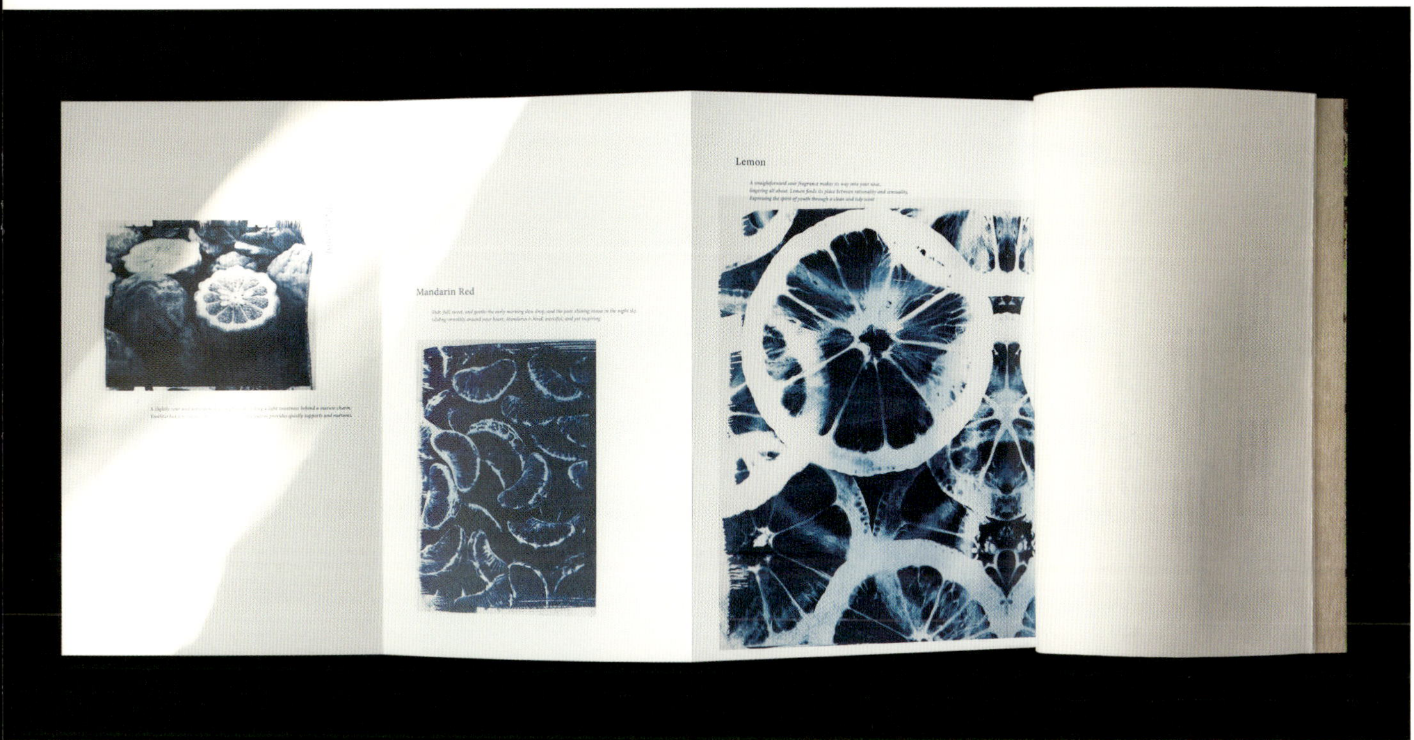

The Surprising Power of Reading

DESIGN
Mistroom

PUBLISHER
Vima House Co., Ltd.

SPECIFICATION
150 mm × 210 mm

BINDING & FINISHING
Paperback with dust jacket

PAPER
Natural wadding paper

TYPEFACE
Hand lettering, MetaSerifLf-BookIta

A book is the map of life. Through a book, readers can link themselves to the next book, a movie, or a rich life. Reading opens up new space for readers, and leads them to places they have never visited and visions they have never seen before. Embarking on the journey of reading, they will meet many beautiful sceneries. This book will make readers confident and will expect them to feel the surprise of freedom, openness, and unlimited extension of life.

06

‘For a book by an author with a unique perspective, the design work will reflect the author’s particular worldview if it is based on an in-depth understanding of his or her ideas.’

What brought you to editorial design?

When we were first hired by the design company, we mainly focused on poster design and the graphic design of exhibitions.

When we had our first editorial design project, we found that the book, as a carrier, was rich in space, time and the sense of touch and so on. These features made editorial design very attractive to us.

Unlike other independent book designers, you work as a duo. How do you work as a team to get conceptual inspiration and direction?

Jui-i: When I start thinking about how to design a book, I feel like a transparent, soft container. I immerse myself in the text of the book, slowly finding the rhythm and becoming synchronised with the author, and then I write down the core idea as well as the design concept. Then I close the book and become aware of living my life with this rhythm. For example, when we are designing a book about mountains, we will take a walk on the mountain, feel its temperature and smell, listen to its sound, observe the people hiking, etc. It is within this process that we find a way to transform the concept into a visual presentation.

Yu-jui: When Jui-i gives me the concept and a proposal of the visual presentation, I would further think about if the visual presentation can connect and resonate with readers. When composing the vision in my mind, the images of the concept will become dynamic like a video, and I will capture a piece of the most appropriate one to present. I think Jui-i’s focus is on the core of the book, and my focus is on building a bridge between the book and its readers.

In the creative process, how do you deal with disagreements?

If there are different opinions, we will stay silent for three minutes. And then we will calm ourselves down and avoid using emotional words. This allows us to express our ideas and listen to the other person’s opinions.

To solve the problem, the best way is to look back at the core idea that has been written at the very beginning. We will try to get rid of our subjective ideas, put ourselves in the shoes of the author, readers and publishers and discuss the solution from their perspectives. Since this is not based on our opinions, we can often reach a consensus during the discussion.

Can you talk specifically about how you presented the concept of ‘free ocean’ in *As Free As the Ocean*? Were there any trials or difficulties?

After deciding to use ‘free ocean’ as the design concept of this book, we began to think about people’s moods and situations when they went to the beach. When readers walked into the bookstore, they were presented with plentiful and complex information and book covers. Therefore, we thought about how they could feel the breeze and calmness of the seaside when they saw the cover of this book in such a situation.

The PVC material used to make the cover is like the vision of the blue sea, and the reflective effect of the material shows a sparkling sea surface. One of the most difficult parts was to present the image of the waves. Each book was designed to have an oblique fore-edge with width differences of 0.06 cm on each page. Since the machine could not do this, we could only carry out the cutting manually. In the end, we completed 5,000 books by cutting pages one by one.

Windy Zone

DESIGN
Mistroom

PUBLISHER
Watyp Publishing

SPECIFICATION
127 mm × 178 mm, 167pp

BINDING & FINISHING
Paperback, jet black hot stamping

PAPER
DuPont Tyvek

TYPEFACE
Hand lettering

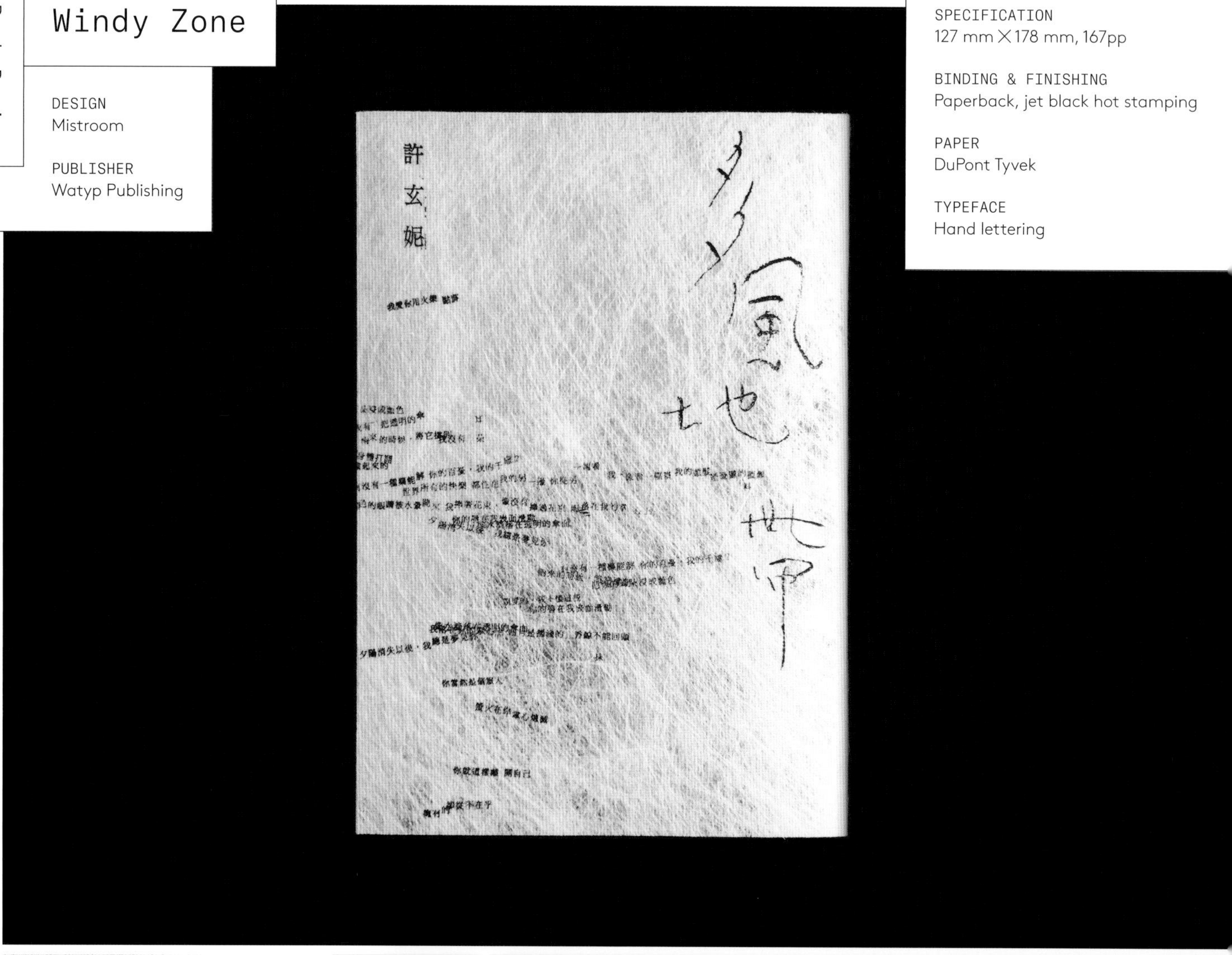

The design is trying to deliver the author's feelings and her thoughts in the book: She liked someone at that time. The person was like a strong wind. Even though this strong wind will blow her to pieces, she still hopes to get closer to the person.

The content and design of *Aroma Island* blend well with your creativity. Before designing a book, what do you do for preparation? How do you build up the characteristics of a book?

For the design preparation, we think it is important to establish a trusting relationship with the author. This is not an easy task because the author thinks textually while the designer thinks visually.

To make the book more special, sometimes we would want part of the design to be completed by the author. Take *Aroma Island* as an example. We asked the author to make a bottle of essential oil for this book based on the book's concept and then we divided the book into three chapters according to the top, middle and base notes of the oil.

The use of special materials and unique binding is a unique characteristic of your work. How do you find a balance between the form and the content?

In the process, we will ask ourselves questions such as 'Does this design decision reflect the content of the book or does it simply highlight the design approach?' This introspection helps determine the most appropriate presentation of the book.

Your works often give readers a fresh feeling both in the design concept and the book's form. How did you break through the comfort zone in style and create a unique design for each book?

Thank you. The most essential part is not about the design, but the content of the book. For a book by an author with a unique perspective, the design work will reflect the author's particular worldview if it is based on an in-depth understanding of his or her ideas.

How long does it take you to design a book? You pay a lot of attention to the intricacy of the design. What do you think of commercial publications that pursue efficiency?

We believe that for the publication of a book, market demand and profitability are part of the business. What we are considering is whether we can bring more cultural thinking into commercial publishing projects. When we started to design books, we usually did cover design only, but in recent years, most of our projects are overall book designs. It takes about half a year for us to design a book and send it to print. We often spend a lot of time in the early stages cultivating and establishing relationships with authors and the book, learning about a new author and understanding a new perspective. It is difficult to separate life from work clearly and to simply calculate our wages by the hour because the nutrients we get in this process are invaluable.

EXPLORE MORE PROJECTS

Lukas/Markus

DESIGN
Lundgren+Lindqvist

PUBLISHER
Il'Editions & Blackbook Publications

SPECIFICATION
200 mm X 223 mm, 82pp

BINDING & FINISHING
Cloth-bound hardcover, embossing, partial hot stamping

PAPER
Arctic Volume White 150gsm, Fedrigoni Sirio Colour Sabbia 115gsm

TYPEFACE
Neue Haas Grotesk 55 Roman

Lukas/Markus is the result of a photographic project spanning over a decade. The project presents a sensitive portrait of architect Sven Brolid's two mirrored chapels, Saint Lukas and Saint Markus and their surroundings, and a portrait of the passing of time as the seasons shift in front of Sanner's lense. The book's clothbound hardcover features an embossing with partial transparent foil, echoing the iconic facade of Sven Brolid's building. When hit by light, the partial foil spells out Gothenburg's area code '031' on the back cover. On the front cover, abstract letters form 'VKG', an abbreviation for Västra Kyrkogården, is also Sanner's working title for the project.

Threads through Time - Archive of Memories

DESIGN
Desislava Danova,
Susana Xavier

PUBLISHER
Self-published

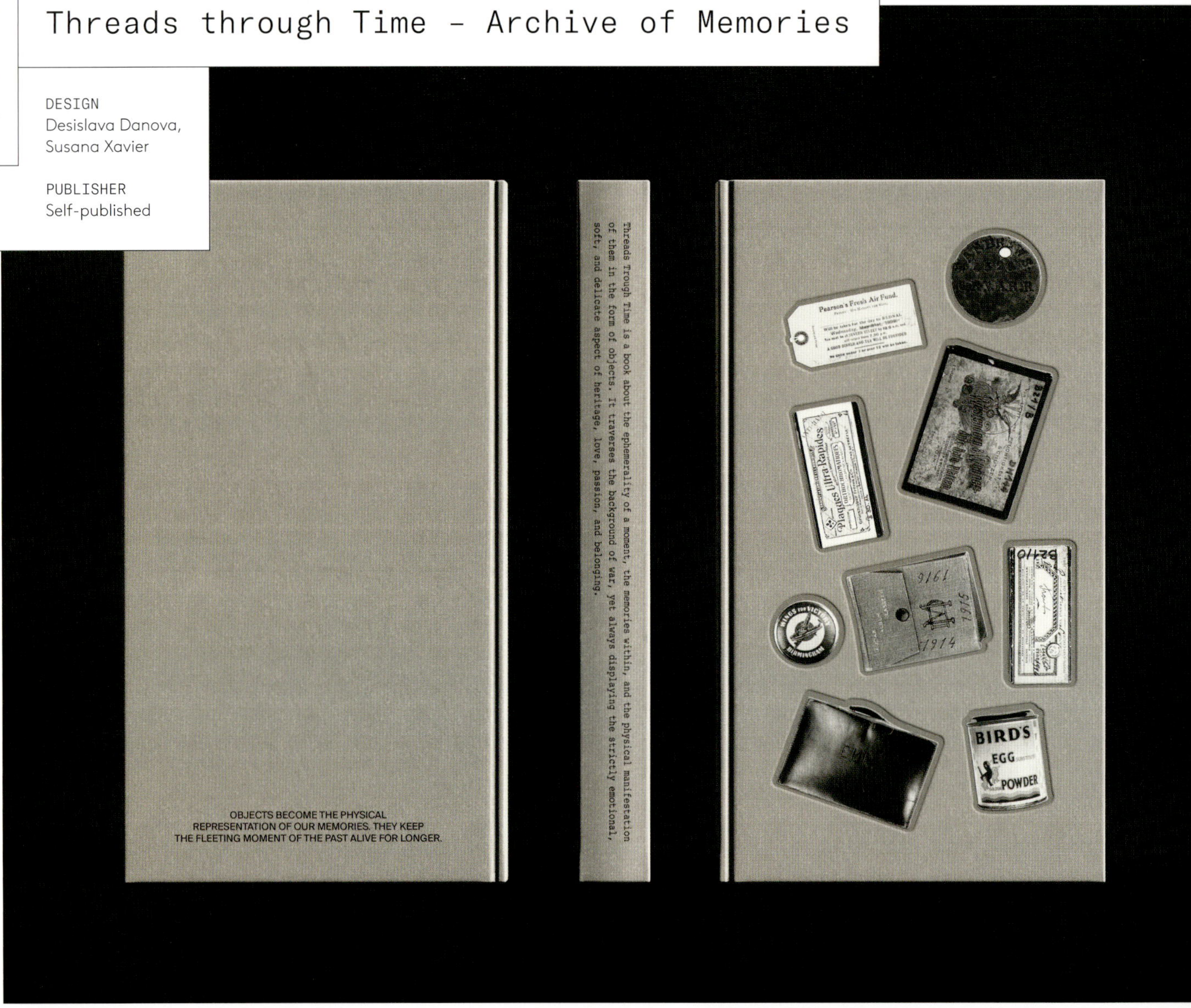

It is a book about the ephemerality of a moment, the memories within and the physical manifestation of the past. The content passes through the topics of love, separation, anxiety and each section of the book is supported by archival documentation of stories, objects, and places. Photography, typography, and design elements echo an archival look, allowing the reader to be deeply connected with the content. The classic and subdued layouts are juxtaposed with the modernity of a narrow hardcover with a subtle debossing on the front cover.

SPECIFICATION
110 mm X 200 mm, 256pp

BINDING & FINISHING
Hardcover, sewn binding, debossing with stickers

PAPER
Fedrigoni Freelife Symbol Gloss 130gsm, Fedrigoni Materica Clay 120gsm, Shiro Echo Natural 90gsm

TYPEFACE
Gascogne, Suisse Int' l, Suisse Works, Courier

Identità oltre il tempo

DESIGN
Riccardo Savioli

PUBLISHER
Self-published

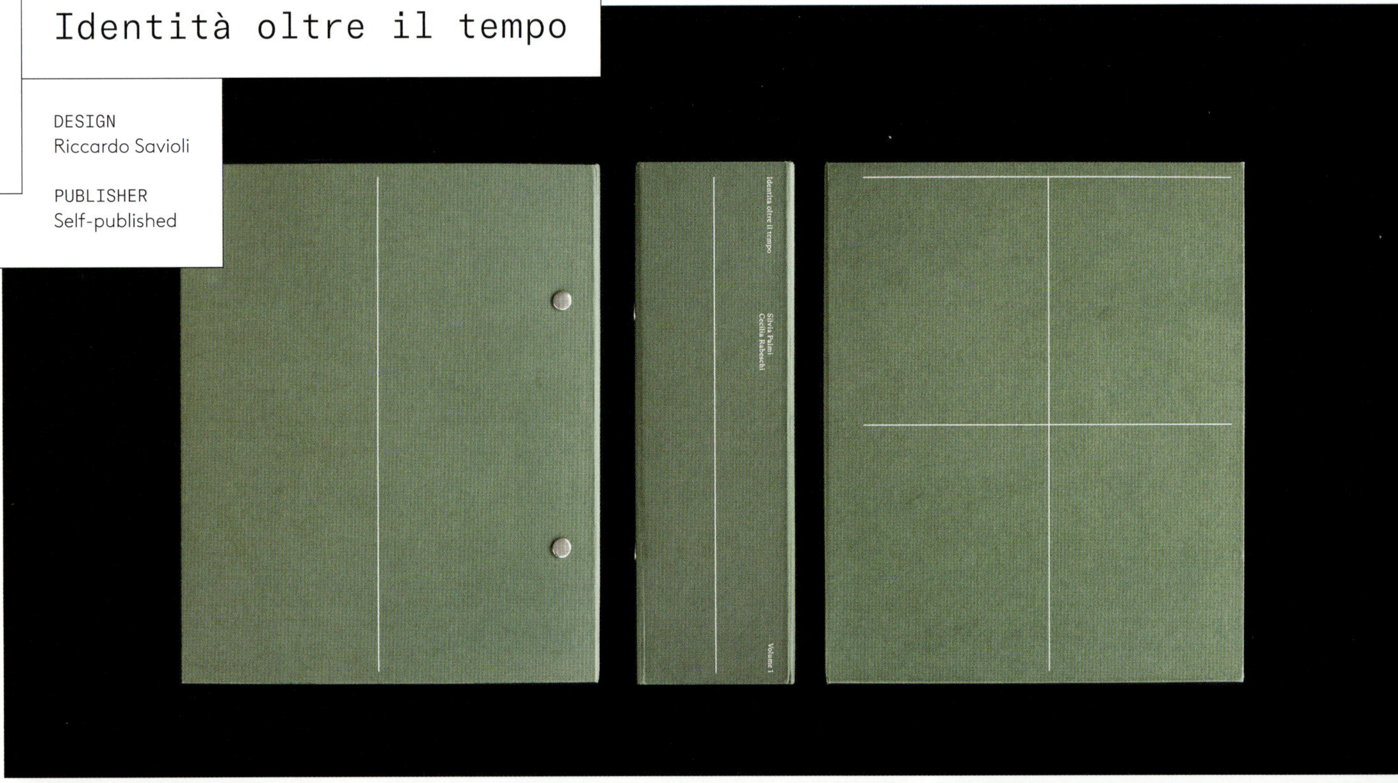

Identità oltre il tempo is a photographic, editorial and exhibition project. It is created to tell the story of the city of Matera. The photographic series follows a path established by the stories of each inhabitant and archival material, implementing visual rewriting of the city. Collected together with a ring binder, the pages of the book are characterised by their individuality in this exhibition. By this approach, all groups of materials are taken together to lead the observer in a labyrinthine structure of the book.

SPECIFICATION
195 mm × 270 mm, 310pp

BINDING & FINISHING
Loose-leaf binding

PAPER
Arcoprint Milk 100gsm

TYPEFACE
Lineto, Bradford

Book Design

Buildings with cour d'honneur in Budapest

DESIGN
Anna Bárdy

PUBLISHER
ARTEM/BOOKS

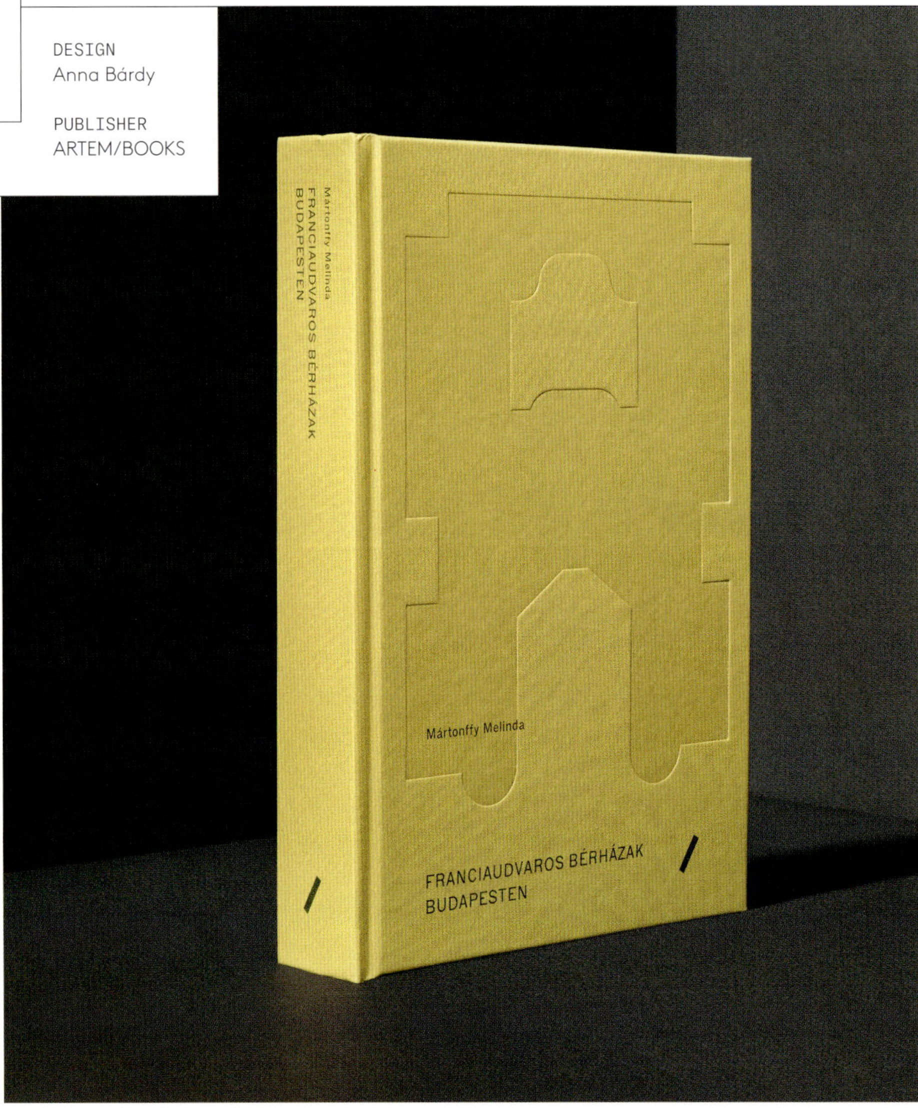

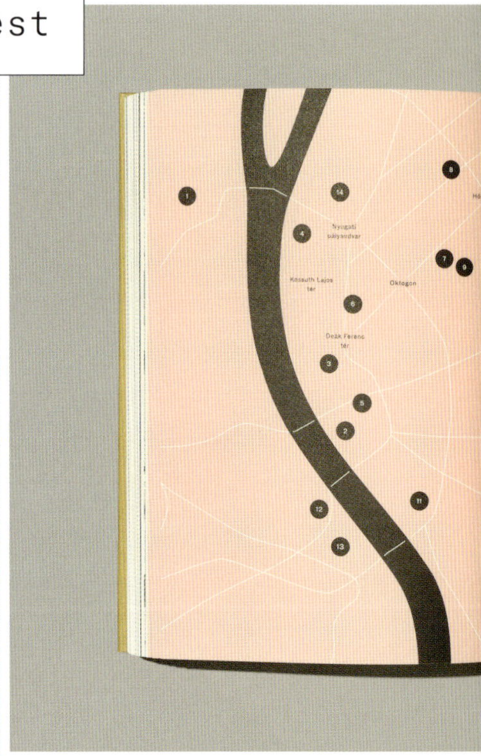

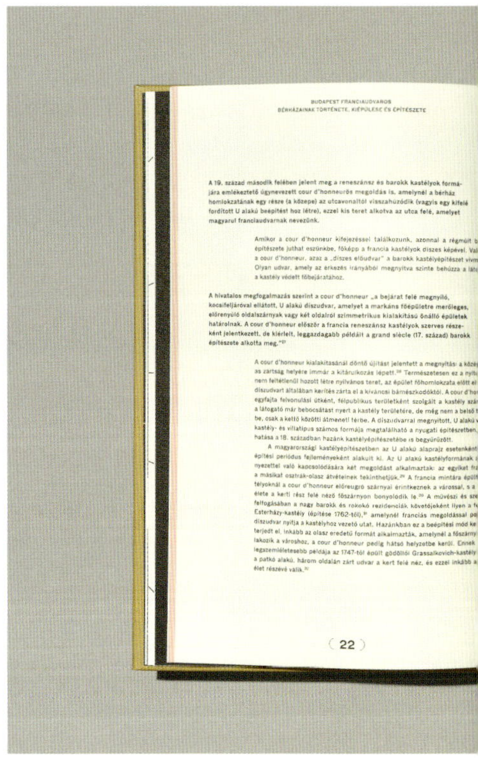

SPECIFICATION
160 mm X 240 mm, 432pp

BINDING & FINISHING
Hardcover, embossing

PAPER
Pergraphica Classic Rough 120gsm

TYPEFACE
Ebuk, Uborka by Hungarumlaut

Buildings with cour d'honneur in Budapest (*Franciaudvaros bérházak Budapesten*) is the outcome of a massive research. The reader was able to explore a less known chapter of the history of the Hungarian capital's architecture on more than 400 pages, accompanied by gorgeous imagery. It is an image-dominated book enriched with archive material, drones, maps and generous line drawings inspired by the originals to loosen up the incredible quantity of the new and exciting information.

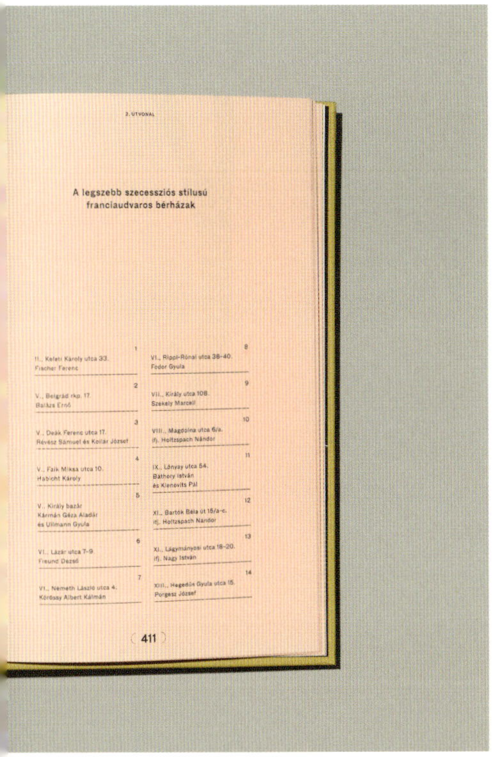

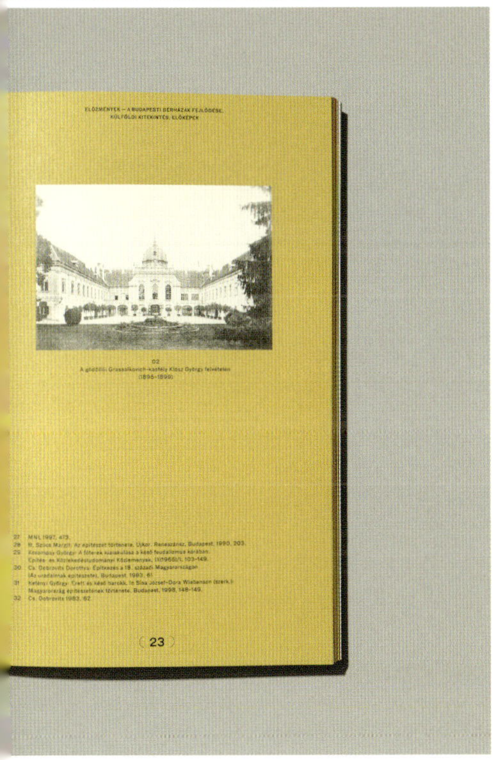

Traços de Gente

DESIGN
Atelier d'alves

PUBLISHER
Amorim

SPECIFICATION
200 mm × 260 mm, 272pp

BINDING & FINISHING
Paperback

PAPER
Materica Pitch 360gsm, Materica Clay 120qsm, Munken Print White 1.8 115gsm

TYPEFACE
Amorim Serif

When the studio started the book design process, they were fully aware that they should not just think about design. Therefore, treating the book as an object was their starting point. Behind the book are the weight of the Amorim cork universe, its roots and its historical legacy. Therefore, they wanted to talk about nature, sustainability, soil, and of course, cork naturally so that people will pick up the book without hesitation. This led them to look for metaphors and sensations through forms and materials.

First of all, the paper. They encoded the idea of nature and warmth through sight (paper tone) and touch (texture). Second, the form. They wanted to create a metaphor 'a glimpse of its inhabitants', for it is very particular to cork, and then appropriated the 'traço' and transposed that through circular cutouts on the cover.

Buch der Körper

DESIGN
Alessia Oertel, Belinda Ulrich, Louisa Kirchner

PUBLISHER
Self-published

SPECIFICATION
297 mm × 420 mm, 30pp

BINDING & FINISHING
Cloth-bound hardcover, screw binding

PAPER
Zigzag folded paper

TYPEFACE
DTL Dorian

Buch der Körper is a study of the body as language and language as a body. It explores the themes of love, pain, confusion, and loneliness. Zigzag folded paper breaks through the single typeface, creating space and increasing the emotional impact of the poem. The book has a classic and solid book cover, contrasting with the open, fragile interior. The folded paper is bound together with golden book screws.

The text is a short poem often ending abruptly. En-dashes and Em-dashes show a change of thought and bridge the related words. For a warm and elegant look, the font DTL Dorian is used. The sand-coloured linen of the cover is reminiscent of a human's skin tone. The poem is printed on soft, structured recycled paper.

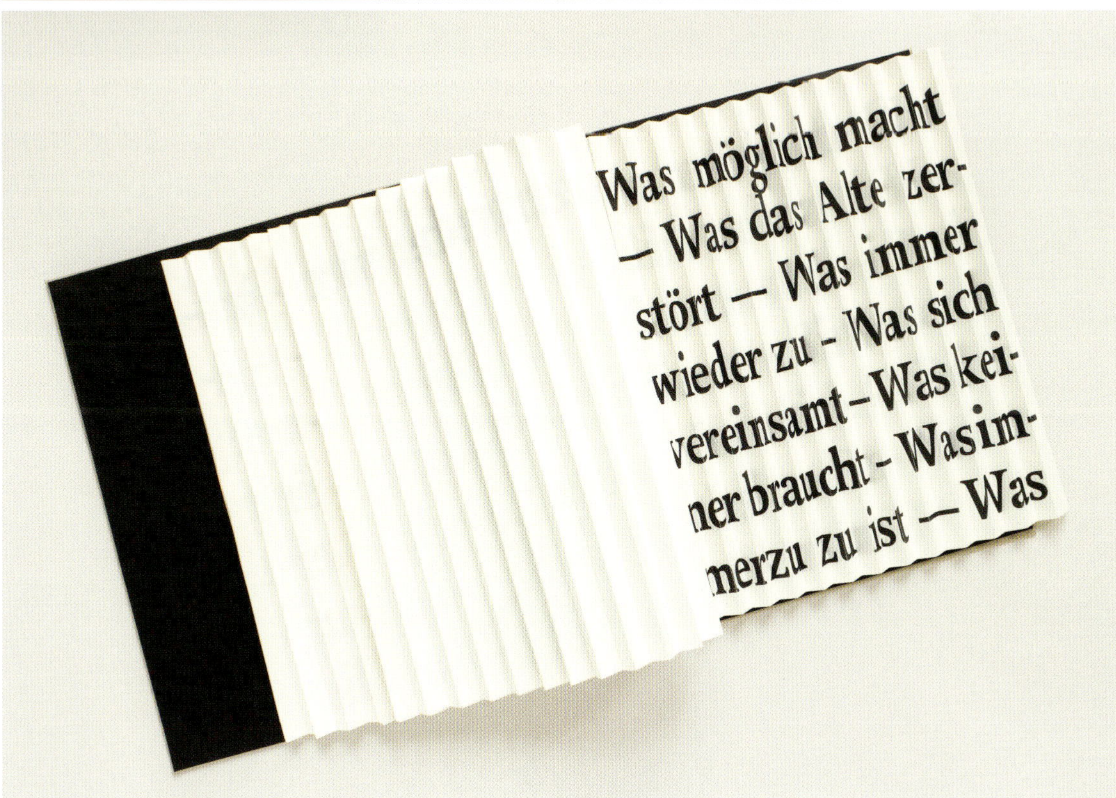

A Garden at Night

DESIGN
Atelier d'alves

PUBLISHER
Rampa

SPECIFICATION
120 mm × 190 mm, 40pp

BINDING & FINISHING
Paperback, accordion folio with mirrored plastic surface

PAPER
Pop'Set Black 240gsm, Munken Lynx 130gsm

TYPEFACE
Stellage Display

A Garden at Night explores the relationship between bodies and landscapes through concepts of trauma, performance and writing. The book is divided into two sides, and they are both formally demarcated. One is a mirrored accordion folio with an interplay between several artistic illustrations and poetic sentences to propose an infinite, unstable landscape; the other is composed of four texts written by four authors: Allen S. Weiss, Pedro Pousada, Nancy Perloff and Tiago Madaleno. The black colour, as the exterior colour, establishes a connection with the 'Night'. The green colour, also the colour of painted trees, portraits nature. And for the silver colour, it reflects the light and echos with the subject.

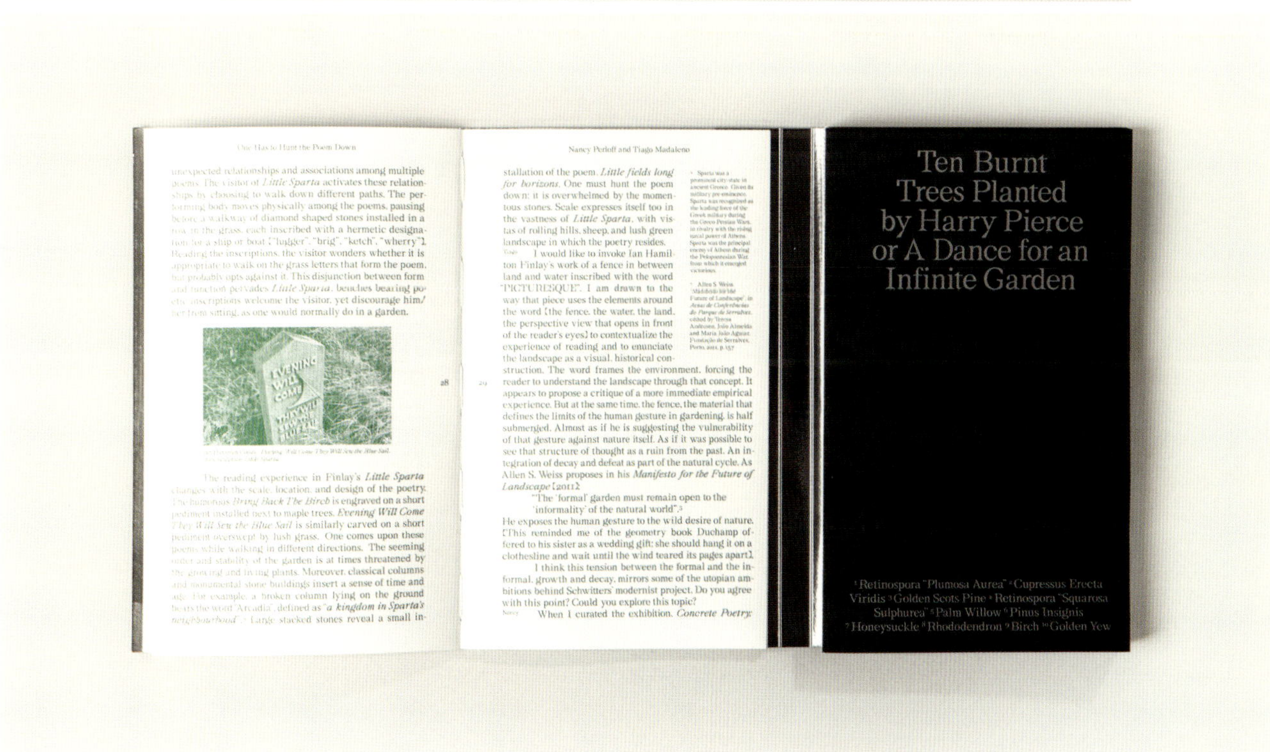

Kyiv Type: Graphic Design & Typography Visual Treasures from Kyiv

DESIGN
Sebastian Schubmehl

PUBLISHER
Self-published

SPECIFICATION
215 mm × 305 mm, 304pp

BINDING & FINISHING
Swiss binding

PAPER
Mohawk Extrarough 300gsm (cover), Munken Pure Rough 150gsm (interior)

TYPEFACE
Suisse Int'l, Suisse Works, Suisse Neue, Euclid Flex by Swiss Typefaces; Kyiv Type by Dmitry Rastvortsev; Kritik by Daniel Stuhlpfarrer; Commune Nuit Debout by Velvetyne Type Foundry; Explanation Serif, Longboy by Sebastian Schubmehl

Kyiv Type is a bachelor thesis focusing on design in Kyiv, the capital of Ukraine. The visual contains design, typography objects and photographs that the author collected during his stay in Kyiv, giving an overview of outdoor design, signage, posters, postcards, print publications in present-day Kyiv. *Kyiv Type* is printed climate-neutral on FSC-certified papers and is designed to be printed on standard oversized A3 sheets, almost loss-free at a low cost. The original texts are published in Russian or Ukrainian. To ensure accessibility for the international audience, all the texts have been translated into English.

God Does Not Play Dice

DESIGN
Kenneth Kuh

PUBLISHER
ArtCenter College
of Design

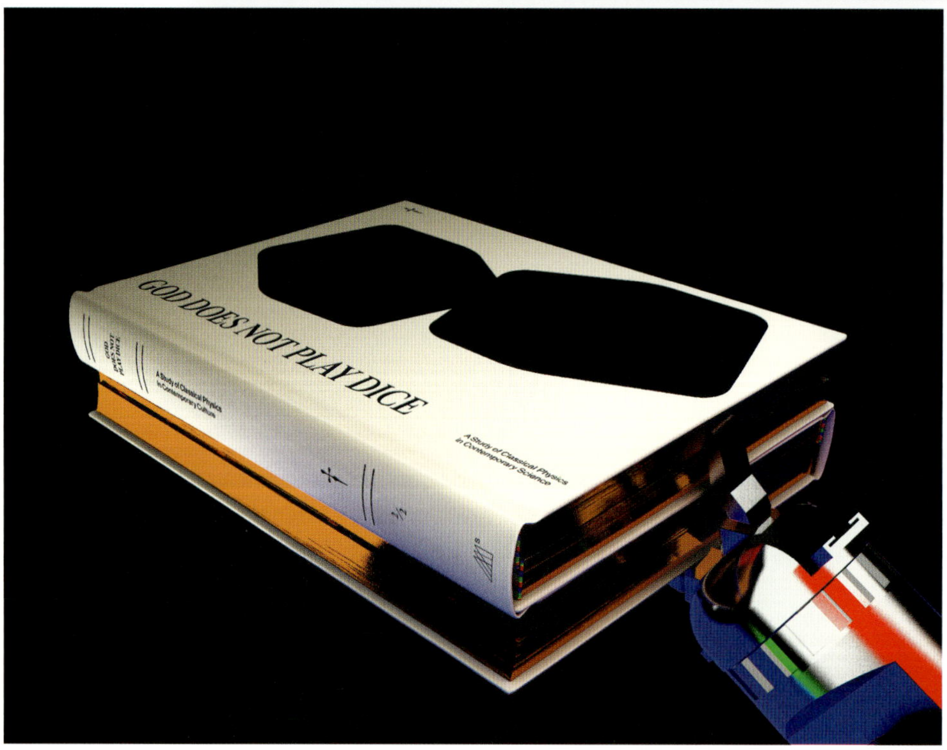

Explore More Projects

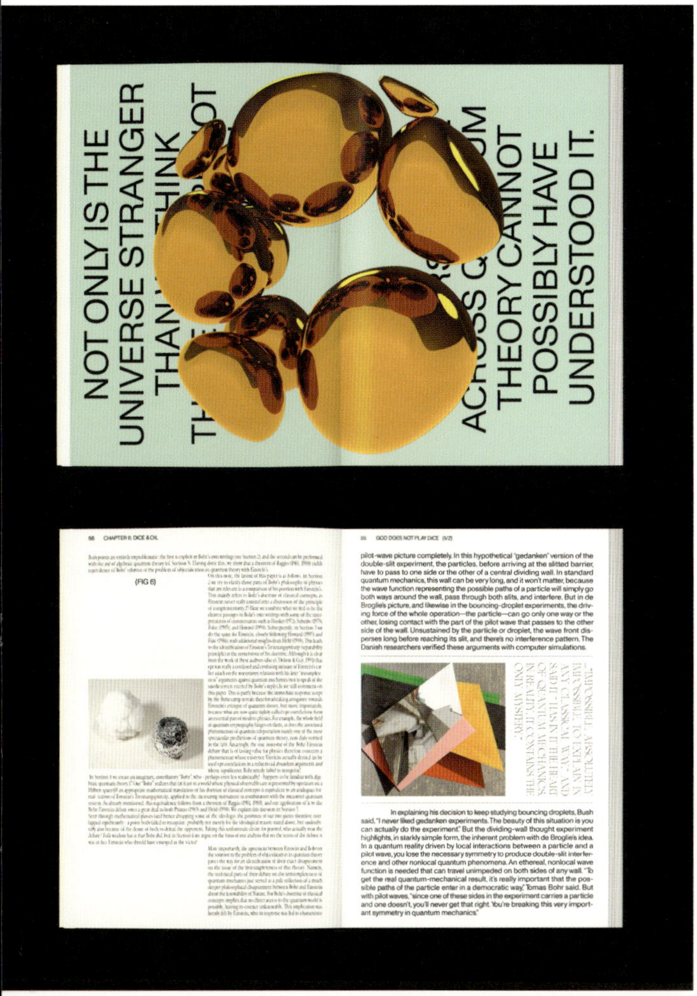

An editorial book that examines the intersection of design and quantum physics, a study of how everything works. Throughout the book, two parallel perspectives on the same subject matter are displayed with different typefaces to establish a neutral visual system for readers to absorb information both efficiently and unbiasedly.

The Monument Grotesk (sans-serif) represents the more modern standpoint from contemporary physics and the Cardinal Fruits (serif) resembles the more old-school classical physics. Cosmic Latte colour is used for the cover as it is the true average colour of the universe. The Dos-à-dos binding allows a dual narrative sequencing for readers to interact with, from different ends of the book. By flipping through the pages from different beginnings, it is as if the readers are performing a tangible time travelling across chapters in chronological order.

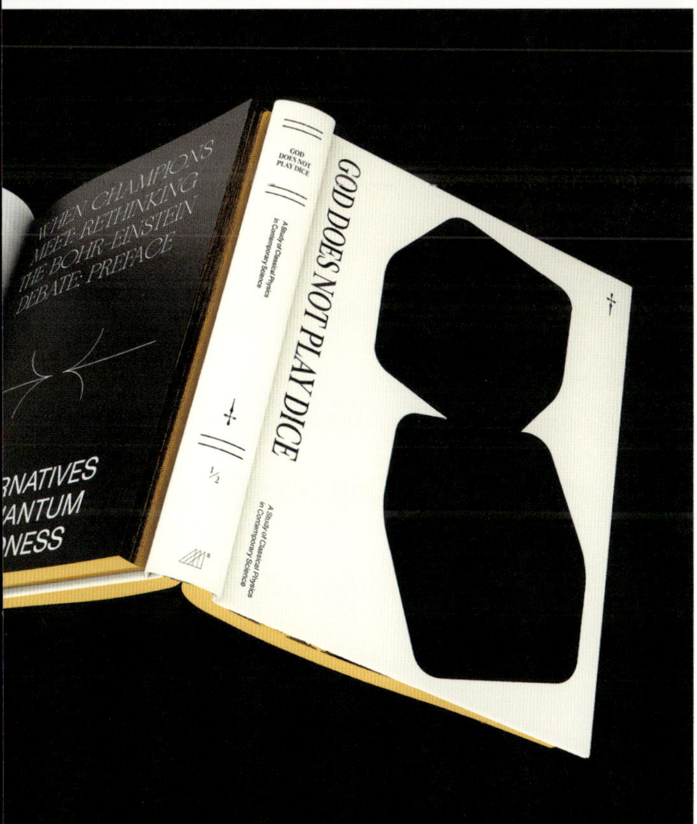

SPECIFICATION
190.5 mm X 280 mm, 418pp

BINDING & FINISHING
Dos-à-dos binding

PAPER
Mohawk Superfine Ultrawhite - Eggshell 80lb

TYPEFACE
Monument Grotesk, Cardinal Fruits, Sometimes Times

Pinocchio - Storia di un Burattino

DESIGN
Luca Longobardi,
Alessandro Latela

PUBLISHER
Self-published (2 copies)

SPECIFICATION
110 mm × 185 mm, 1142pp

BINDING & FINISHING
Sewn binding

PAPER
Cyclus Offset 70gsm

TYPEFACE
Tiempos by Klim Type,
Sharp Grotesk by Sharp Type

There are several interpretations of Carlo Collodi's text, one of which is from Carmelo Bene, who declared 'When Pinocchio learns to read, he becomes a mediocre being.' From this interpretation, the design idea to present the book as a fake pocketbook which is disproportionate and almost unusable came up. The 'IO' (In Italian, I) on the cover, as in the story, is a puppeteer who orchestrates the child's holy unconsciousness. The text tends to vanish and indicates the loss of innocence that distinguishes the protagonist in the first chapter, giving back the idea of oppression as the concept of the book.

La Xarxa al Bosc. Joan Brossa i la Poesía Experimental, 1946-1980

DESIGN
Todojunto

PUBLISHER
Barcelona City Council &
Joan Brossa Foundation

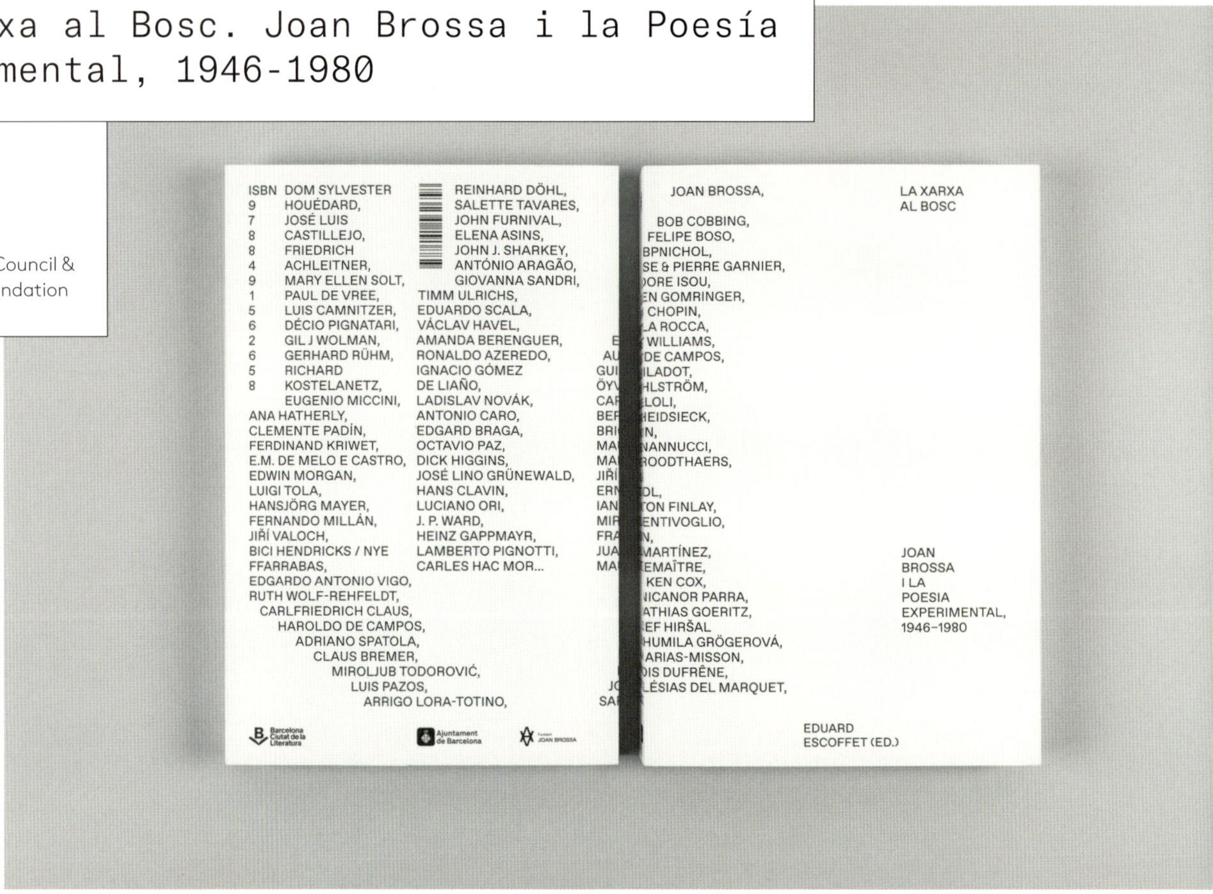

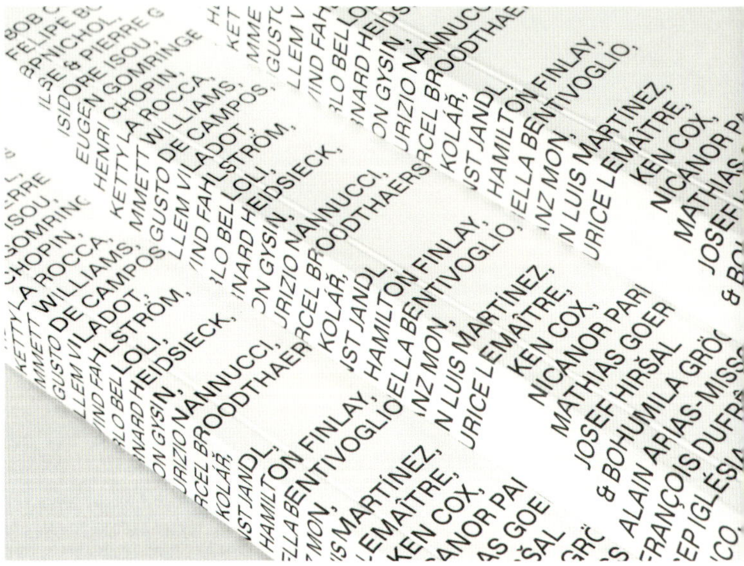

SPECIFICATION
160 mm X 240 mm, 228pp

BINDING & FINISHING
Perfect binding, extended book flap covering the fore-edge of the text block

PAPER
Munken Lynx Rough

TYPEFACE
Favorit

This is a book published for the exhibition of experimental poetry curated by Barcelona-based poet Eduard Escoffet in the Joan Brossa Foundation. Most of the pieces from the exhibition are visual poems by authors around the world. The designers wanted to pay tribute to the typographic works of all these masters by treating the book as a tactile and cohesive piece of print work, using Dinamo's Favorit typeface, and carefully caring about the layout of each spread on the book.

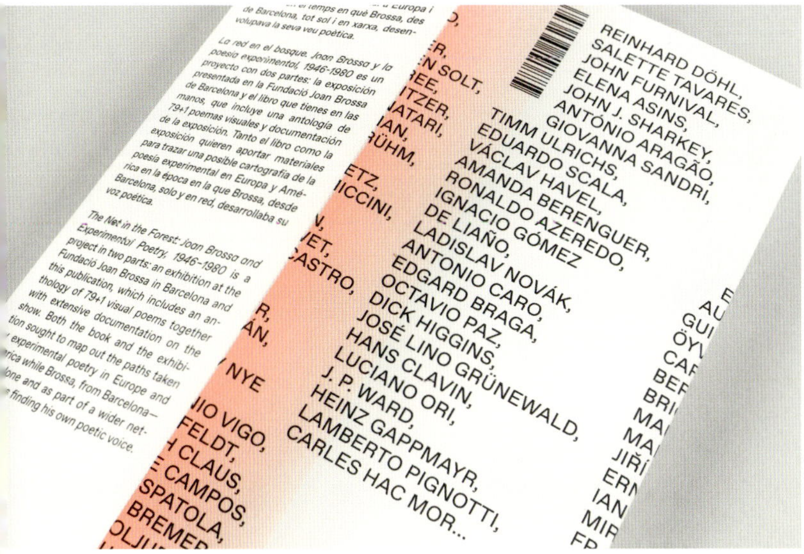

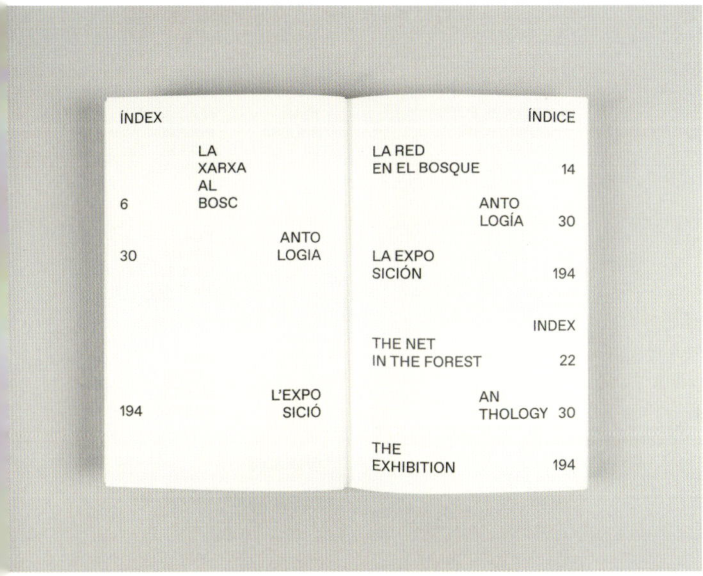

Cinematograph

DESIGN
Tsai Chia-hao

PUBLISHER
Houlang; Guizhou People's Publishing

The main theme and subtitle of the book emphasise film directing. The author is a director, therefore the design focuses on the director's perspective. The director's megaphone is used as the imaginative element, disassembled into the geometric patterns on the front cover of the dust jacket. In addition, the megaphone icons are also placed on the cover and the belly band deliberately. The repetition of stills represents the montage of the film. The compression, expansion, and deformation of the geometric patterns symbolise the various angles of the director. And the shaded facial expressions of the characters provide the viewer with imagination of the faces, expressions, and actions of the actors, which are one of the main focuses of this book. The book title and the geometric shapes on the dust jacket are separated across the front and back of covers for readers to discover.

SPECIFICATION
148 mm × 216 mm, 248pp

BINDING & FINISHING
Hardcover

PAPER
Eco-friendly cotton paper 176gsm,
Eco-friendly fine pattern paper 118gsm

TYPEFACE
Noto Sans

Book Design

Dr. Mary's Monkey

DESIGN
Tsai Chia-hao

PUBLISHER
Faces Publications

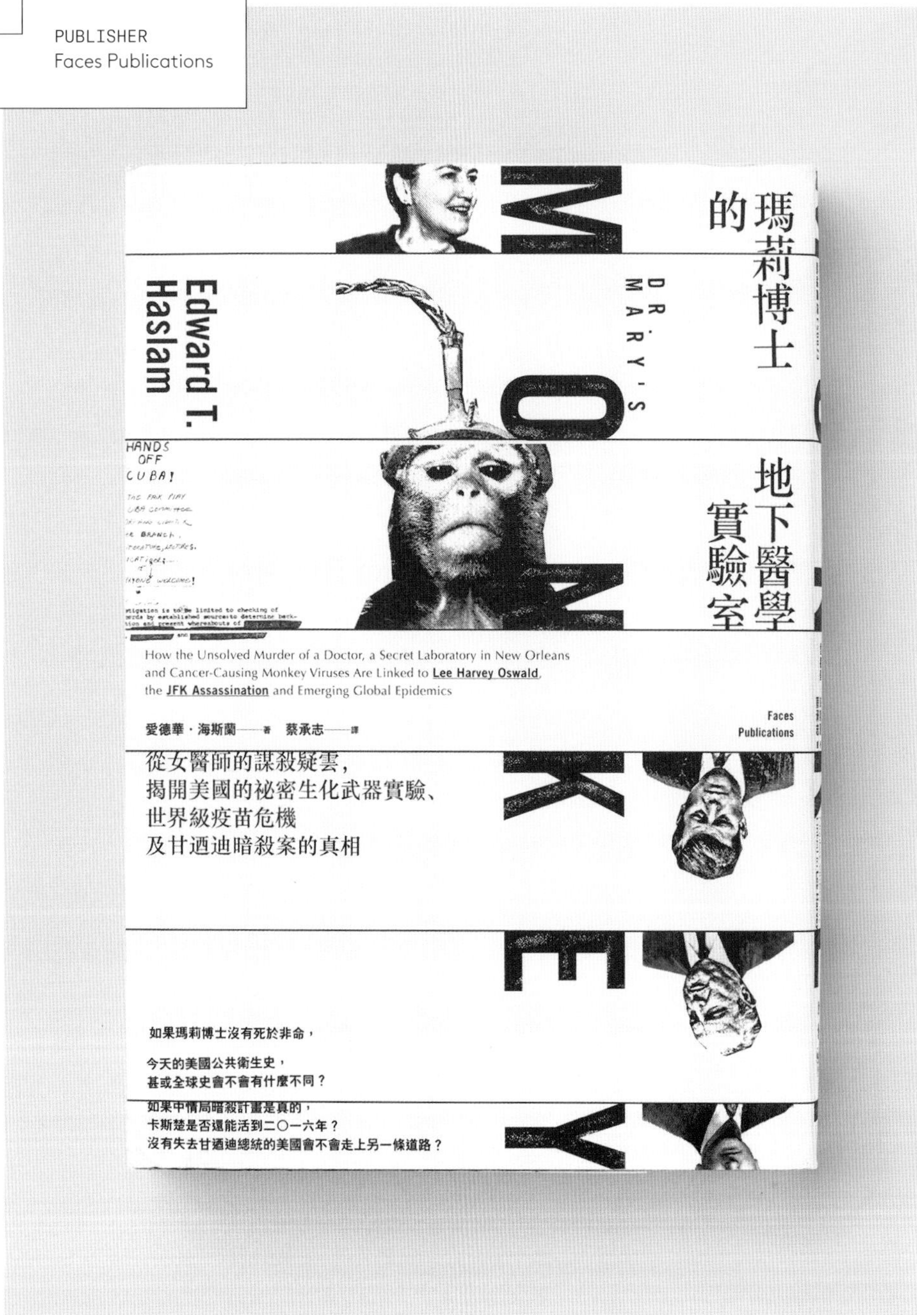

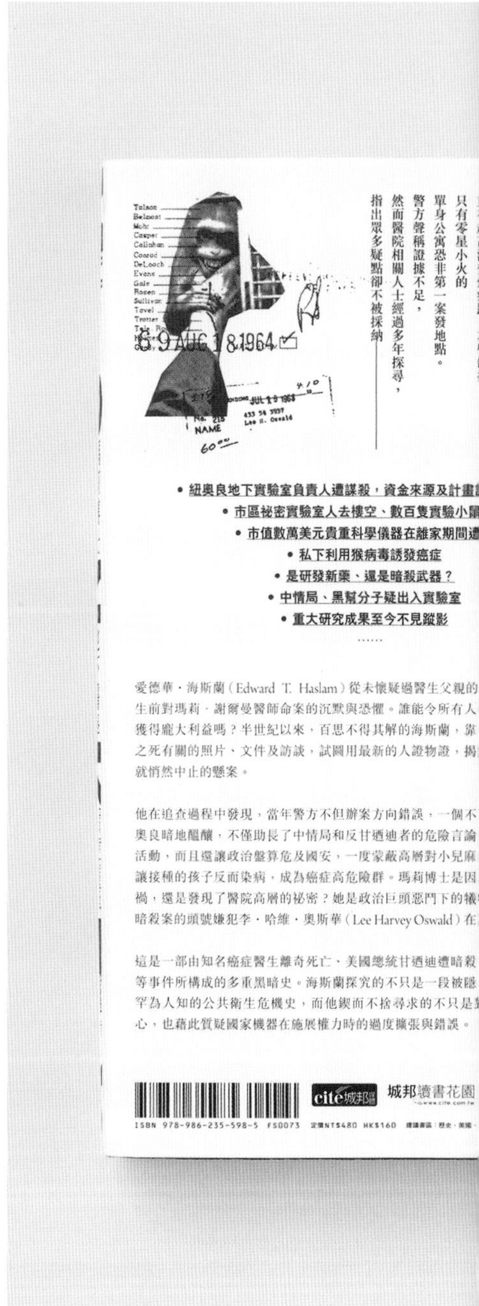

SPECIFICATION
148 mm × 210 mm, 424pp

BINDING & FINISHING
Paperback

PAPER
ThePaperOne Plain paper (ZZ1601)
135gsm

TYPEFACE
Trade Gothic

Each line on the cover is to illustrate an idea of checking the clues one by one. There are four pictures of people's heads in addition to the monkeys in the initial design and the website references for different channels. However, one of them was accidentally deleted by the printing plate maker during the printing process. The designer did not notice until he had the second review carefully. Although it is an annoying and careless printing mistake, it became an interactive design to test readers' capability of reviewing clues.

Gesellschaft Eine Insel

DESIGN
Daniel Zenker

PUBLISHER
Self-published

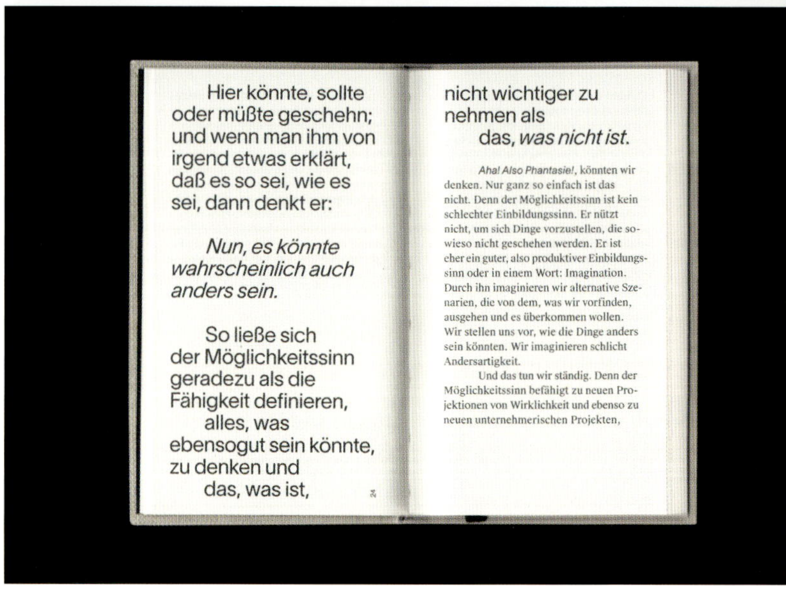

SPECIFICATION
95 mm × 155 mm, 124pp

BINDING & FINISHING
Hardcover, section sewing, hot stamping, natural linen cover, bookmark

PAPER
OKASTAR glossy 115gsm, Holmen TRND 80gsm

TYPEFACE
Lausanne by Nizar Kazan, Suisse Works by Swiss Typefaces

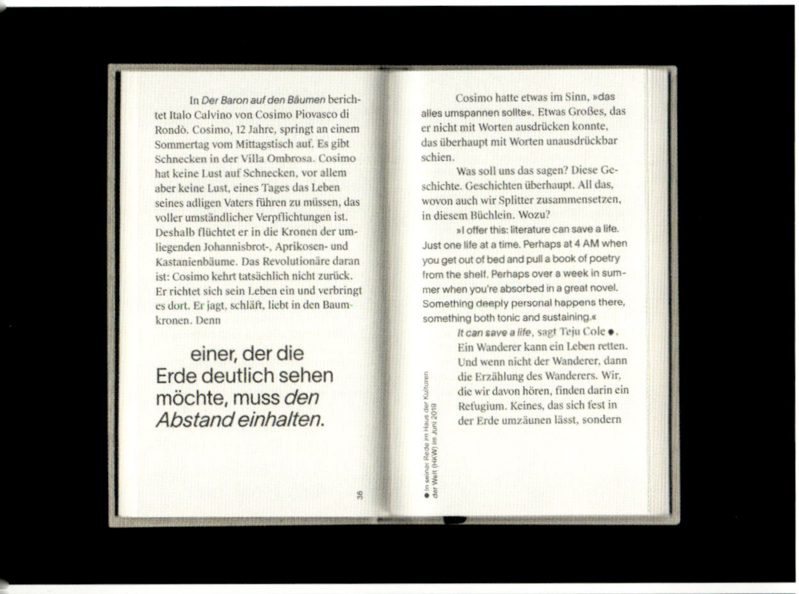

This book is the written observation of a business congress from the viewpoint of literature: the language of entrepreneurship encountered the language of culture. This mixing of viewpoints is reflected in the typographic composition of the book: body text in a rather traditional but modern serif font combined with a likewise classic but contemporary grotesque for expressive headlines, literary quotes and emphases. This high contrast between font sizes is balanced with well-dosed white space in spacing and edges to ensure a dynamic, inviting yet subtly guiding reading experience.

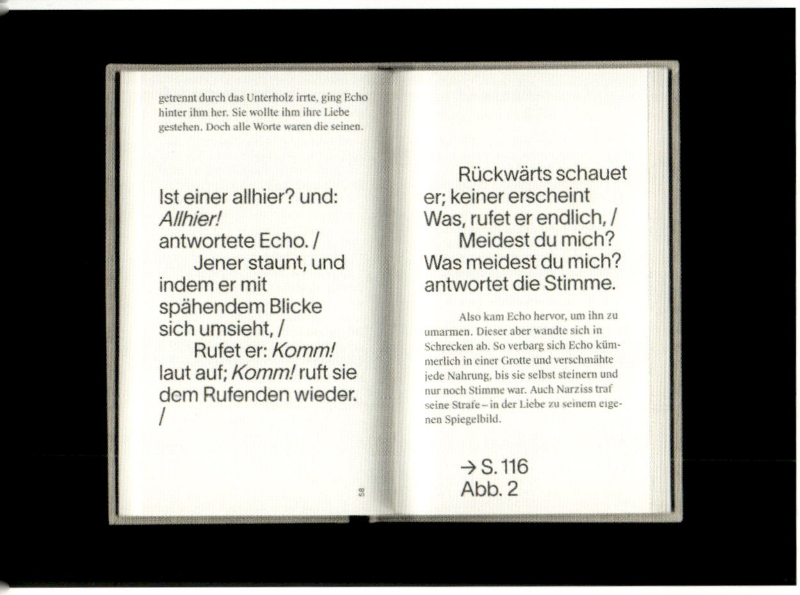

The Lives of Paintings/Życie obrazów

DESIGN
Renata Motyka

PUBLISHER
Stefan Gierowski Foundation

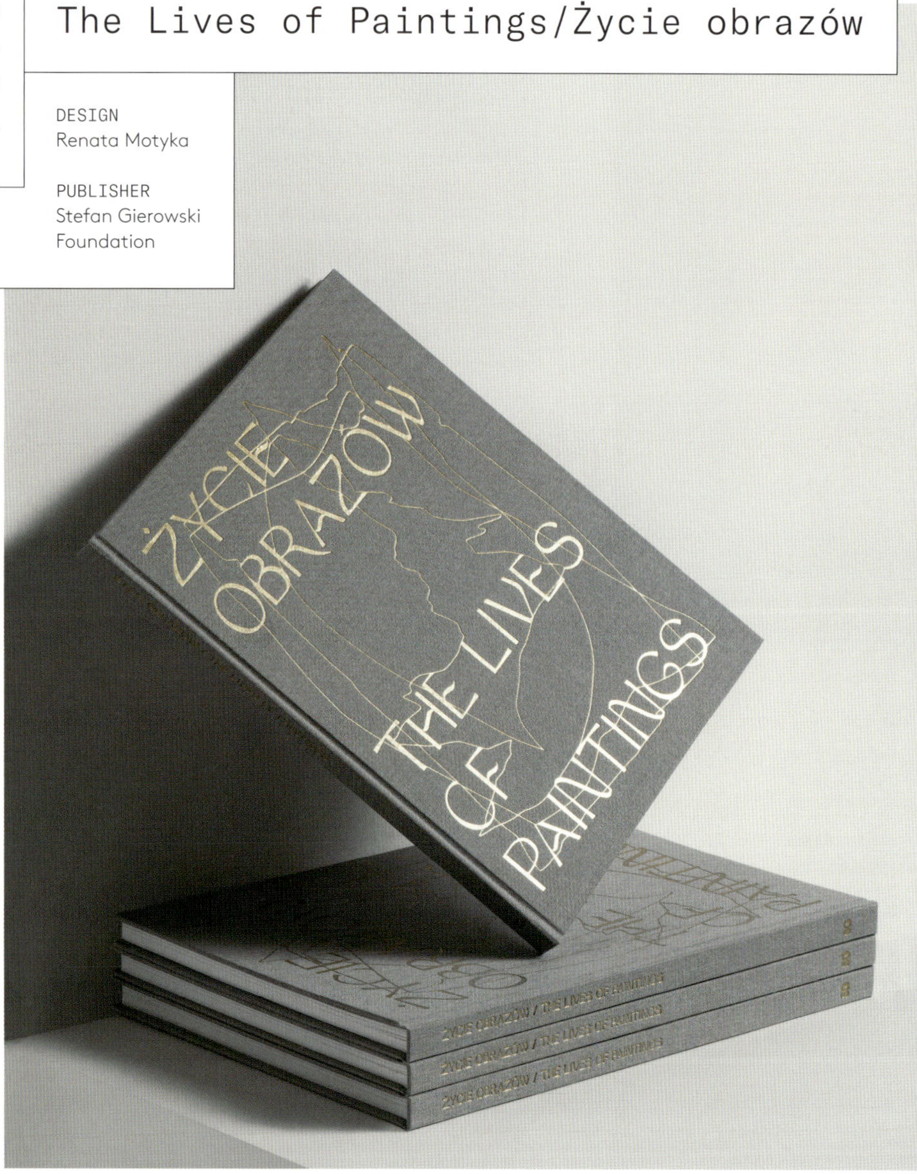

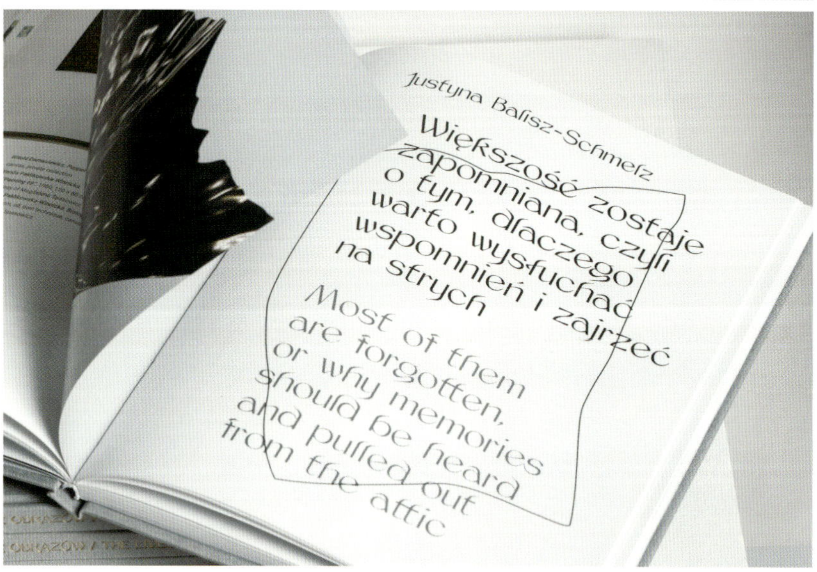

SPECIFICATION
215 mm X 275 mm, 140pp

BINDING & FINISHING
Hardcover, hot stamping

PAPER
Novatech Matt

TYPEFACE
Monarch, Merriweather, Roboto

The catalogue accompanying the exhibition The Lives of Paintings/Życie obrazów includes photographic documentation of the exhibition, reproductions of paintings and texts. The project The Lives of Paintings/Życie obrazów deals with the issue of the disappearing artistic works in Poland, which is a common cultural heritage. It tries to draw the public's attention to the severity of the material and symbolic loss of these works.

Visual identification is based on the theme of a painting – a damaged, old, forgotten work of art. In the project, it appears as a levitating, shape-shifting, three-dimensional object against a grey neutral background. It brings to mind objects and forgotten works of art that are covered with grey dust and show up in a dark and grey cellar. The object is sometimes replaced by its outline as a memory of the presence of this work.

100% Porto

DESIGN
Oscar Maia

PUBLISHER
Porto City Theatre

SPECIFICATION
155 mm × 240 mm, 268pp

BINDING & FINISHING
Perfect binding, rectangle mirror paper

PAPER
Fedrigoni Arcoprint Milk 90gsm, Pop'set Apricot 80gsm

TYPEFACE
FK Display, Fortescue, Plaak

For the design, large typography contrasted with the smaller text blocks emulates the idea of boldness versus detail. This distinction reflects the character of Porto's inhabitants, known to have a very outgoing personality, easygoing, welcoming, and warm-hearted.

The names of the 100 participants on the cover is a way of representing their existence as elements of the city and icons for the project. The mirror on the back includes the readers as a part of the project, and has this idea imprinted in their minds as they finish the book and see their reflections on it.

Fonts SK – Digitised Type Design in Slovakia

DESIGN
CarnokyType

PUBLISHER
Slovak Design Center;
CarnokyType

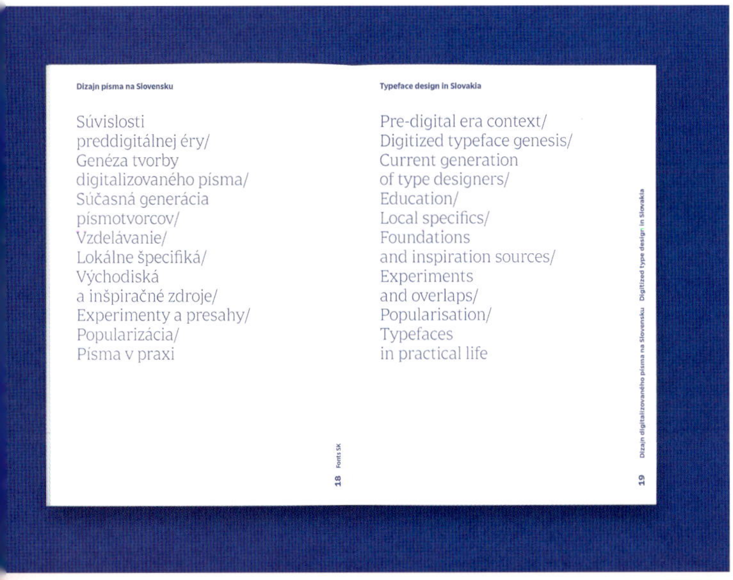

Fonts SK maps the digitised type design in Slovakia. Its open-bound softback and minimalist cover design are hidden underneath a dust jacket in several versions, all referring to the variety of content and, with the help of a pangram in the Slovak language, to the specifics of local diacritics. The most extensive part of the book is the chronological presentation of the types, all typographically set through short descriptions. Two primary colours (red and blue), combined with white paper is a metaphor for national identity. The result is a coherent gesamtkunstwerk, with the author being not just an editor of the publication, author of texts, co-publisher and graphic designer, but also a type designer who set the whole book with authorial fonts.

SPECIFICATION
170 mm X 240 mm, 412pp

BINDING & FINISHING
Paperback, bare spine

PAPER
Olin Rough High White 300gsm, 130gsm

TYPEFACE
Zin Serif, Zin Sans, Zin Slab, Zin Display

Post-foundational Book Cover Series

DESIGN
Genis Carreras

PUBLISHER
Gedisa

Book series explore new ways to understand politics through the lens of the most important thinkers of the 21st century. Each cover reduces the core idea behind each book of this collection to a single abstract icon and colour.

SPECIFICATION
131 mm × 195 mm, 80-150pp

BINDING & FINISHING
Paperback with flaps,
matt lamination

PAPER
Offset paper 240gsm (cover),
80gsm (interior)

TYPEFACE
Apercu Bold

Age of Union

DESIGN
Baillat Studio

PUBLISHER
Anteism

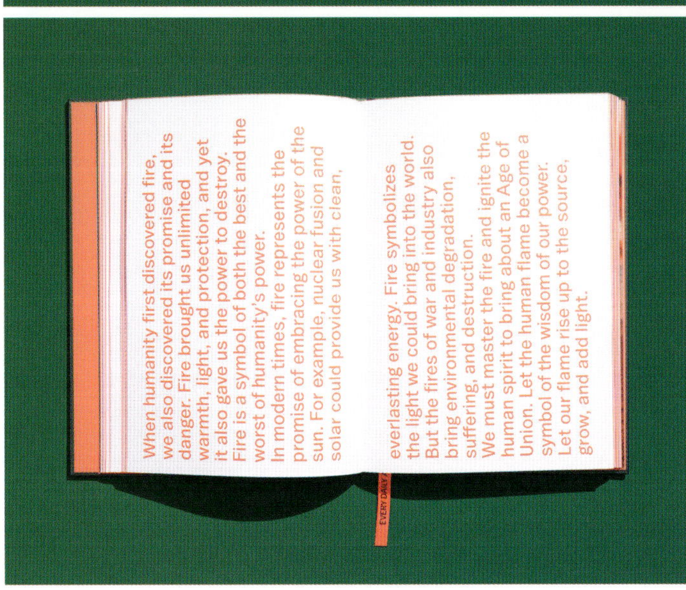

SPECIFICATION
195 mm × 270 mm, 210pp

BINDING & FINISHING
Swiss binding, hot stamping, debossing, edge printing

PAPER
–

TYPEFACE
Du Nord by Playtype

The book draws on the author's personal and philosophical viewpoint to initiate positive progress in the world. Nine contemporary artists from varying fields of practice were brought together through a dozen of seminal pieces. The striking colours in each piece, combined with those found in the other works, produce a powerful chromatic experience.

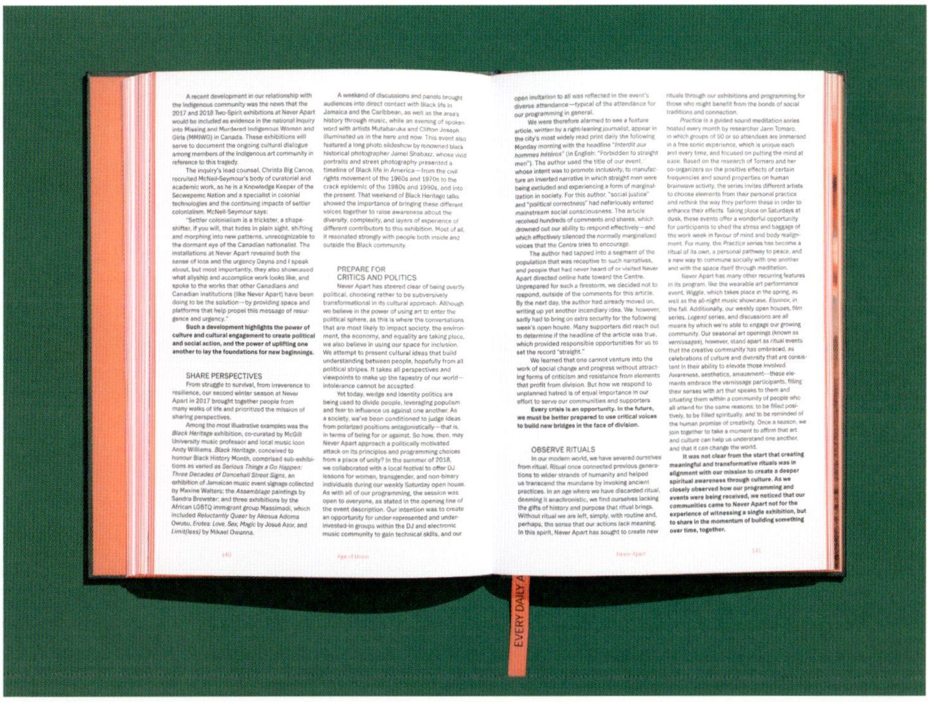

The Bird Project 2006-2017

DESIGN
Lundgren+Lindqvist

PUBLISHER
Il'Editions

SPECIFICATION
207 mm × 280 mm, 208pp

BINDING & FINISHING
Paperback, section sewing, foil embossing (cover), high gloss UV coating

PAPER
Arctic Silk 250gsm, Arctic Silk 130gsm, 576 mm × 750 mm fold-out poster

TYPEFACE
Neue Haas Grotesk 55 Roman

Stockholm-based artist Erik Berglin wheatpasted 4982 hand-cut images of birds in nature in twelve cities around the world. This book features 101 plates printed in a complex process with fluorescent colours instead of their CMYK counterparts. The plates are silkscreen coated with high gloss UV varnish, adding to the vividness of the colours. An index of Latin names of the 4982 birds and their addresses is included in a folded poster. 30 copies of the special edition are divided into three sets, each in a fluorescent acrylic glass slipcase.

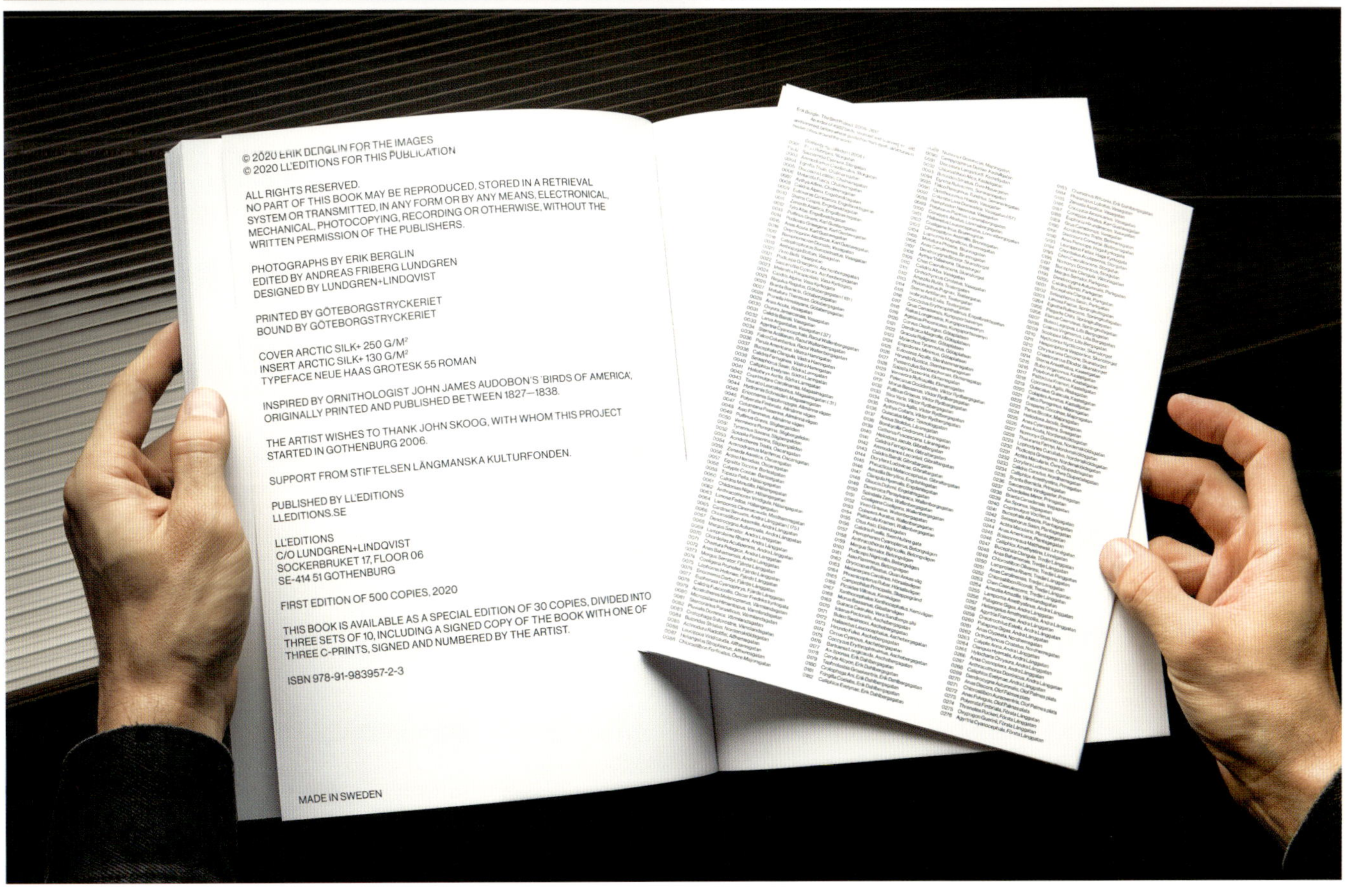

Makers Bible - Human Space (Black Edition)

DESIGN
Melville Brand Design

PUBLISHER
Melville Brand Design

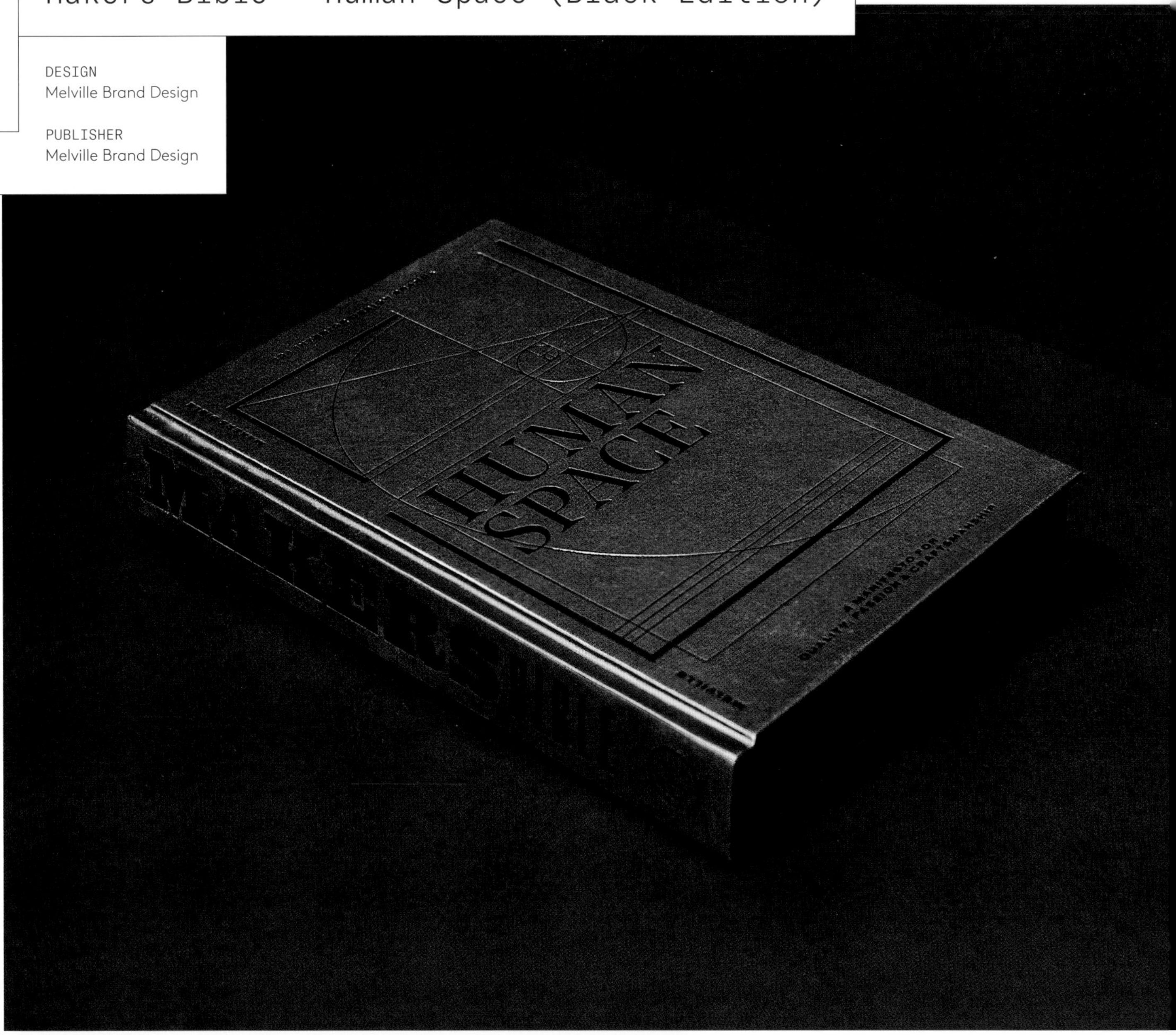

SPECIFICATION
160 mm X 240 mm, 376pp

BINDING & FINISHING
Hardcover, sewn binding

PAPER
Winter & Company Corvon (cover), IGEPA Salzer touch 120gsm (interior)

TYPEFACE
Sharp Grotesk (headings), Noe (body)

Makers Bible – Human Space is a story-telling book featuring 101 passionate makers and crafter brands in interior design and architecture. This edition serves as a guide for readers who are looking to add the human touch to their living spaces and thus seeking sustainable alternatives and inspiration. The black edition is a special edition. While the content remains unchanged, the black edition comes in a completely black finish, with matt black cover, shiny black embossing and a black colour cut.

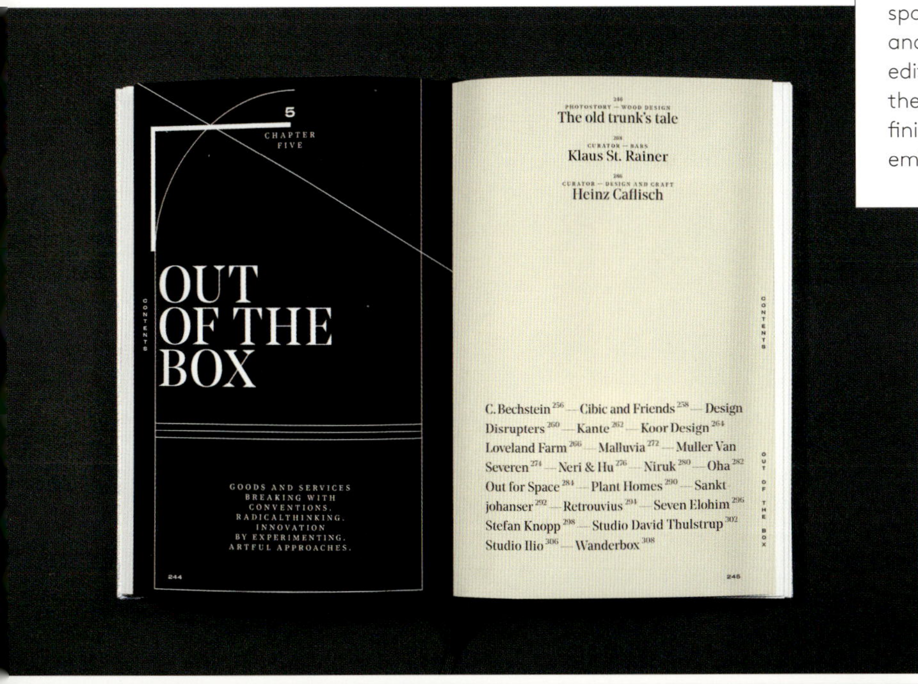

Carcasse: The Butcher's Kitchen

DESIGN
Tim Bisschop

PUBLISHER
Hannibal books

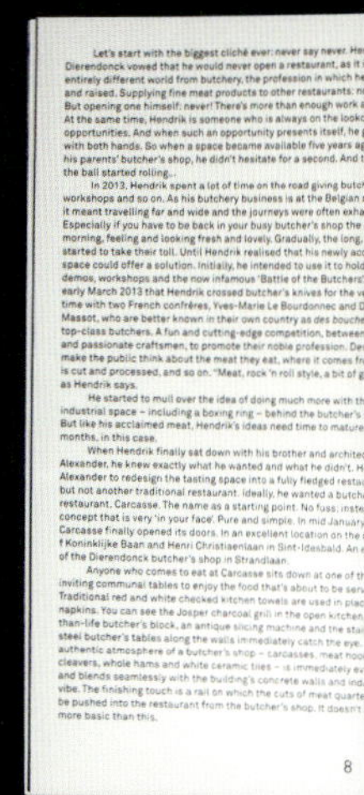

SPECIFICATION
232 mm X 271 mm, 192pp

BINDING & FINISHING
Hardcover, bare spine, pre-drilled hole for a meat hook

PAPER
Munken Rough

TYPEFACE
Peter & Brandon Grotesque Bold

A book with recipes and the story about the restaurant Carcasse. Carcasse is a meat-lovers mecca and owner Hendrik Dierendonck is a meat connoisseur. This book tells the story of where great quality meats come from and includes the best recipes from Carcasse, each created with Dierendonck's passion for quality and perfection. The book is designed with a bare spine and a pre-drilled hole for a meat hook.

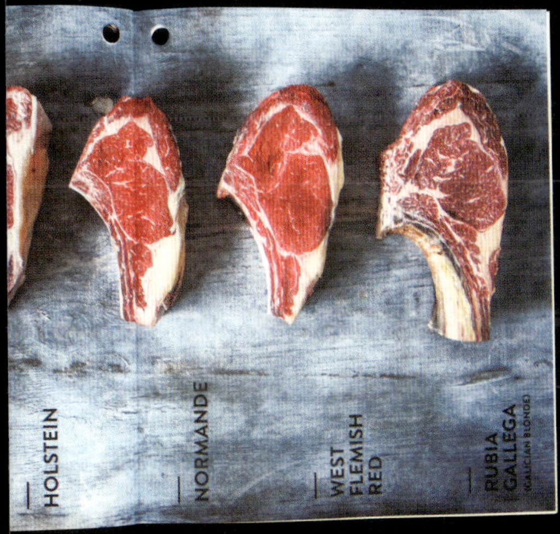

Wish/Wonen in Stadshart

DESIGN
Studio de Ronners

PUBLISHER
GRAS Uitgevers i.c.w.
Gemeente Groningen

The book looks like a manageable red block. The colour refers to the city heart. Besides, the book block is a nod to the typical red brick that can be found everywhere in Groningen – baked from the Groningen clay. The cover symbolises the theme of the manifestation: the attractiveness of the city heart, the relatively high density that characterises the inner city and the seemingly limited space for new developments. On the cover, the designers played with the limited space and it offered more than imagination. In addition to space for a title, the cover presents all architects included, and the images offer a glimpse into the interior of the building. On the cover, the designers presented the 'blurb' of the book. As such, what the book is about becomes apparent immediately.

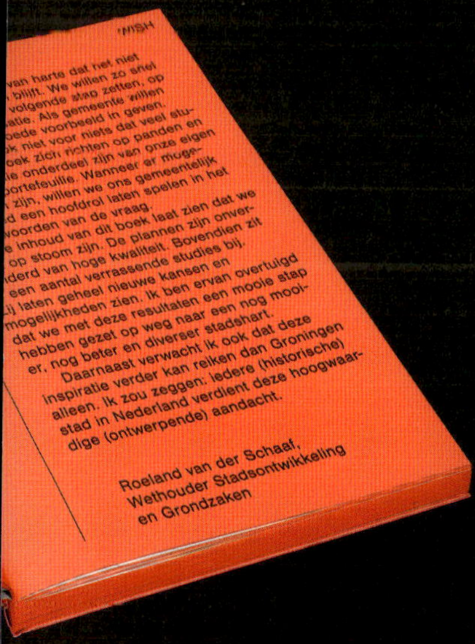

SPECIFICATION
171 mm × 252 mm, 267pp

BINDING & FINISHING
Sewn binding, edge printing

PAPER
Uncoated paper Velvet 1.5, Symbol Freelife 130gsm, paper bract-coated with Wibalin Dove Grey

TYPEFACE
Nimbus Sans Regular; Plantin MT Italic, Regular and Bold

Wanderspace/Zwerfruimte

DESIGN
Sarah Schrauwen

PUBLISHER
nai010 publishers

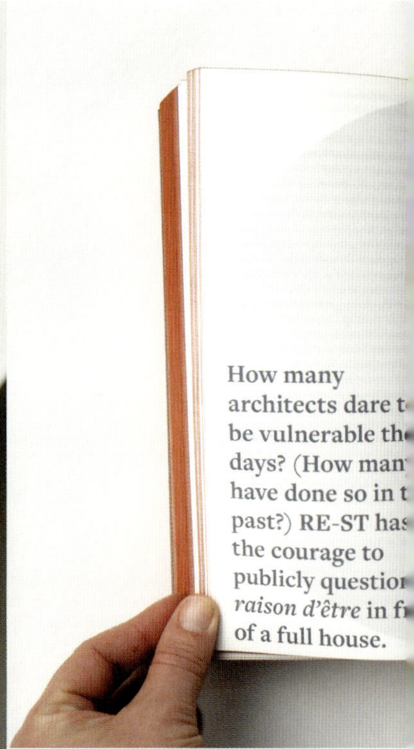

SPECIFICATION
100 mm × 210 mm, 384pp

BINDING & FINISHING
Flush-cut hardcover, debossing, edge printing

PAPER
Wibalin Recycled (cover), EOS 2.0 90gsm (interior)

TYPEFACE
Larsseit, Freight Text

RE-ST Architecten, the authors and editors of *Wanderspace/Zwerfruimte*, had the concept of a brick-sized book in mind from the very beginning. This idea was inspired by an artwork by the Belgian artist and architect Luc Deleu, called 'De Laatste Steen van België' or 'The Last Brick of Belgium', which embodies their philosophy of re-using empty and forgotten spaces rather than building or developing new ones. Metaphorically, this book could be the 'last brick' of Belgium. It was the starting point of the design and the production process.

Építész Stúdió 1990-2020

DESIGN
Ákos Polgárdi

PUBLISHER
Építész Stúdió

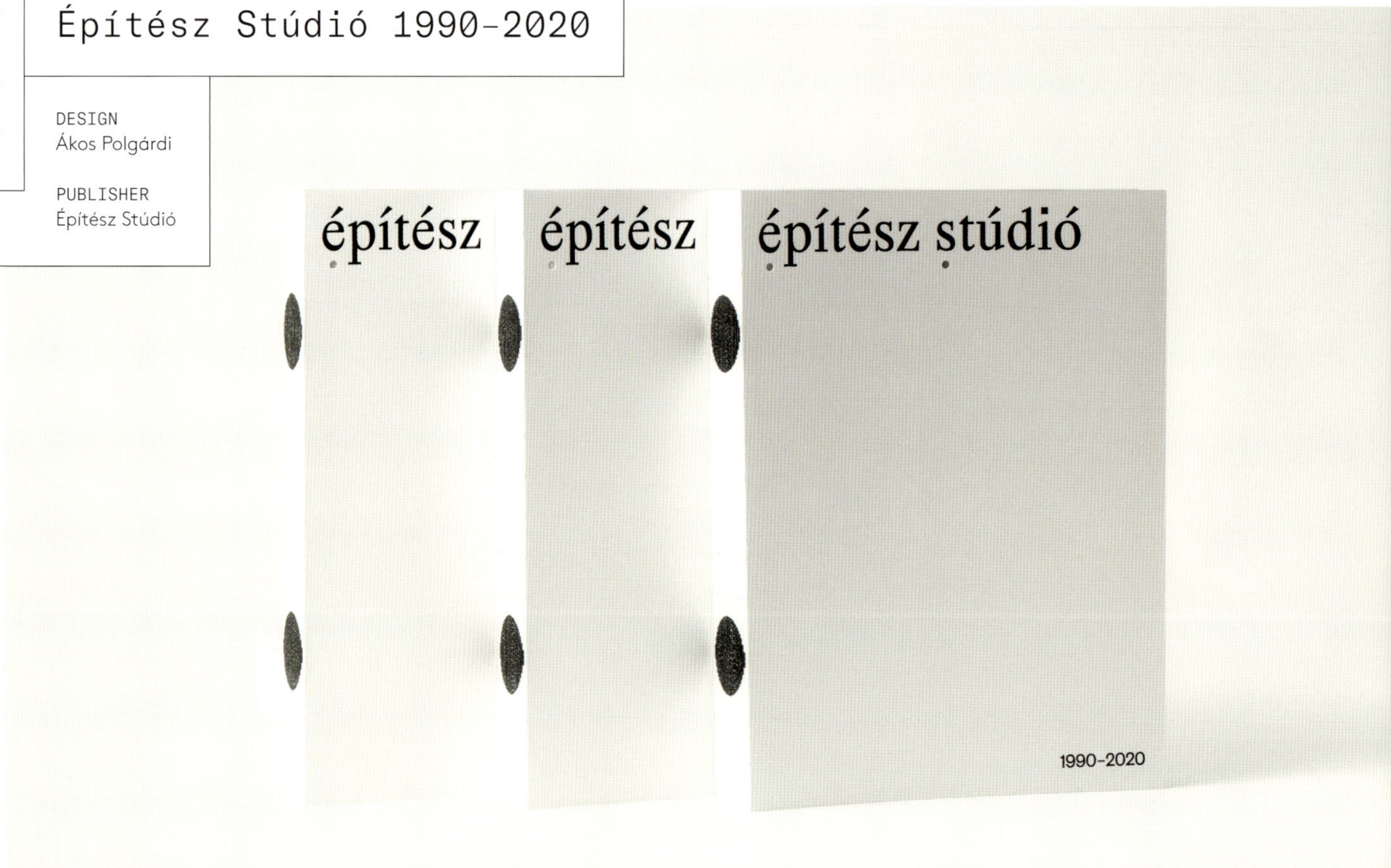

SPECIFICATION
220 mm X 290 mm, 464pp

BINDING & FINISHING
Paperback, hot stamping,
die cutting (cover)

PAPER
Curious Matter Goya White 270gsm,
Munken Polar Smooth 120gsm

TYPEFACE
Founders Grotesk, Happy Times at
the ÉS

Építész Stúdió 1990–2020 lists all 476 projects completed to date by leading Hungarian architecture practice Építész Stúdió. Some of them are presented in details (featuring plans, photos, renderings), while some just their basic project data (serial number, date of design, final phase reached, contributing architects). The book was launched at the és30 exhibition opening where visitors were invited to draw, paint or leave their marks on the blank covers. Those attending the finissage were asked to choose their favourite cover design and bring it home.

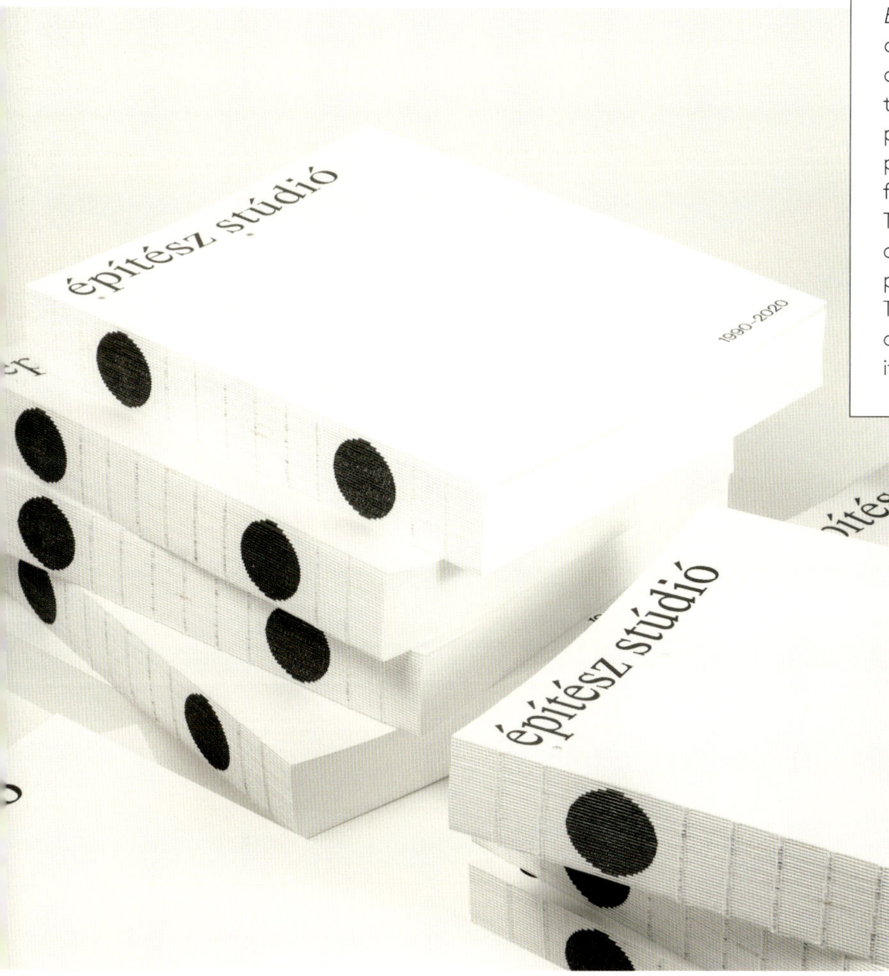

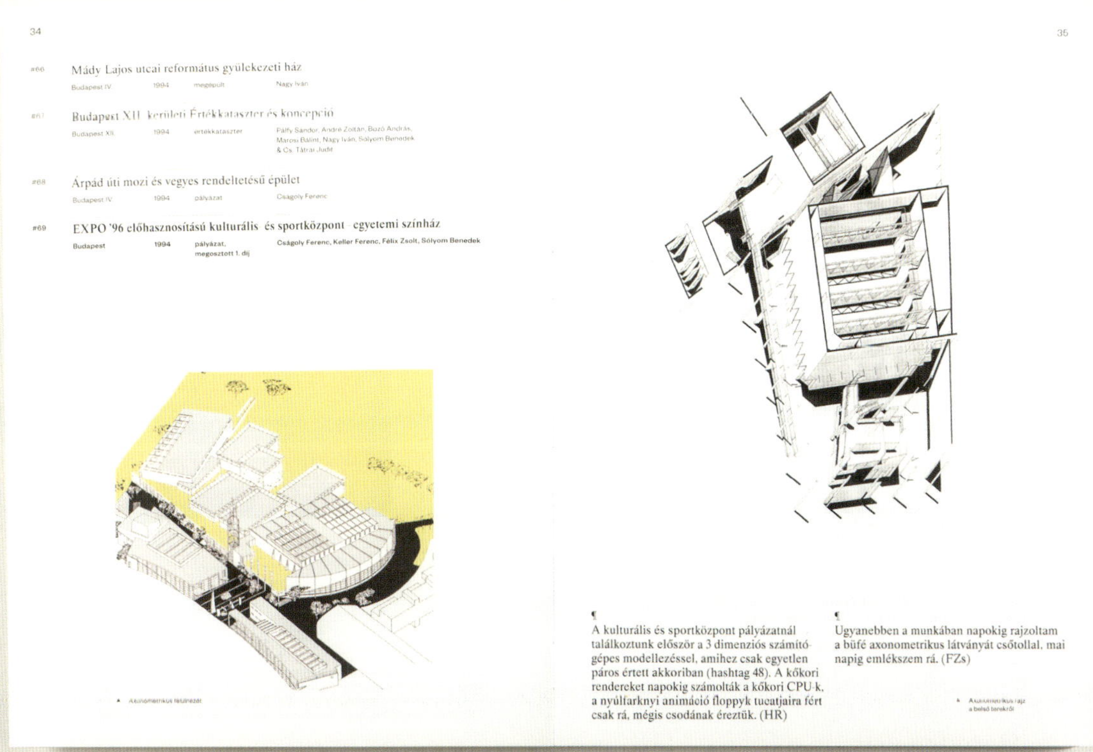

J.D. Salinger's Works

DESIGN
Ákos Polgárdi

PUBLISHER
Európa Könyvkiadó

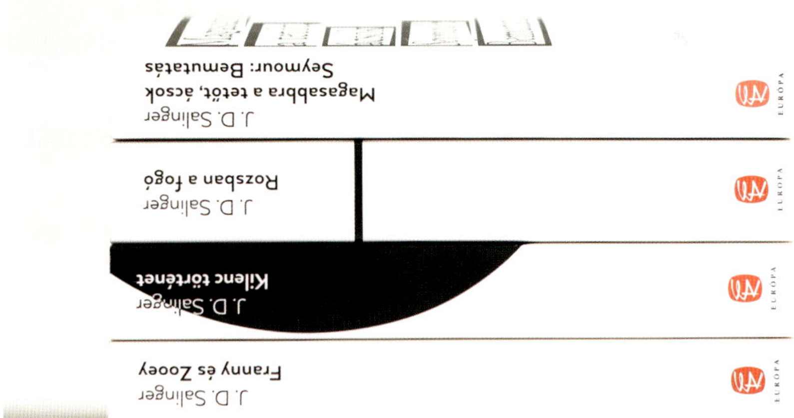

SPECIFICATION
110 mm × 185 mm, 268pp~308pp

BINDING & FINISHING
Paperback with French flap

PAPER
Uncoated paper

TYPEFACE
Custom, Centaur

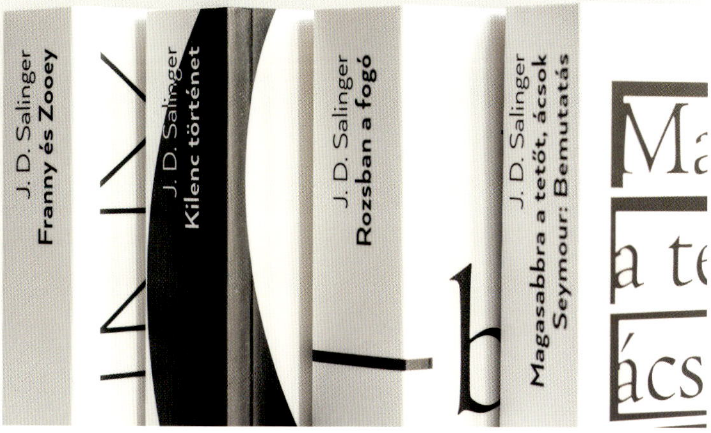

The designer was commissioned by Hungarian publishing house Európa Könyvkiadó to design covers for J. D. Salinger's works. Salinger gave strict instructions regarding the cover designs for his books and forbade any illustrative elements, which is why a purely typographic approach seemed justified.

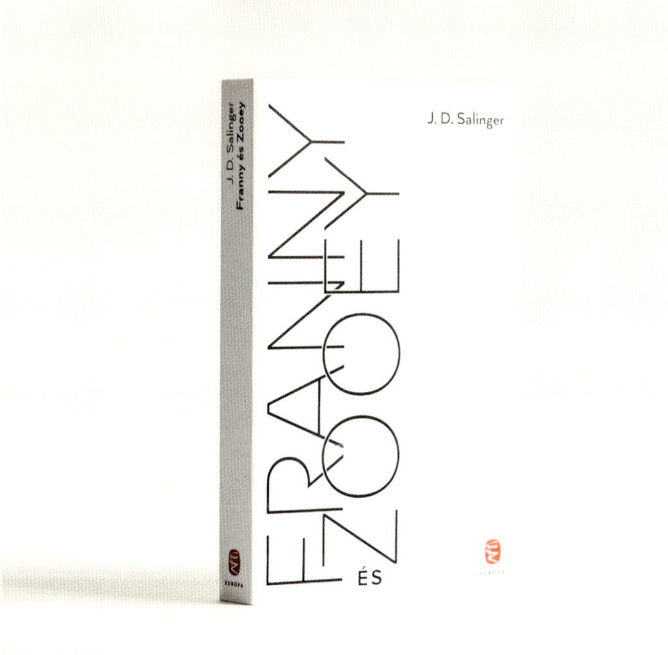

Made in Fukushima

DESIGN
Moby Digg

PUBLISHER
METER Group

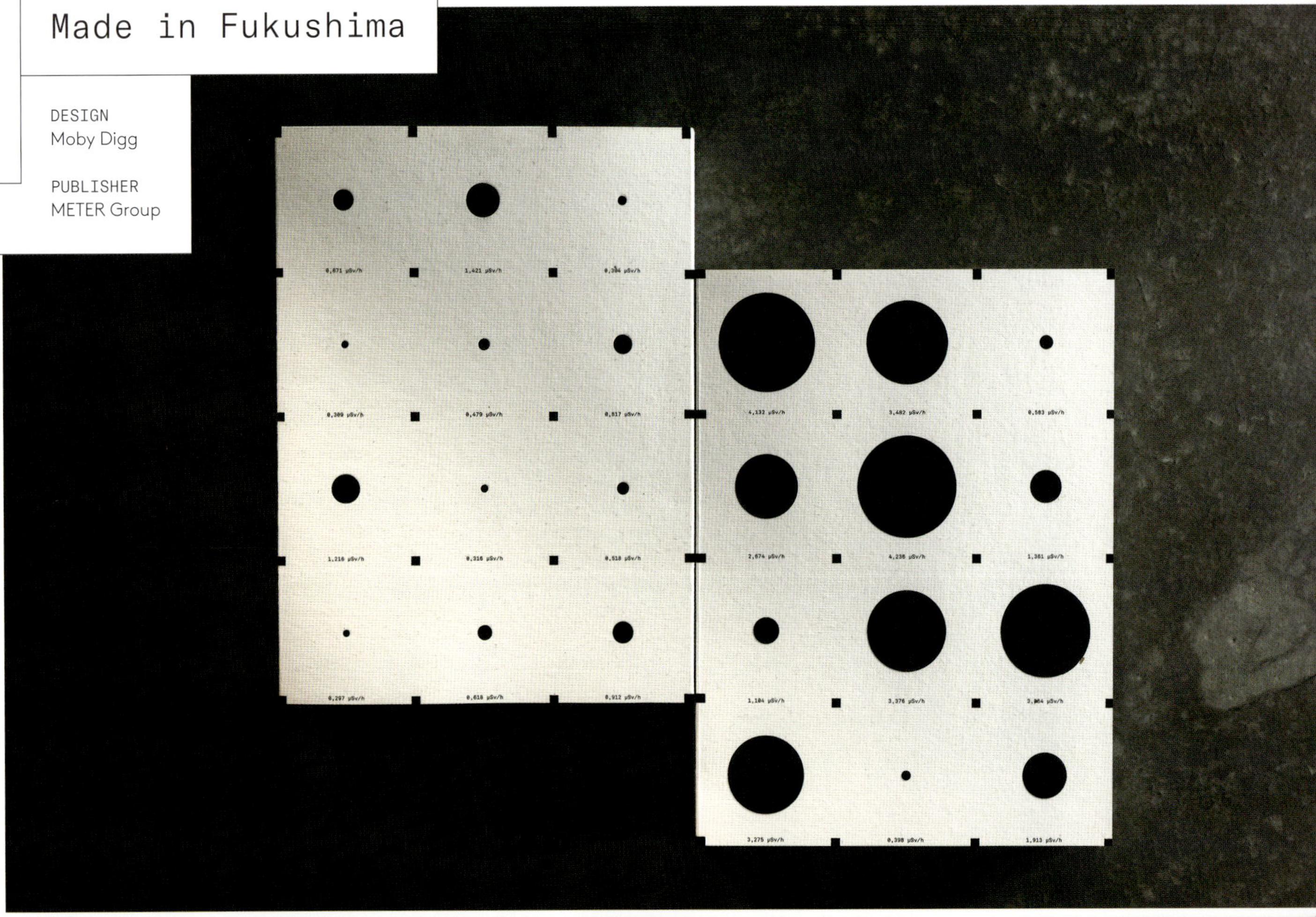

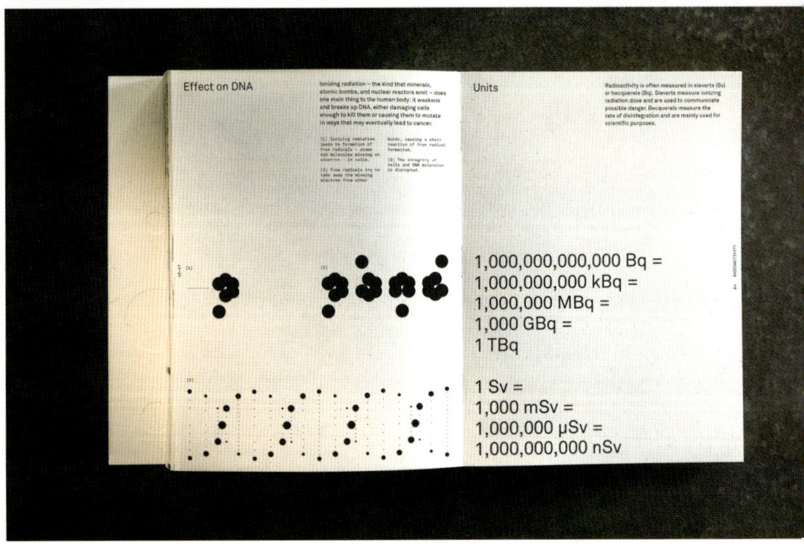

SPECIFICATION
175 mm × 230 mm, 232pp

BINDING & FINISHING
Japanese and Swiss binding, embossing, debossing, flaps, coloured thread

PAPER
Paper made from decontaminated rice straw by Gmund papier

TYPEFACE
Akkurat

More than 25,000 hectares of farmland were contaminated after a tsunami hit the Fukushima Daiichi Power Plant. Scientists developed a method to grow safe rice. However, no one bought the rice because of the stigma. To help people understand, the designers turned science into something tangible. Paper made from rice straw from the decontaminated fields was produced by papermakers from Fukushima and Gmund Papier. With this paper, they printed a book that tells the story of the decontamination, the farmers and their products – using photography, interviews, background information and data visualisation.

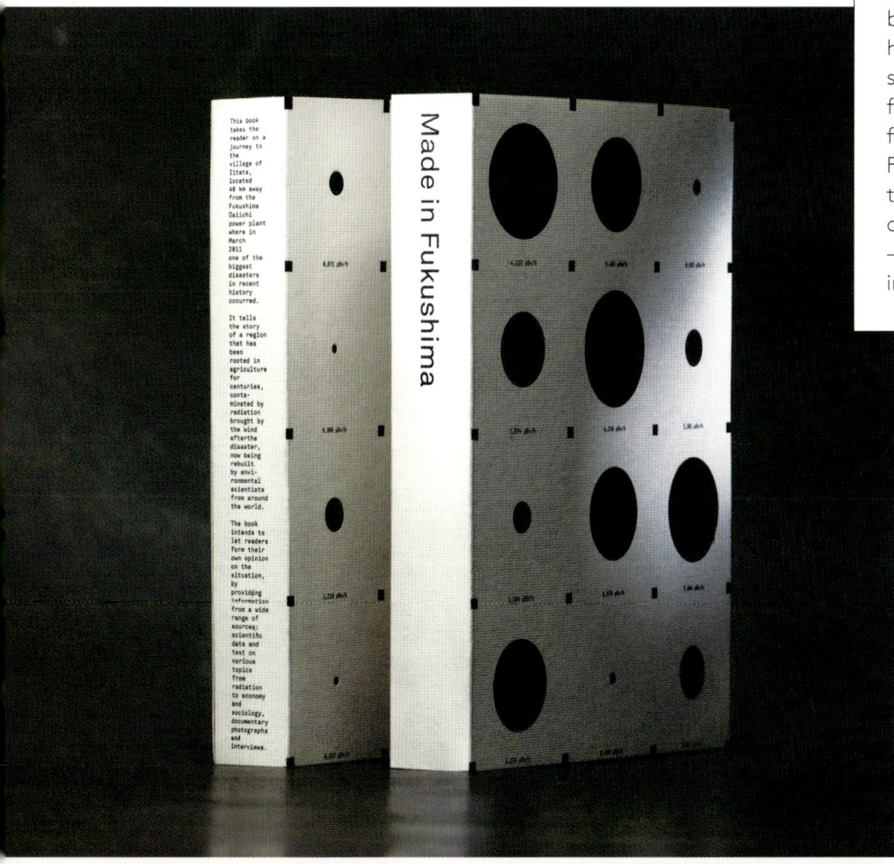

Arts Development Plan Hannover 2030

DESIGN
Bureau Hardy Seiler

PUBLISHER
City of Hanover

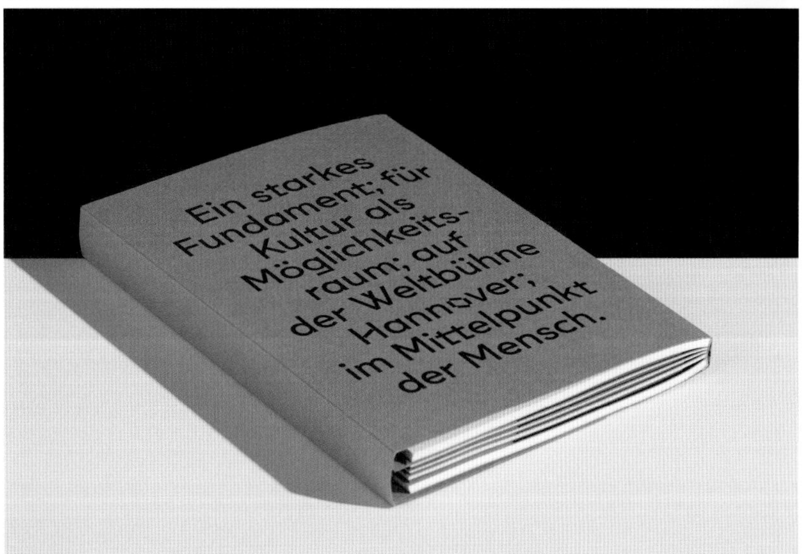

SPECIFICATION
170 mm × 240 mm, 168pp

BINDING & FINISHING
Sewn binding, cover flaps, silver hot stamping, die cutting, 5 Leporellos

PAPER
Fedrigoni Tintoretto

TYPEFACE
Kurt by Letters Begin, Centra No.1 by Sharp Type

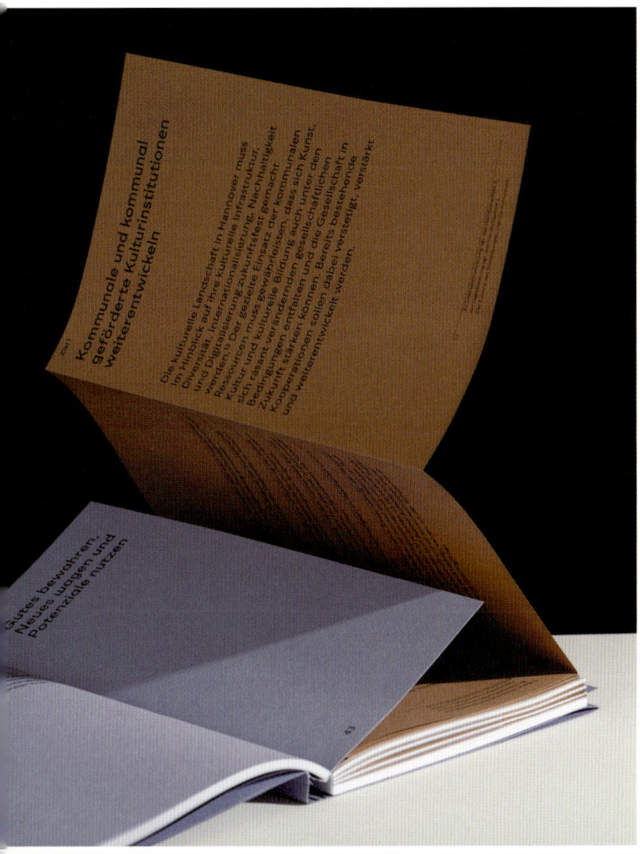

The design of this future-oriented publication is inspired by Kurt Schwitters, but with a contemporary interpretation of the basic principles. Registers separate each section and provide a perfect orientation for readers. The pages about objectives and actions are folded and all objectives are placed on shortened pages. FSC-certified papers in different weights, colours and sizes are used to separate chapters. The silver hot foil allows the appearance of the cover to change constantly. The custom font 'Kurt' makes this publication fairly unique.

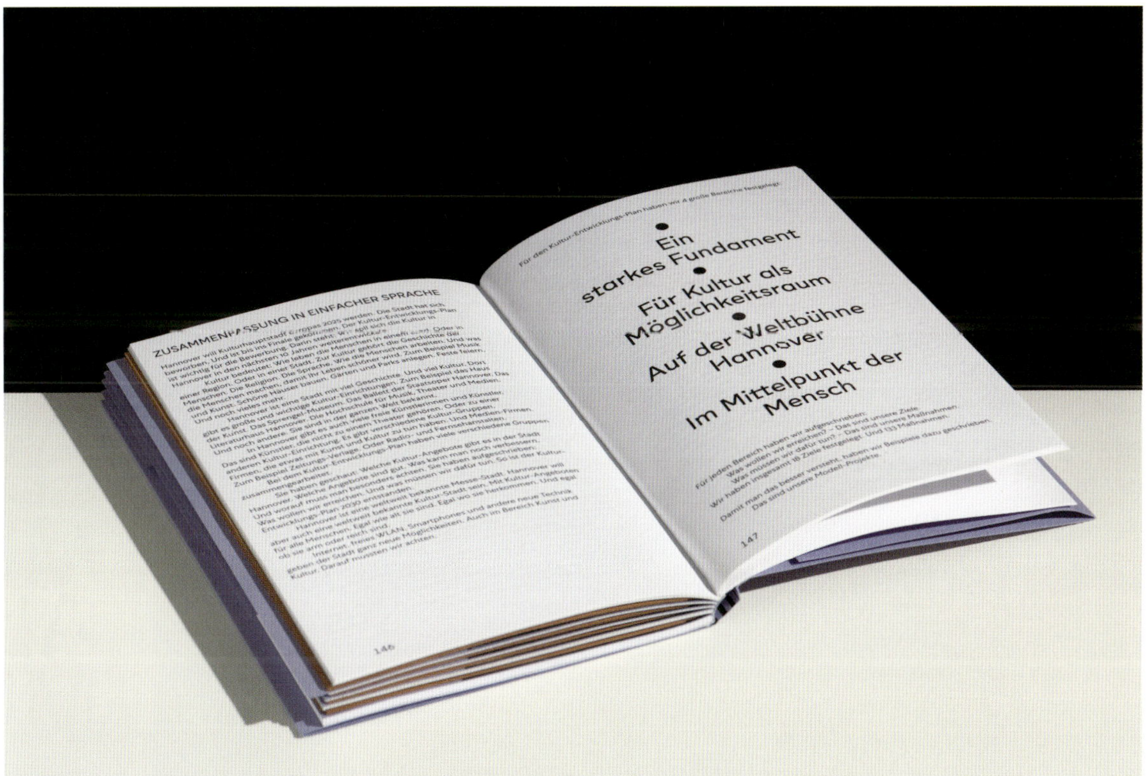

Pasatiempos Modernos

DESIGN
Rebeka Arce Studio

PUBLISHER
@putosmodernos

SPECIFICATION
130 mm × 165 mm, 156pp

BINDING & FINISHING
Perfect binding, UV coating

PAPER
Shiro Echo Bright 120gsm

TYPEFACE
Uxum Grotesque by Bureau Nuits

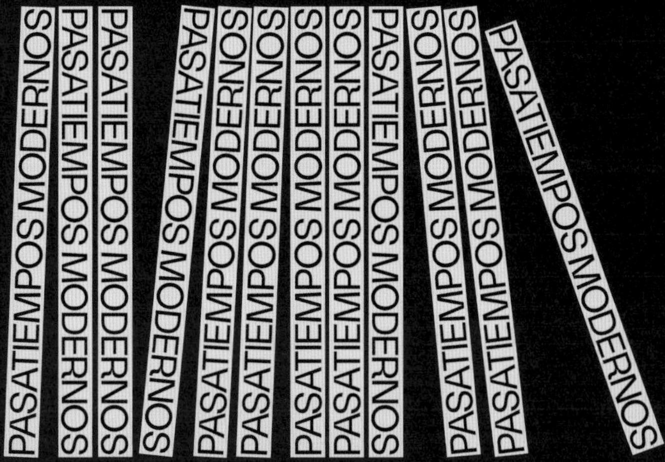

Pasatiempos Modernos is a book part of the new brand refreshment made for PutosModernos in 2020. The studio defined a new visual system based on text stripes, a quirky sans-serif typeface, a fresh photographic style and a bright colour-coded product range. *Pasatiempos Modernos* is a remix of the crossword, the naval battle and other classics along with many new games adapted to modern life. More than 70 challenges and games for adults are included in this volume, such as a gluten-free alphabet soup, a millennial dictionary, visual acuity tests to distinguish the runner from the impostor and the seven differences between two versions of the iPhone and so on.

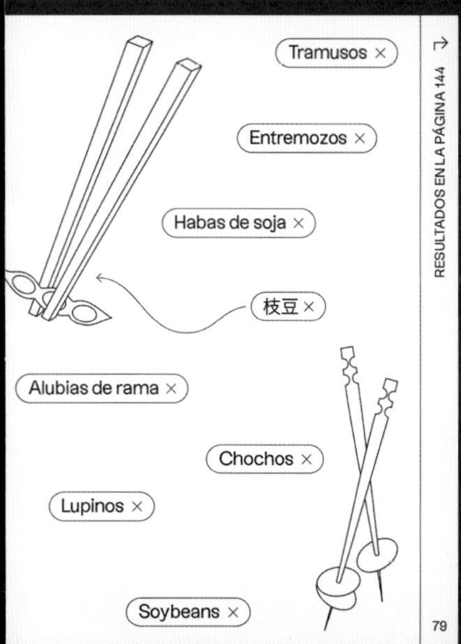

Inside Muses

DESIGN
Toby Ng Design

PUBLISHER
K11 MUSEA

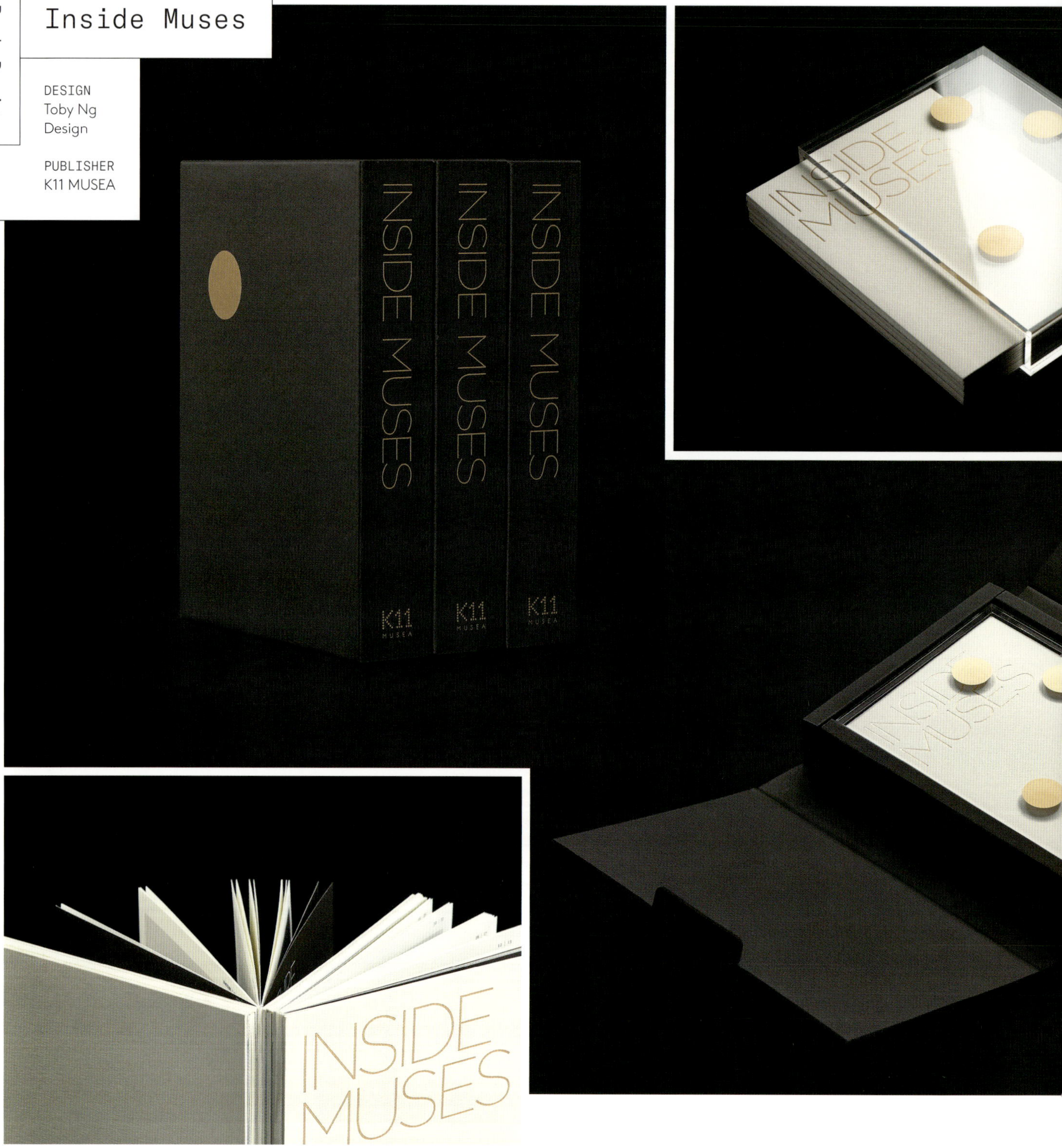

SPECIFICATION
148 mm × 205 mm

BINDING & FINISHING
Hand-sewn saddle stitching, gold hot stamping, die cutting

PAPER
Olin Rough Cream

TYPEFACE
Gotham, Plantin

Reflecting the spirit of discovery, *Inside Muses* is designed to evoke an explorative and engaging experience through an unconventional book format. Referencing the K11 brand and logo, circle graphics on the cover represent the sensuous spheres of the four muses. Both regular and executive editions of the book are exquisitely crafted to depict the fine quality of K11 MUSEA. The regular edition is assembled with intricately hand-sewn binding while the executive hardcover edition is encased in a premium crystal acrylic box, reminiscent of vitrines displaying objects d'art. The unique reading experience of *Inside Muses* draws elements of surprise, igniting curiosity, as readers are encouraged to journey through adventure and discovery in K11 MUSEA.

Slash: Between Identity and Differences

DESIGN
E. Bovio, M. Murano, L. Ritorto, F. Zivoli

PUBLISHER
Graduation project

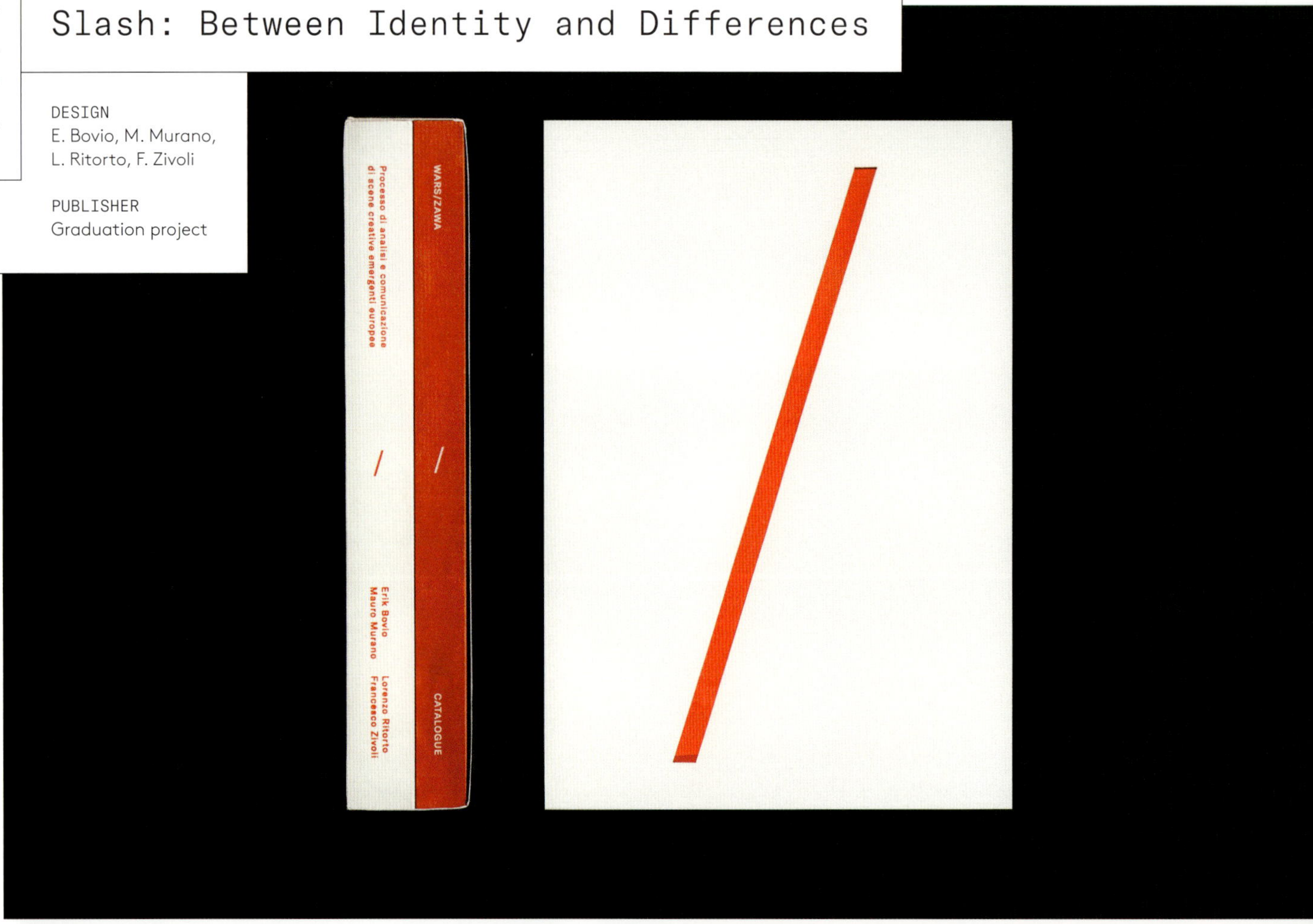

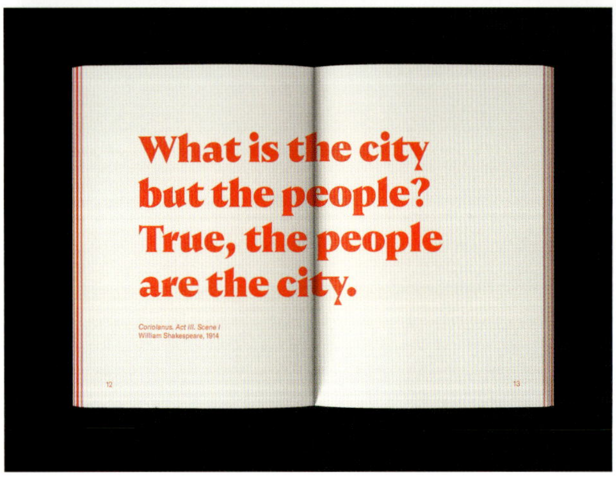

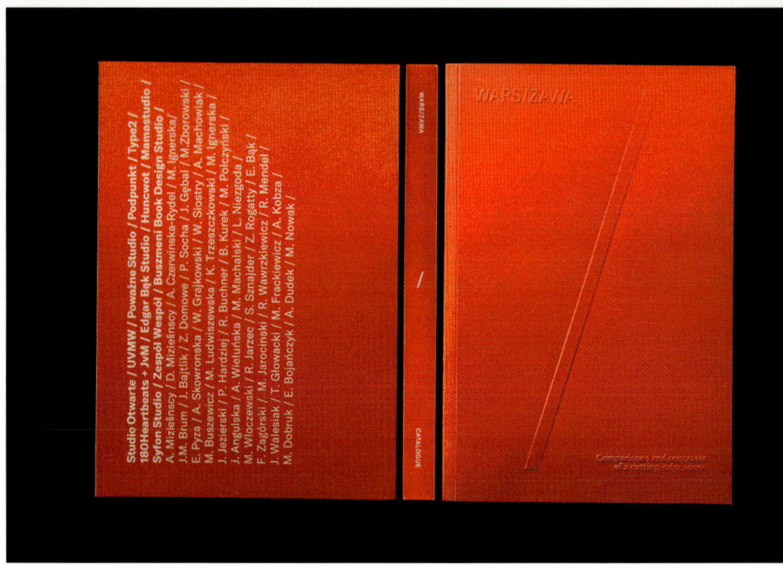

SPECIFICATION
158 mm × 225 mm,
256pp (vol.1), 195pp (vol.2)

BINDING & FINISHING
Perfect binding, embossing

PAPER
Fedrigoni Ispira 300gsm,
Favini 100gsm

TYPEFACE
GT America, Nocturne Serif

As a bachelor's degree project in the major of Design and Visual Communication of Politecnico di Torino, the project aims to diffuse a common awareness on the emerging European graphic design scenes. It is also to weave a network – starting from Warsaw – that unites the creative communities giving space and voice to the emerging ideas of young professionals. This also shows how their emerging creativity is the forerunner of their rise.

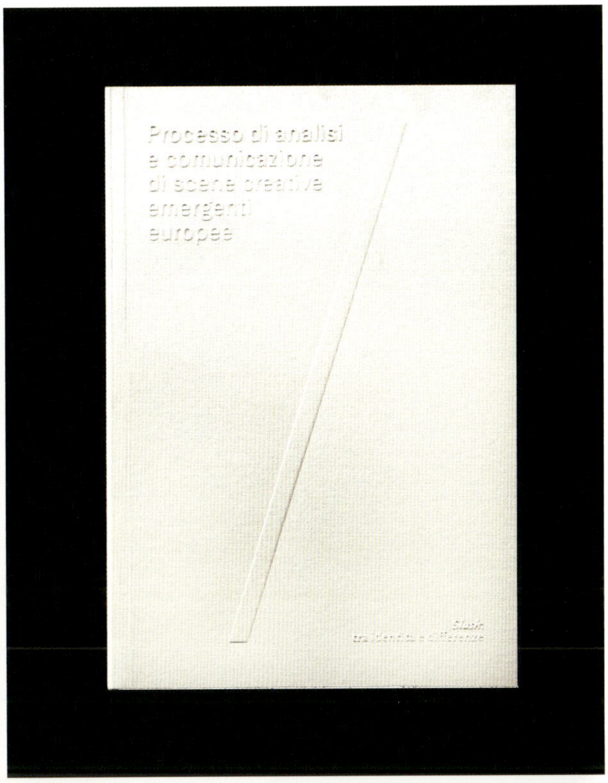

Visuality of Schizophrenia

DESIGN
Adrienn Császár

PUBLISHER
Self-published

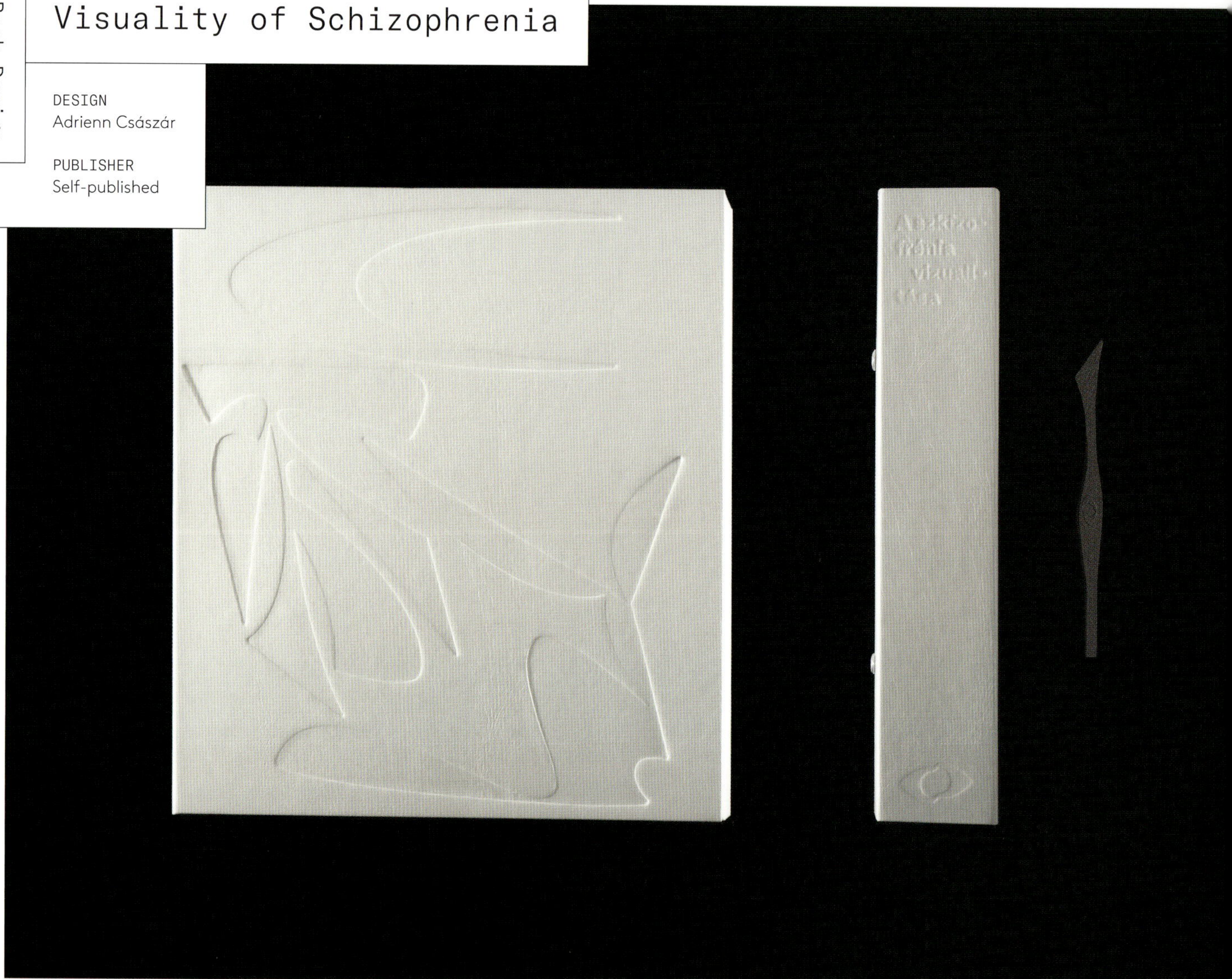

Nowadays, one in hundred people is diagnosed with schizophrenia. Unfortunately, stigmatic and negative stereotypes are common towards this mental illness. This project is to present schizophrenia in a precise and versatile way, starting from psychodiagnostic basics to visual artistics. All graphic details of the book present the characteristics of schizophrenia and make the readers interact with the book. In this way, they will get familiar with schizophrenia and this might erase their negative prejudices towards this illness.

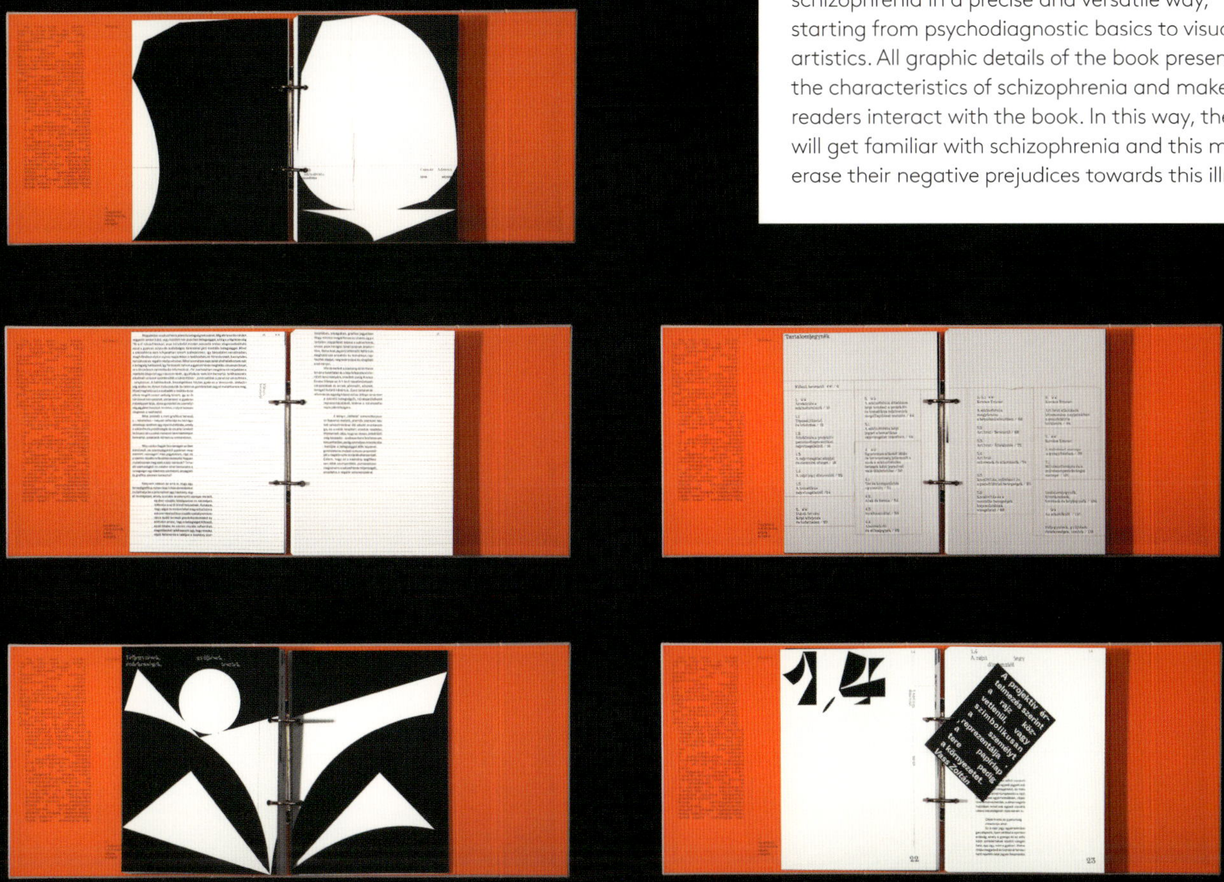

SPECIFICATION
215 mm X 235 mm, 189pp

BINDING & FINISHING
Loose-leaf binding, debossed leather cover

PAPER
Colour Style leather (pristine white 00) 300gsm, Pergaphica Classic Rough 240gsm

TYPEFACE
Totentanz Backslanted, Whyte Inktrap

Global Climate Change

DESIGN
Carla Cabras

PUBLISHER
Self-published

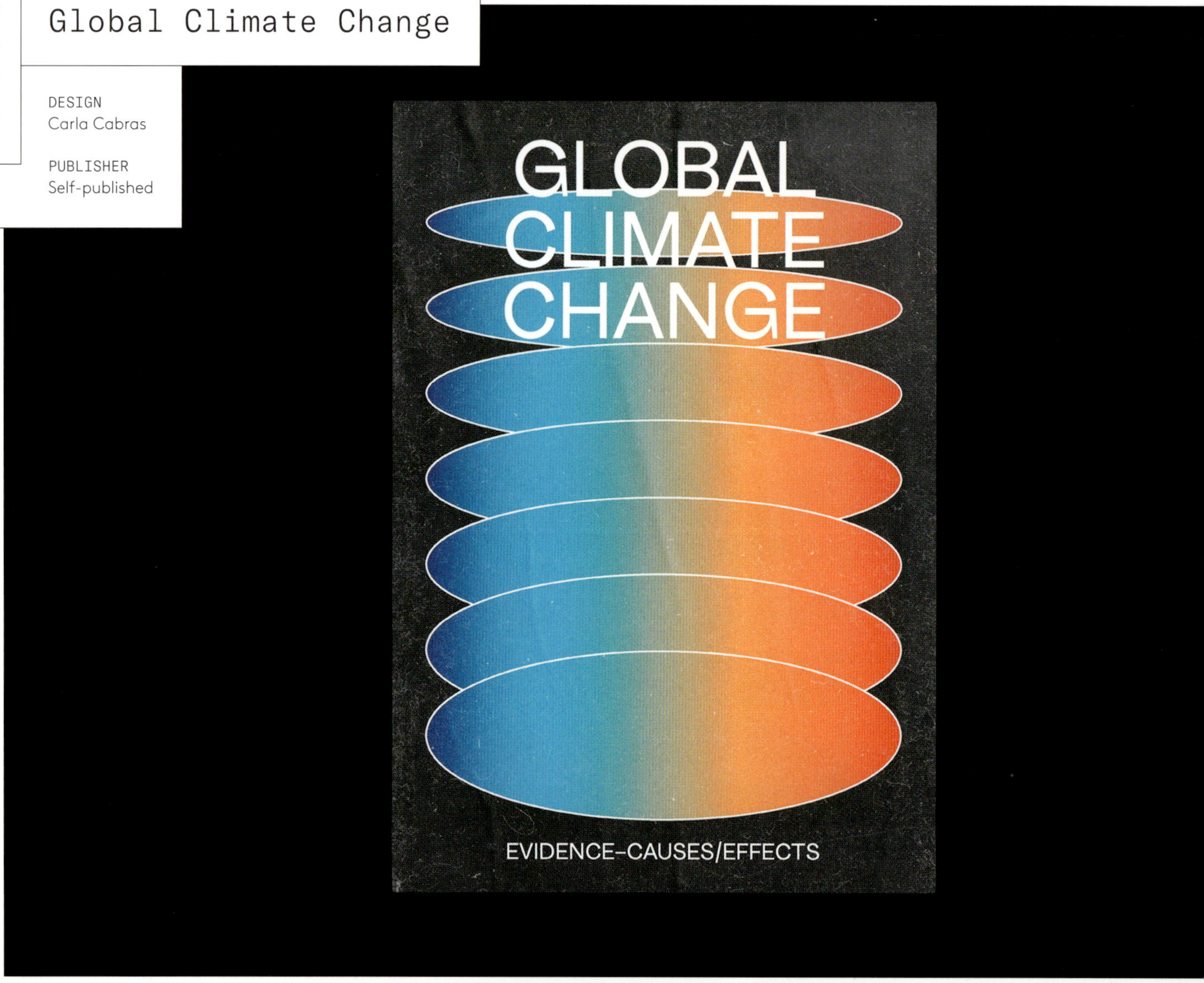

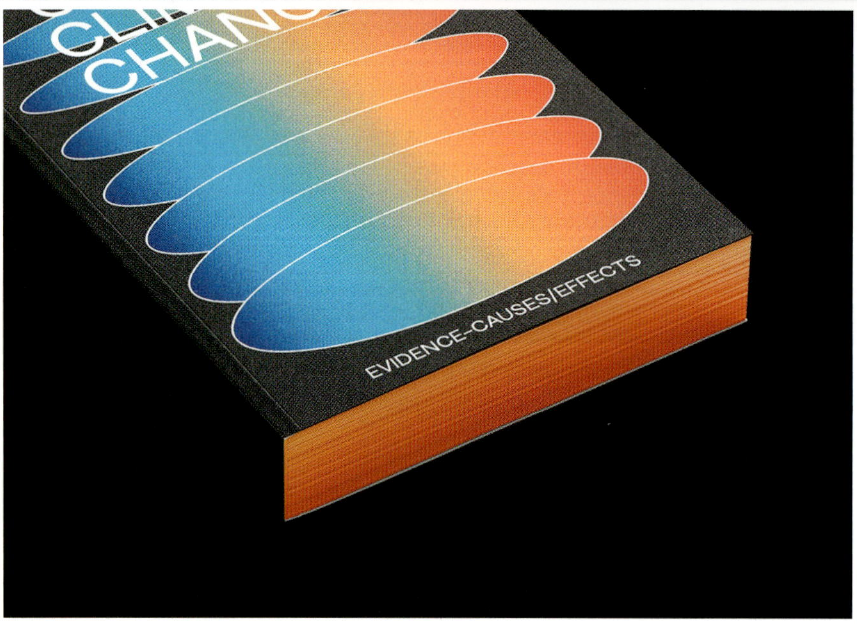

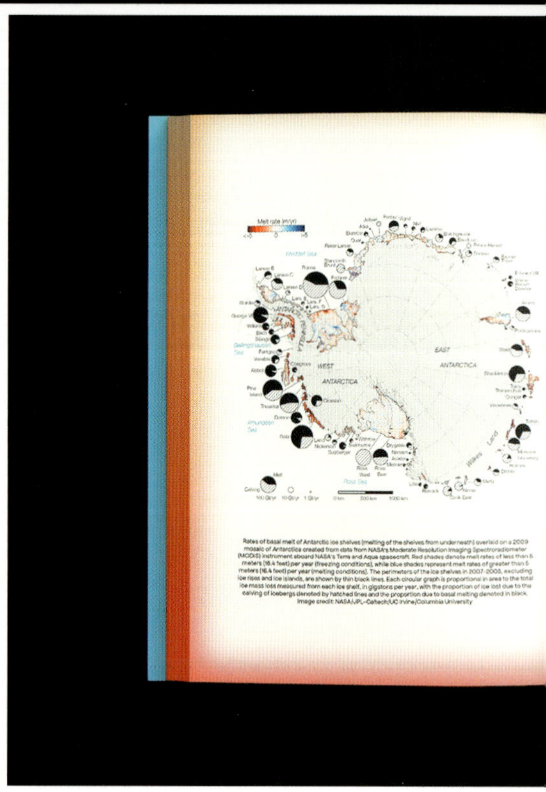

With this project, the designer wanted to give voice to a great problem of our times: climate change. For the book, she not only focused on the causes and the consequences but also wanted to give space to the possible and innumerable solutions to change this process. As for the graphics, she wanted to simulate global warming by using red shades on the pages. The paper used is recycled and other materials used are sustainable.

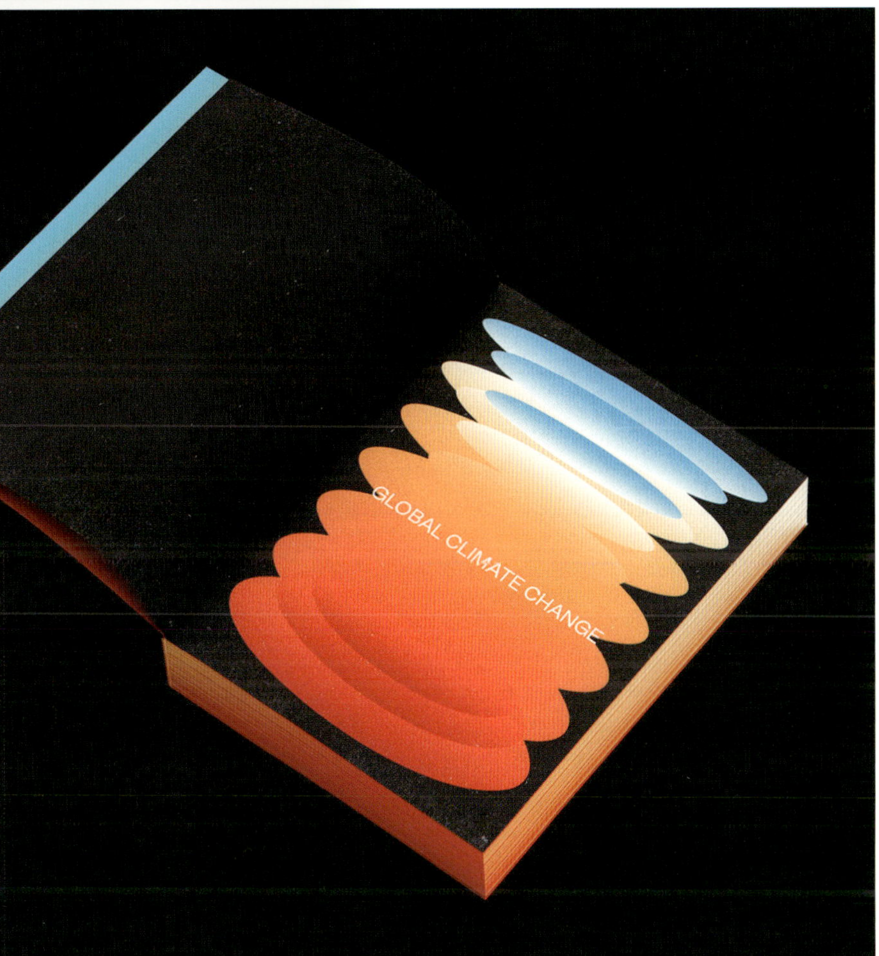

SPECIFICATION
115 mm × 210 mm, 320pp

BINDING & FINISHING
Paperback

PAPER
Recycled coated/uncoated paper

TYPEFACE
Apfel Grotezk

Cuenca Debajo de la Segunda Farola – Erasmus Book

DESIGN
Péter Morvai

PUBLISHER
Self-published
(2 copies)

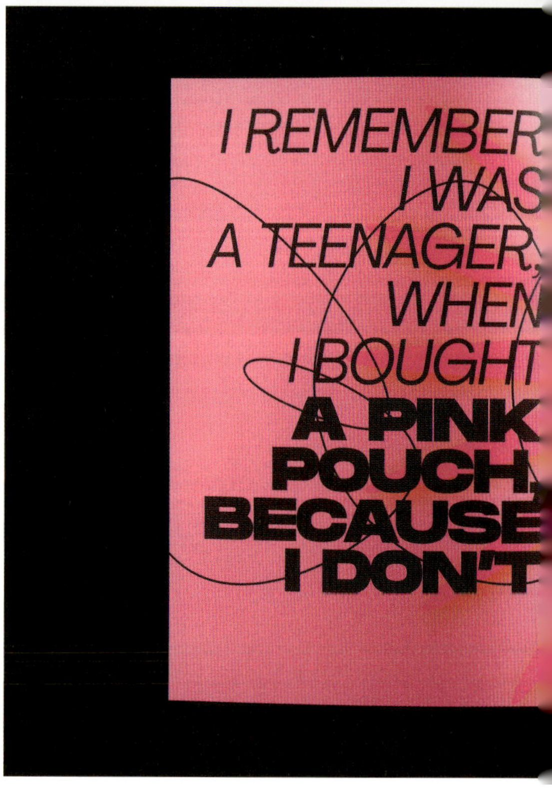

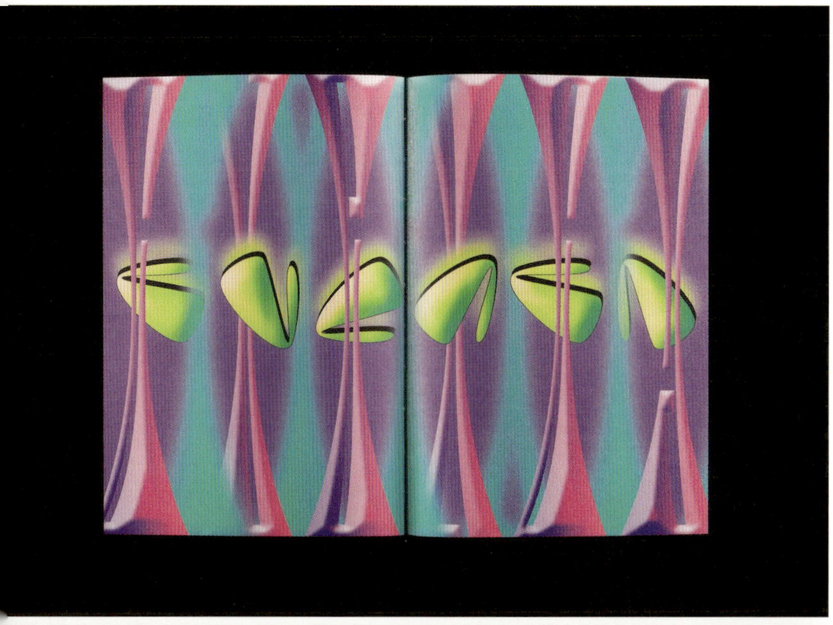

In Cuenca (Spain), the designer tried to experience every moment as a flow experience, then transferred that flow to his work using a book as the medium. It is an attempt to visualise intangible and inexplicable feelings in physical space through typography and photography. These two are narrated through the conscious and free organising principle of the flow experience, and thus help to create an impression about the city and the designer's journey.

SPECIFICATION
148.5 mm × 210 mm, 224pp

BINDING & FINISHING
Bare spine

PAPER
Papyrus Rainbow offset paper 230gsm (cover)

TYPEFACE
Agrandir, Formula Condensed, Monument Extended, Grafler, Neue Machina, Gatwick, Cirka, Hatton by Pangram Pangram Foundry

Velado

DESIGN
Marc Villalba

PUBLISHER
Unpublished photobook

SPECIFICATION
152 mm X 210 mm, 144pp

BINDING & FINISHING
Hardcover, sewn binding, two books bound together by the back cover

PAPER
Black plastic endpapers, Munken Kristall Rough 120gsm, inserts in different sizes, folded poster

TYPEFACE
Helvetica

The photographic work *Velado* brings together some of the things that the designer's father kept during his years in an advertising agency as a graphic designer. All these objects, found some time after he died, somehow constitute his presence and a starting point of his narrative. The photobook is structured in two parts, which can be read individually or together. Presence and absence work together to create a story that speaks in the language of intuition and metaphor, instead of rational discourse. Using this language, the book delves into universal concepts such as loss, memory, the passage of time and acceptance. The book is completed to construct an object book that offers the possibility of obtaining different readings. Its binding allows its being read as a single volume or as two facing pieces.

Insight Independent Bookshop

DESIGN
Huang Wan-eng

PUBLISHER
Association for Independent Bookshop Culture

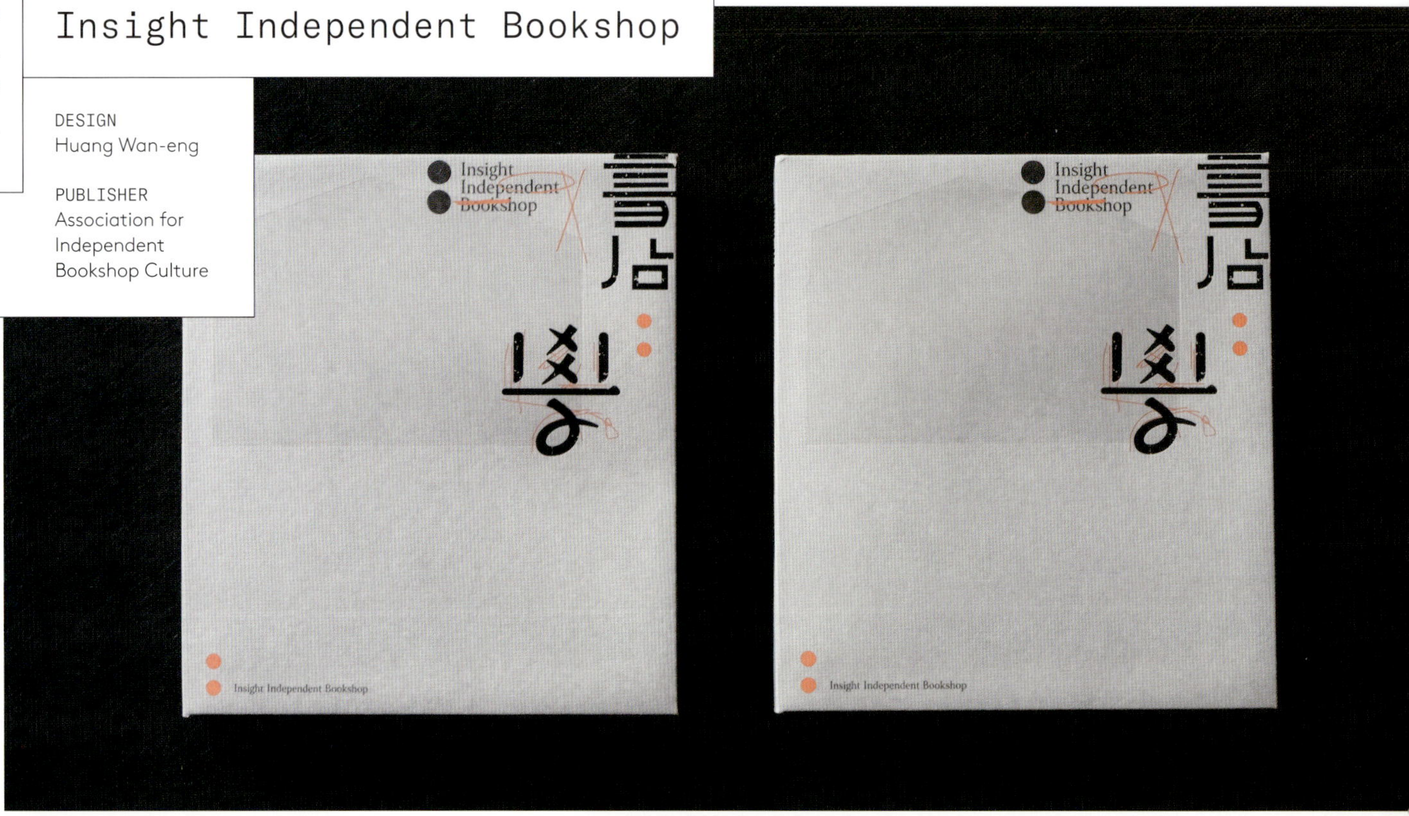

SPECIFICATION
150 mm X 165 mm (box),
140 mm X 150 mm (interior), 36pp

BINDING & FINISHING
Manual gluing and machine gluing, EVA foam inserts, sewn binding, black hot stamping, transparent hot stamping

PAPER
DAYA PAPER black cardboard 400gsm, Dongjiu Puzhen Paper CG 300gsm (box); Dongjiu Puzhen Paper CG 115gsm (interior)

TYPEFACE
Kozuka Mincho Pr6N, MS Mincho

This is a CD booklet including interviews of 16 local independent bookstores. *Insight Independent Bookshop* emphasises the concept of 'insight'. The colon symbolises the state of learning to run a bookstore, and further, that the knowledge of bookstores is evolving. To combine the image of a book with the character ' 書 ', the vertical strokes of the standard character ' 書 ' is discarded but horizontal lines are retained to present the appearance of the book. The idea of 'learning' is constant throughout the editorial design. ':', an important symbol of the entire visual design, is presented after modification, smearing, and marking. This conveys a message that every independent bookstore survives by constantly modifying itself. The modification is also a process of continuous revision, adjustment and learning.

Book Design

Cheers Book Covers

DESIGN
A Black Cover Design

PUBLISHER
Cheerspublishing

SPECIFICATION
130 mm × 184 mm

BINDING & FINISHING
Perfect binding

PAPER
Yan si-Qiu xiang paper, premium print paper, Brisk paper

TYPEFACE
Lantinghei by FounderType

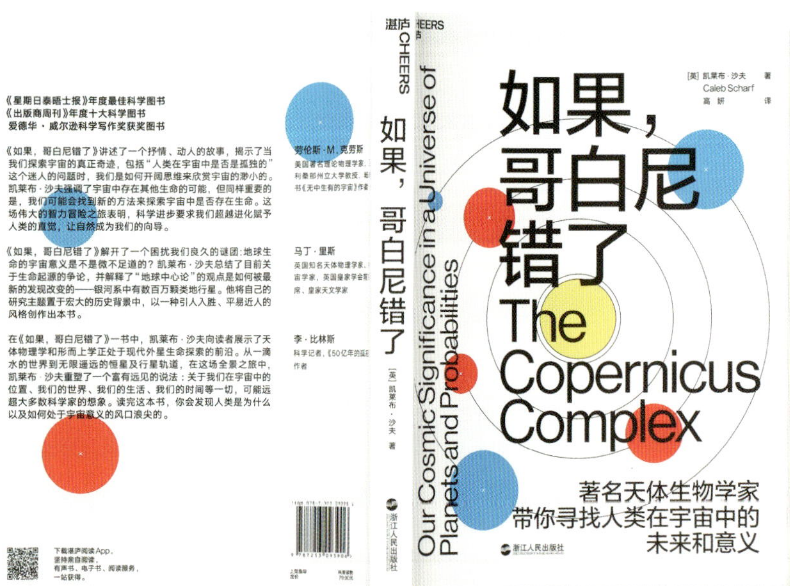

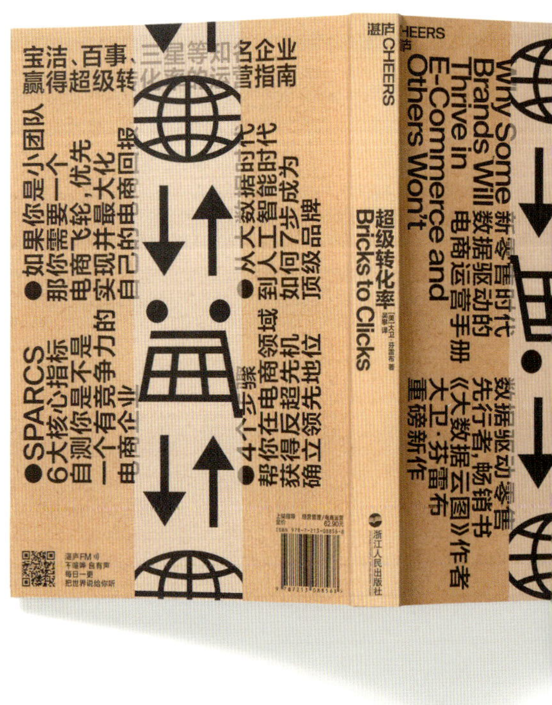

After one year of cooperation with Cheerspublishing, the design agency has established a clear visual identity for its brand and products. This visual identity is developed and refined based on the idea of 'information goes first', the principle Cheerspublishing has been emphasising in the overall brand concept. Through layout design of both Chinese and English, the cohesive arrangement of information, and the restrained use of decorative design, books by Cheerspublishing have distinctive and unique appearances among similar publications of the same kind. It is proved that Cheerspublishing, after the upgrade, has led more young people to discover and then to fall in love with reading.

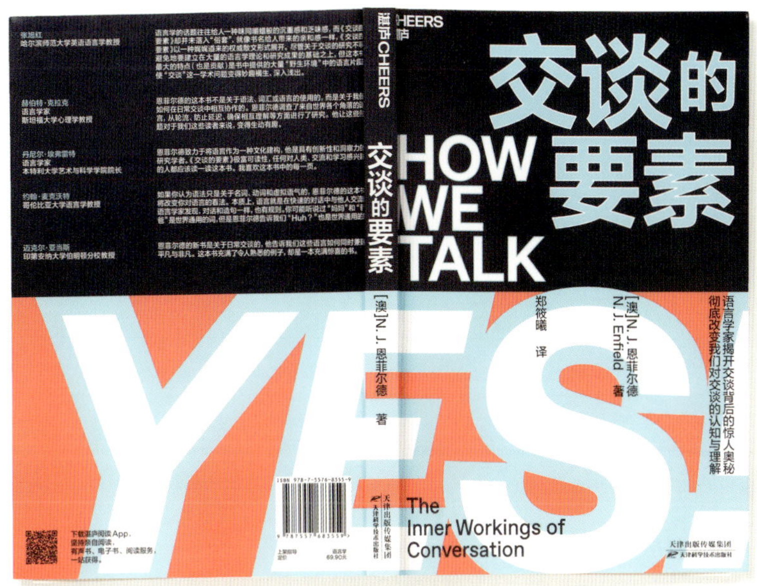

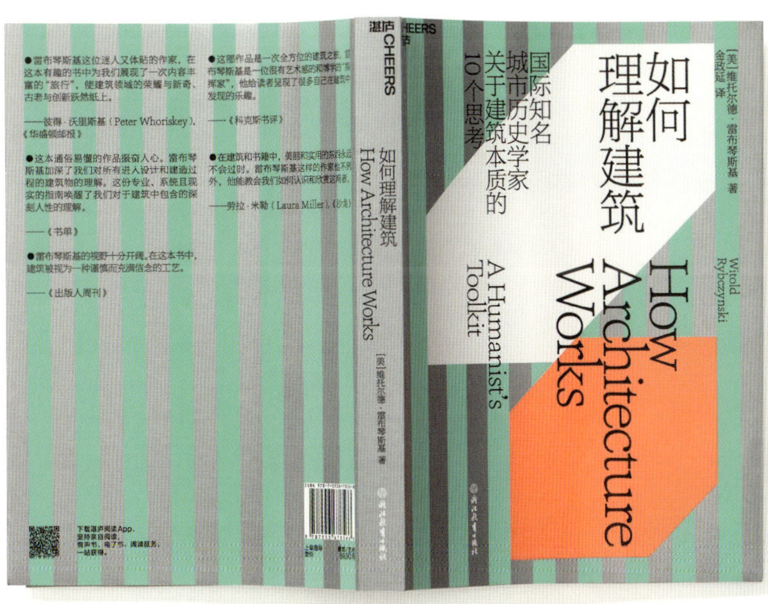

Globe in Motion 1–2

DESIGN
Matúš Hnát

PUBLISHER
Institute of Ethnology and Social Anthropology, Slovak Academy of Sciences

In today's increasingly interconnected world, international migration has become a reality that affects nearly every corner of the globe. A large number of studies with various graphs, charts and diagrams are included. Contributors submitted their infographic sets in different graphic styles and colour schemes. The main challenge within the clear and bold design concept was to unify the individual infographics into a single colour scheme consisting of the basic black and the additional neon Pantone colour.

The printing impact is supported by coated Arctic Volume White paper. The design is supplemented with one typeface used in both volumes, unifying lines and graphic elements. The interior design concept follows the cover design, where a simple icon of the globe is transformed with an imaginary infographic style, representing an interconnected world and movement.

SPECIFICATION
165 mm × 235 mm, 216pp (vol. 1), 156pp (vol. 2)

BINDING & FINISHING
Flexo binding, anti-scratch matt lamination with hot stamping, ribbon bookmarks

PAPER
Arctic Volume White 115gsm

TYPEFACE
GT America

Efforts in Aesthetic Movement

DESIGN
Alien Wu

PUBLISHER
Reading Times

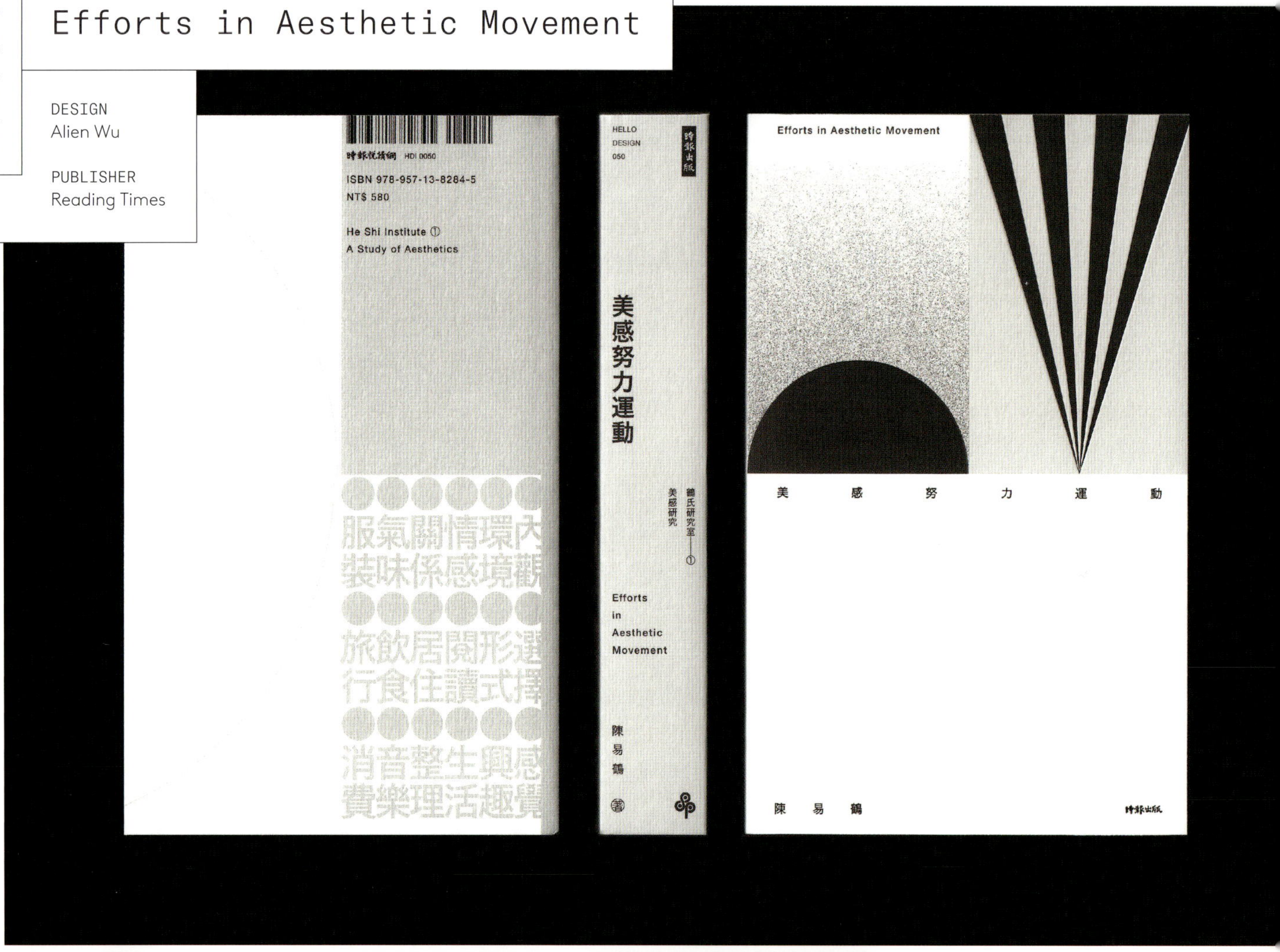

SPECIFICATION
120 mm × 190 mm, 448pp

BINDING & FINISHING
Paperback, black hot stamping, debossing

PAPER
TAKEO ARAVEAL-FS snow white 186gsm, TAKEO NT RASHA-174C 116gsm

TYPEFACE
Hiragino Kaku Gothic Pro

The 'movement' in the title means 'action'. To deliver this meaning, it would be plain to use solely dynamic images to present the state of movement, so the designer had the idea of comparing movement with a static state.

The cover is cut into two blocks. The upper half is composed of dots, lines and planes to give a sense of 'movement', while the lower half creates a static atmosphere as if rationality and sensibility both occupy half of the consciousness. The cover constitutes a balance between the dynamic and static states through this contrast, through which aesthetics is delivered. The inner pages are designed for a pleasing reading experience. Words in each unit are as concise as possible to leave white space in a layout, relieving the burden on readers to absorb information as much as possible.

Thing-ology

DESIGN
Flowing Design

PUBLISHER
Locus Publishing

SPECIFICATION
148 mm X 210 mm, 320pp

BINDING & FINISHING
Hardcover, hot stamping, die cutting

PAPER
Pimex white kraft paper (dust jacket), premium wood-free uncoated paper (cover)

TYPEFACE
Ku Mincho

The book title 'thing-ology' means 'learning from objects'. Therefore, the book is treated as an object in the design. The multi-layered dust jacket covering the book is designed with the inspiration of wrapping paper to emphasise the book as an object. To present the idea of 'from', as it is in Chinese '裡', die cutting is used to dig a hole into the book cover. At the same time, the character '裡' is deliberately covered slightly to illustrate the concept – learning from objects.

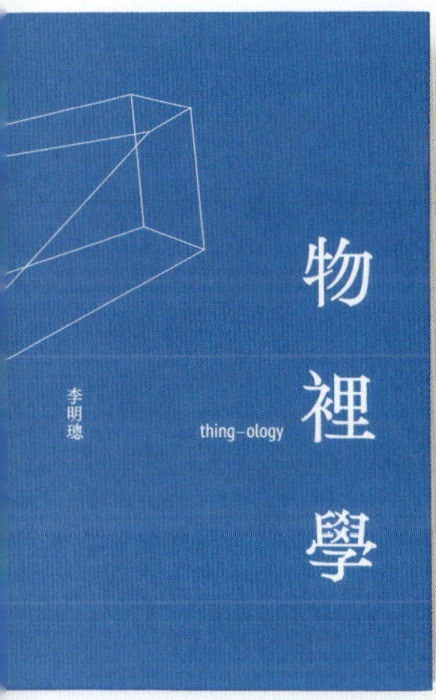

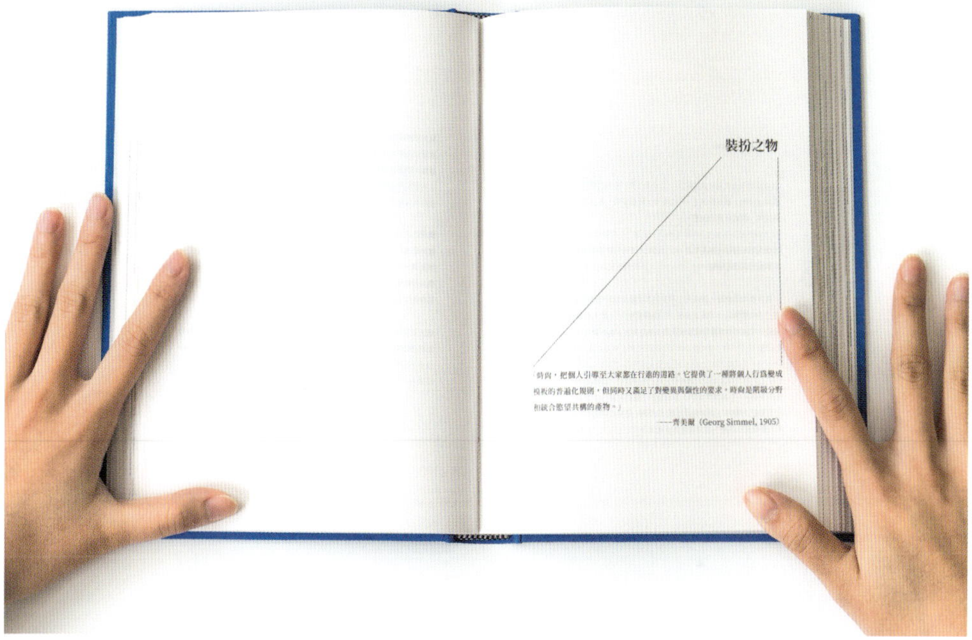

I Think I'll Be Fine after Eating Ice Cream

DESIGN
Wu Chia-lin

PUBLISHER
Squirrel Culture

SPECIFICATION
130 mm × 190 mm, 352pp

BINDING & FINISHING
Sewn binding, dust jacket, embossing, gold hot stamping

PAPER
Light-coated paper (jacket), Simili paper (interior), different papers within the book

TYPEFACE
Mincho

From the perspective of a child, wife, mother, teacher and woman, the author collects the scenes and writes poems as she has insomnia at night. She captures the moment in youth, love and life with gentle, delicate and private words.

The cover illustration is consistent with the title and the concept of this book. In addition, it means that there is nothing ice cream cannot solve. If there is, then get more. The bar code, usually on the back cover, is placed on the ice cream cup on the front cover. When scanning the bar code to buy the poetry collection, it is like readers are buying a cup of ice cream and make peace with the world at the same time.

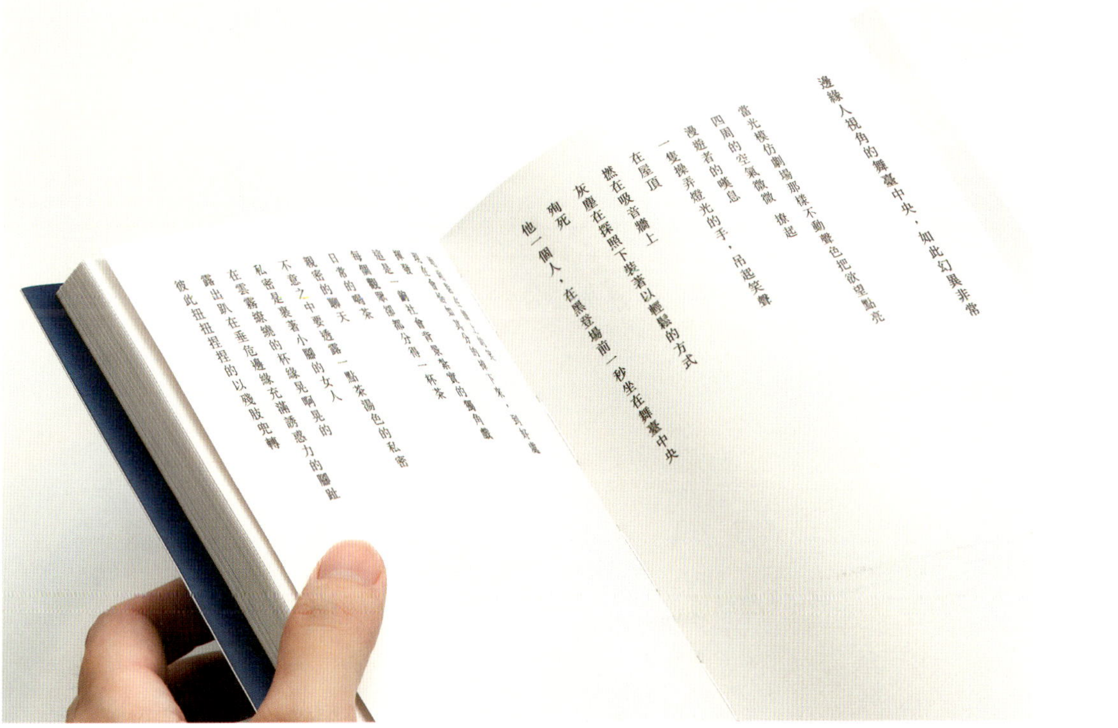

To Say Goodbye Is to Die a Little

DESIGN
Wu Chia-lin

PUBLISHER
Reading Times

SPECIFICATION
148 mm X 210 mm, 240pp

BINDING & FINISHING
Perfect binding, dust jacket, debossing, red hot stamping, reverse-side printing

PAPER
Light-coated paper (dust jacket), Kraft Carton (cover), wood-free uncoated paper (interior)

TYPEFACE
Mincho

'In fact, we have been saying goodbye for a long time. We will know more and more clearly that what we wait for is the end of the goodbye itself.' This book is a mixture of many kinds of literature. Death is a heavy topic, but the designer wanted to interpret it lightly. Debossing the title of book is a simple way to present her idea. As readers touch the dust jacket, they will know even if it seems to be nothing, it is still not easy to stop people from feeling sorrowful.

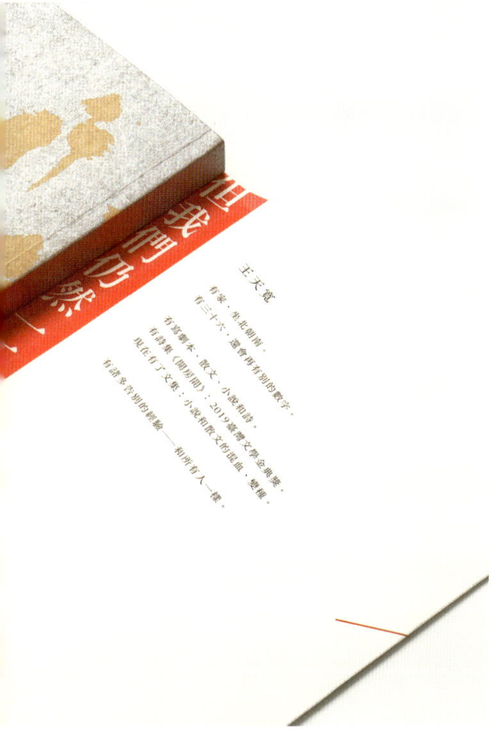

Possible Anatomies

DESIGN
Ana Resende

PUBLISHER
Corpo Atelier

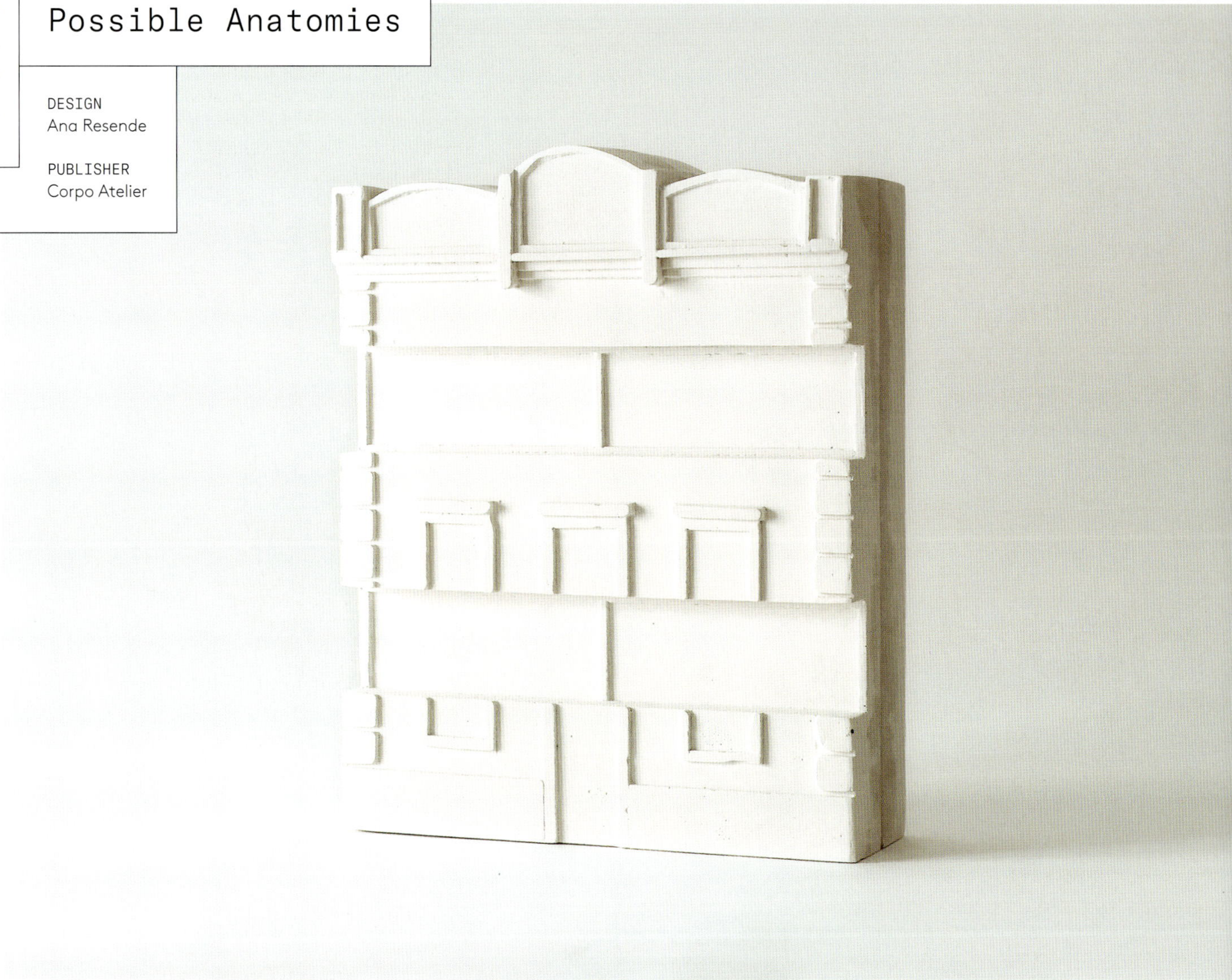

SPECIFICATION
158 mm × 230 mm, 176pp

BINDING & FINISHING
Hardcover with canvas, hot stamping, plaster model

PAPER
Symbol Tatami White 115gsm

TYPEFACE
Saol Text

This work is created to catalogue a series of drawings and models into a book that presents a loss of the physical experience they provide. Such experience of scale, materiality and weight cannot be properly translated into a printed medium. *Possible Anatomies* is embedded in a plaster sculpture. By making it unavailable, the book is presented as an abstract idea, with no correspondence to the physical reality of the future reader. To confirm its existence, readers must destroy the sculpture.

Cacaform Birds

DESIGN
Zhu Yingchun,
Huangfu Shanshan

PUBLISHER
Guangxi Normal
University Press

SPECIFICATION
170 mm X 245 mm, 288pp

BINDING & FINISHING
Section sewing, hollow back, die cutting, dotted line cutting (keys)

PAPER
Cotton wool paper 220gsm (cover, belly band), Munken paper 100gsm (interior)

TYPEFACE
Song Yi, Qidixiaokai, Lantinghei by FounderType

Cacaform Birds began in 2014 upon Zhu Yingchun's fortunate encounter with bird droppings. The book derives creative inspiration from the mundane, combining painting and photography to transform the common traces of everyday life.

Bird-like droppings are re-imagined as fantastical cacaform birds which are compiled in this book in three sections: images, catalogues and keys. Readers are invited to follow the instructions and the design of the book to read front to back and then back to front, before unsealing the central section to reveal the origin of these remarkable creatures. The book's design arouses great curiosity in its readers, bringing together content and form to express the core value that creativity comes from life and stems from discovery.

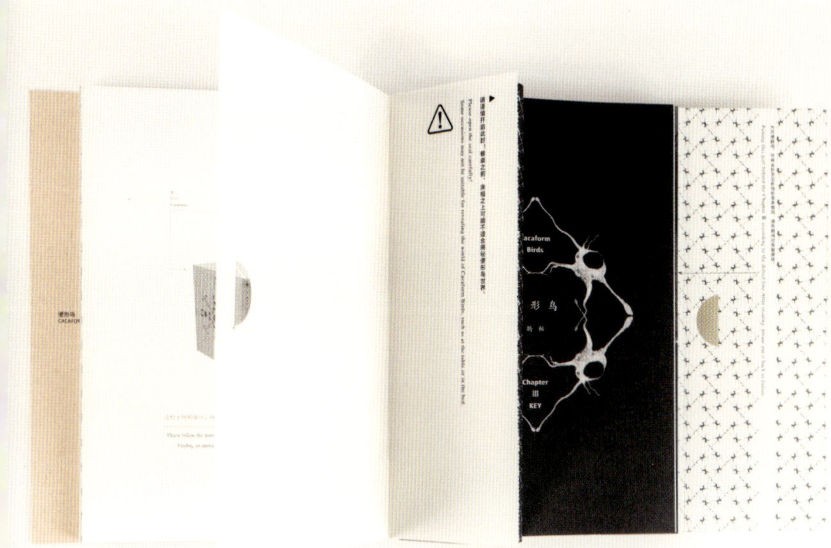

Bug's Book

DESIGN
Zhu Yingchun,
Huangfu Shanshan

PUBLISHER
Guangxi Normal
University Press

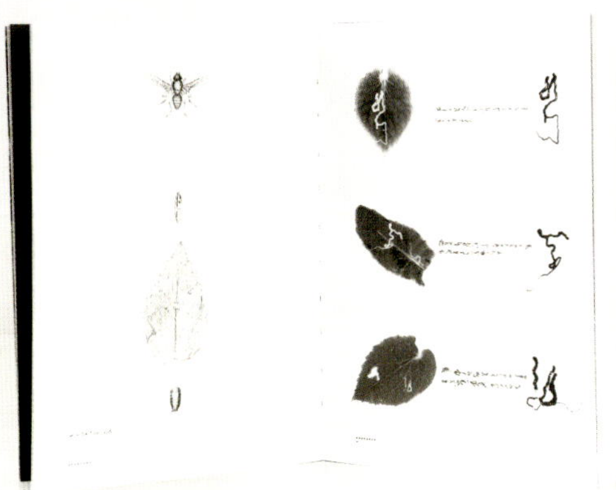

Bugs' Book is a major work of Zhu Yingchun's and the result of several years of painstakingly observing the wildlife around his studio. Seemingly a book with text, the book does not in fact contain a single word. Rather it is a mysterious creation of the bugs themselves making Zhu Yingchun not a creator, but a discoverer and compiler.

The traces of snails, earthworms, stink bugs and other insects, to which many turn a blind eye, are the subject of Zhu Yingchun's gaze and his ever-expanding curiosity and marvel. Like Chinese calligraphy or landscape painting, the work of each bug has a distinctive style, from the cursive script of the leaf-miner flies to the earthworms' apparent seal script, the dry brushwork of the stink bug to the long-horned beetles and their dotted textures.

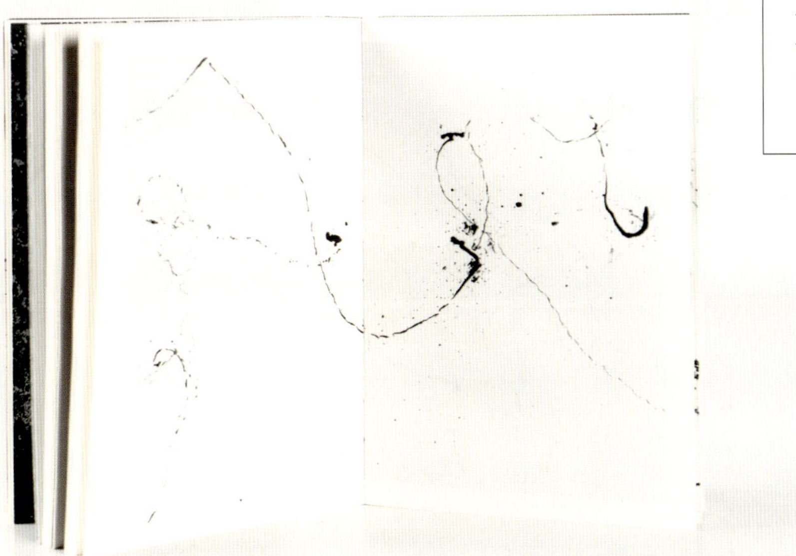

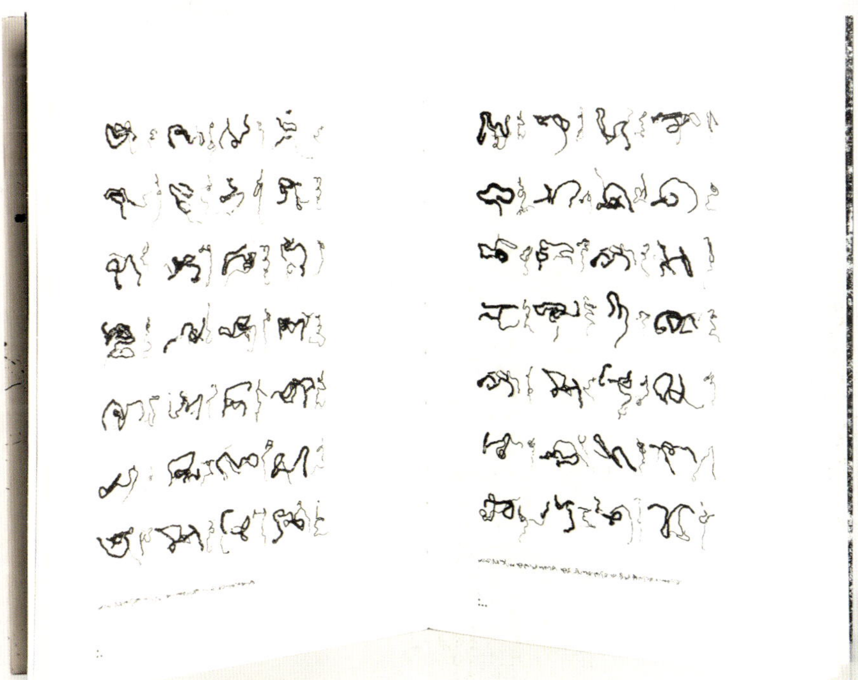

SPECIFICATION
140 mm X 200 mm, 312pp

BINDING & FINISHING
Section sewing, bare spine with cloth

PAPER
Antalis Curious Collection Beige 135gsm (cover), Xuanqing paper 105gsm (first half), Munken paper 100gsm (second half)

TYPEFACE
–

Craftsman

DESIGN
Zhu Yingchun,
Luo Wei,
Yang Xiaofang

PUBLISHER
Minzhu yu Jianshe
Publishing House

This book tells the story of fifteen village craftsmen and reveals the changes in traditional Chinese lifestyle and artisan culture. Each story has a title page on which the craftsman's trade is written using materials related to their trade. The bamboo craftsman's trade was written using bamboo. A round-headed brush was used to write the title of 'Blacksmith' and the heading 'Pot Repairer' was scattered with ash from the underside of pots. The cover is dark and weighty, while the title was made from a woodblock print whose lack of clarity reflects the ambiguity of a craftsman's identity.

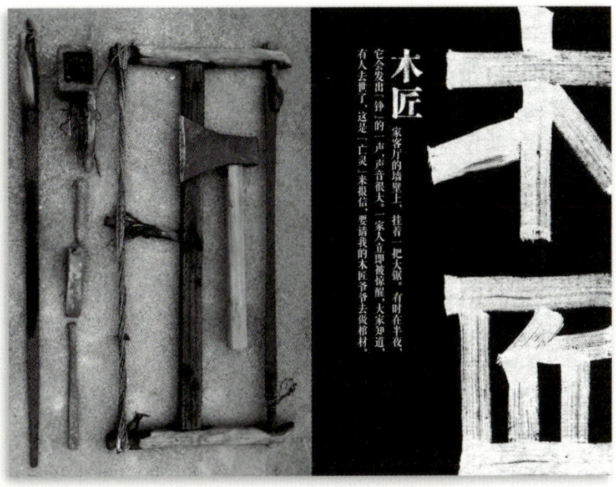

SPECIFICATION
140 mm X 210 mm, 320pp

BINDING & FINISHING
Sewn-binding, debossing, trimming, black spray paint

PAPER
Kraft paper, Munken paper

TYPEFACE
Hei Ti, Kai, Shu Song by FounderType

A Study on Hong Kong Beiwei Calligraphy & Type Design

DESIGN
Mak Kai-hang

PUBLISHER
Joint Publishing

Type Design distilled the research progress in dissecting the arts and the spirit behind the traditional calligraphy style – Beiwei Zansyu by Hong Kong type designer Adonian Chan. Archiving a comprehensive research journey, the book reveals the traditionality and originality behind this intangible gem.

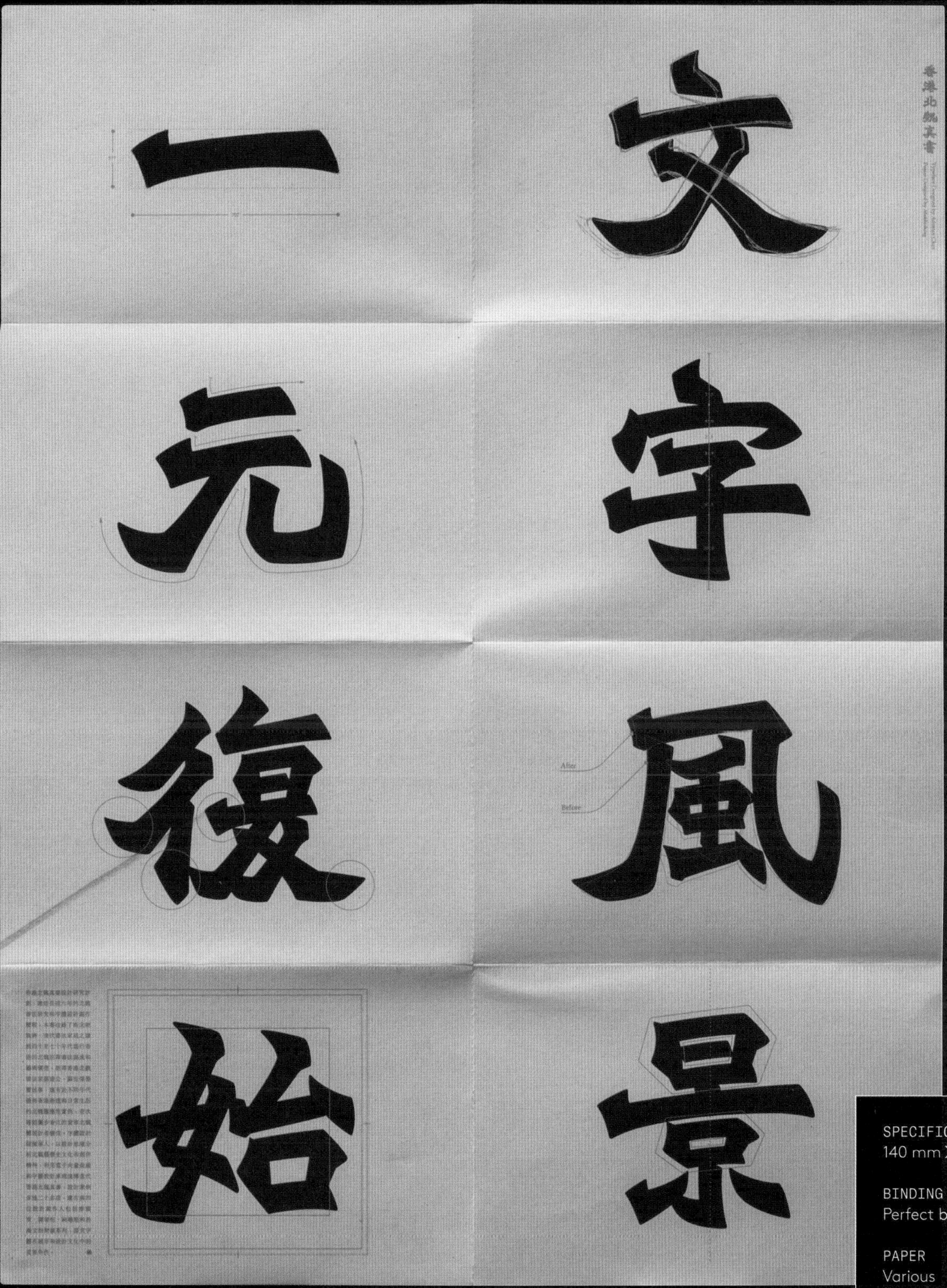

SPECIFICATION
140 mm × 200 mm, 344pp

BINDING & FINISHING
Perfect binding, hot stamping

PAPER
Various

TYPEFACE
Literatura

Asia-Pacific Design No. 16

DESIGN
Mak Kai-hang

PUBLISHER
Sandu Publishing

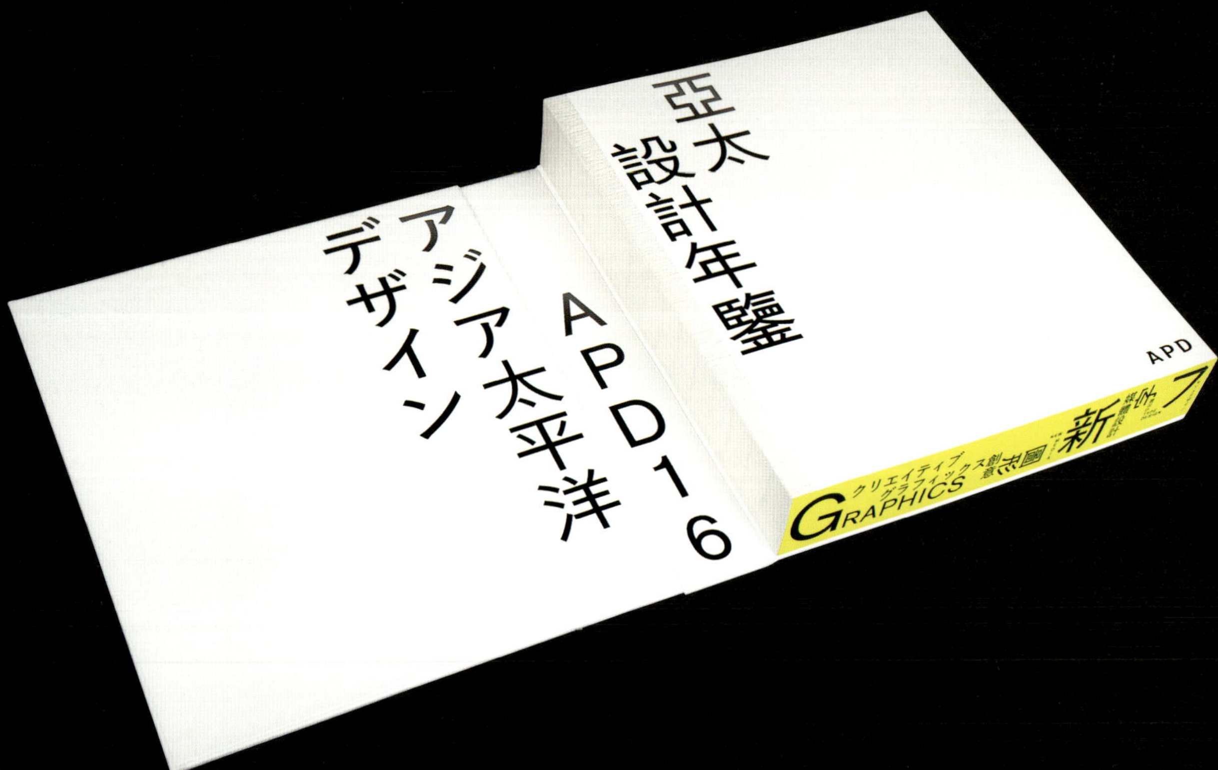

Asia-Pacific Design (APD in short) is the most authoritative professional design yearbook in the Asia-Pacific region, which has been published 16 years in a row by Sandu Publishing and Design 360° – a concept and design magazine since 2005. With the theme of 'Integration of Design', Mak Kai-hang pushed the boundary of typographic design by deconstructing a bulk of texts into the rhythmic arrangement, challenging readers' usual reading habits via the art of typesetting.

SPECIFICATION
248 mm X 290 mm, 488pp

BINDING & FINISHING
Perfect binding, hot stamping, screen printing on edges

PAPER
Fedrigoni Old Mill Premium White 130gsm, Antalis Olin 120gsm, Tonli Fantasy 120gsm

TYPEFACE
Akzidenz-Grotesk Pro

Book Design

Typographic Design in China

DESIGN
Pan Yanrong

PUBLISHER
Sandu Publishing

The publication explores the position of Chinese character design in the current design context. Three sections of the book are skillfully combined into one, and the book's binding builds a multifaceted reading space and enhances the reading experience.

SPECIFICATION
130 mm × 170 mm

BINDING & FINISHING
Hardcover, hot stamping, edge printing

PAPER
Canvas, IK coloured paper, Tonli Fantasy 120gsm, Antalis Massiva Beige 80gsm

TYPEFACE
Song

Yu-ichi Inoue/Shiko Munakata/Kazuo Yagi

DESIGN
Qu Minmin &
Jiang Qian

PUBLISHER
The Commercial Press

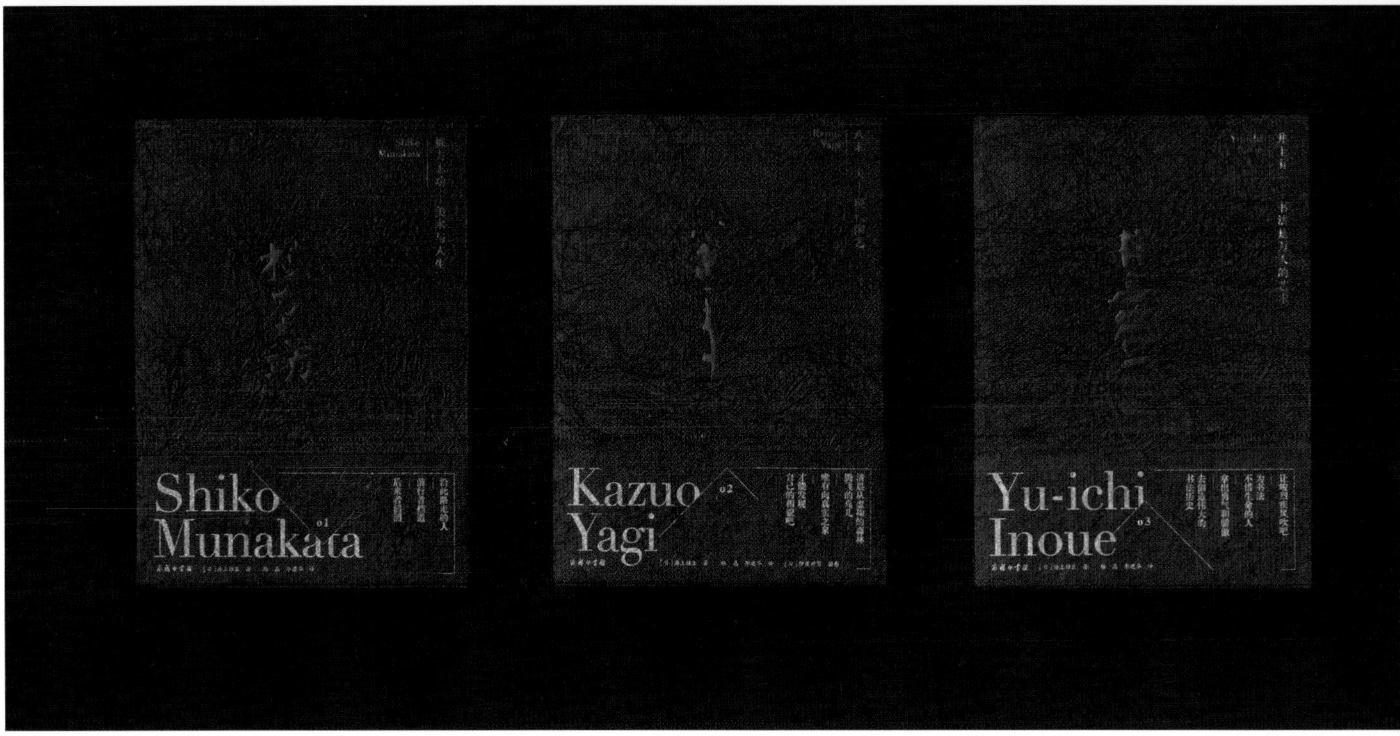

SPECIFICATION
130 mm × 180 mm,
552pp/392pp/562pp

BINDING & FINISHING
Hollow back

PAPER
Handmade paper

TYPEFACE
Kai, Shu Song by FounderType

This is a series of books about three representative Japanese artists of the twentieth century. At that time, they were in the important transition period of Japanese art and had an essential influence on Chinese modern artists in the same cultural circle.

The cover is made of handmade paper. The whole book is printed in two colours. And the paper is soft and light, giving readers a quiet reading experience.

Unknown

DESIGN
Pan Yanrong

PUBLISHER
Jianyu Graphics Lab

SPECIFICATION
300 mm X 300 mm

BINDING & FINISHING
Hardcover, UV coating, hot stamping

PAPER
Canvas, Antalis Curious Matter 120gsm, Touch paper 120gsm

TYPEFACE
Shu Song by FounderType, Source Han Sans

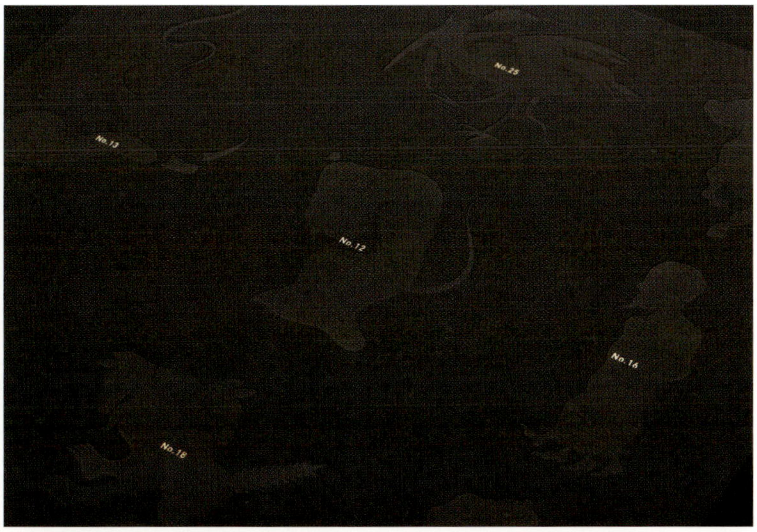

The 36 images in the book illustrate monsters in the darkness. The designer created a group of creatures after he got inspiration from *The Classic of Mountains and Seas* – an ancient Chinese fiction. UV coating and bronze foil are employed on the matt black paper to create mystery. The illusional images and the tinge of bronze foil are vague yet mysterious, which invite readers to read and discover the book.

The Codices of the Masters

DESIGN
Pan Yanrong

PUBLISHER
Jiangsu Phoenix Fine Arts Publishing House

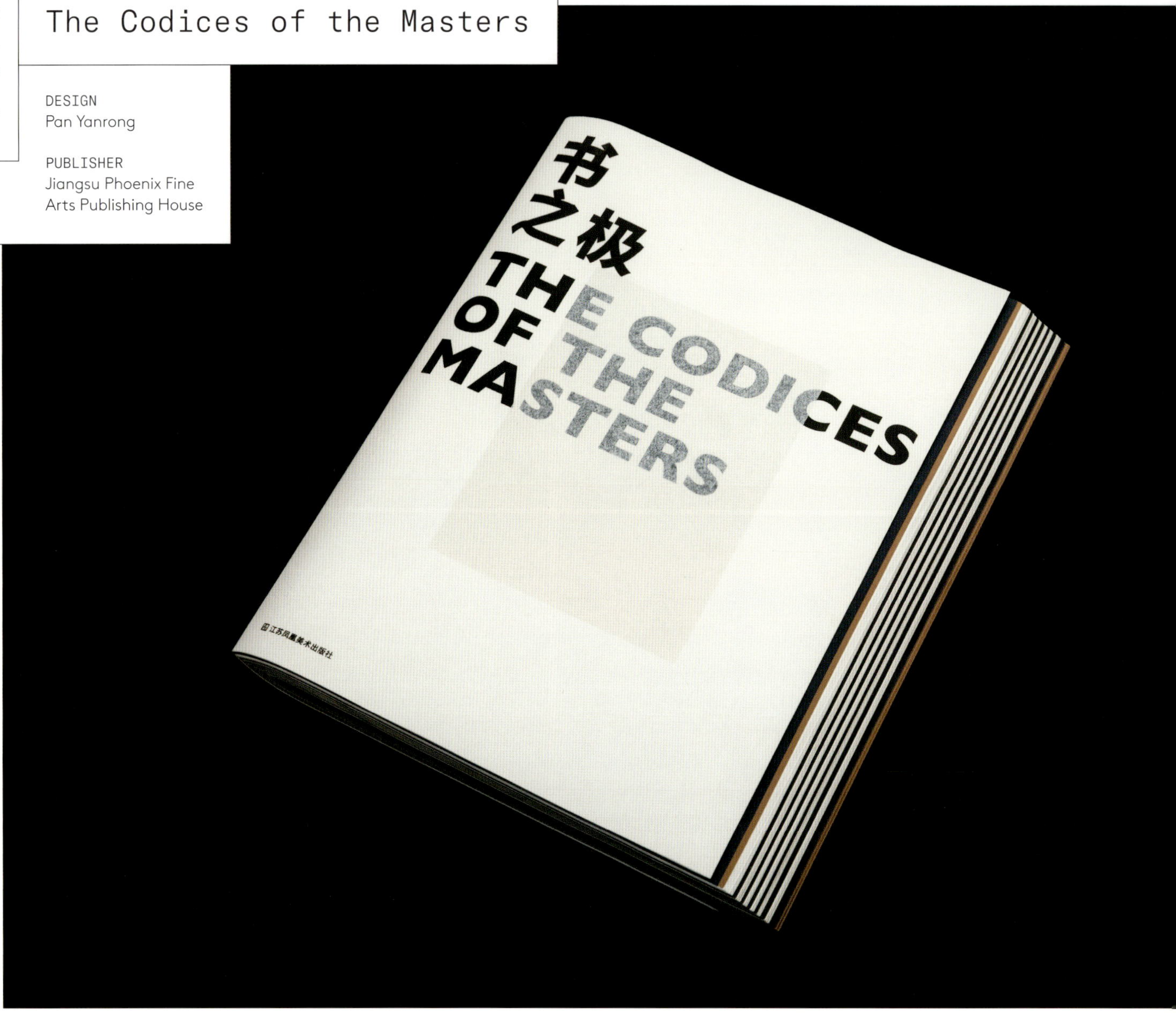

SPECIFICATION
280 mm X 330 mm, 580pp

BINDING & FINISHING
Sewn binding, embossing

PAPER
Uncoated paper, art paper

TYPEFACE
Source Han Sans, Gill Sans

The Codices of the Masters is a publication about hand-made books by artists. The author selected 24 books, including hand-made books by contemporary artists such as Dalí, Henri Matisse, Marc Chagall, Zao Wou-ki and Chu Teh-chun. He tells the stories of the works, explaining the meaning of these hand-made books in the artists' careers and analysing their techniques of making books and their artistic characteristics. The book is bound with folded sheets, which gives readers a relaxing and soft reading experience.

Pleasure of Learning

DESIGN
Qu Minmin &
Jiang Qian

PUBLISHER
Jiangsu Phoenix Fine
Arts Publishing House

The book reflects eastern aesthetics, and the book is wrapped with a felt always used for Chinese painting. The title is printed with a seal on the edge of the book.

In an ancient Chinese layout, the book is read from left to right. The vertical text and the irregular layout bring out a beautiful sense of rhythm. From the start to the end, the repeated black and white calligraphy connects the content and chapters. Beginning with white pages, the book develops through repeated black and white calligraphy and ends again with white pages. The whole process expresses the author's attitude: learning is a process of insistence and repetition.

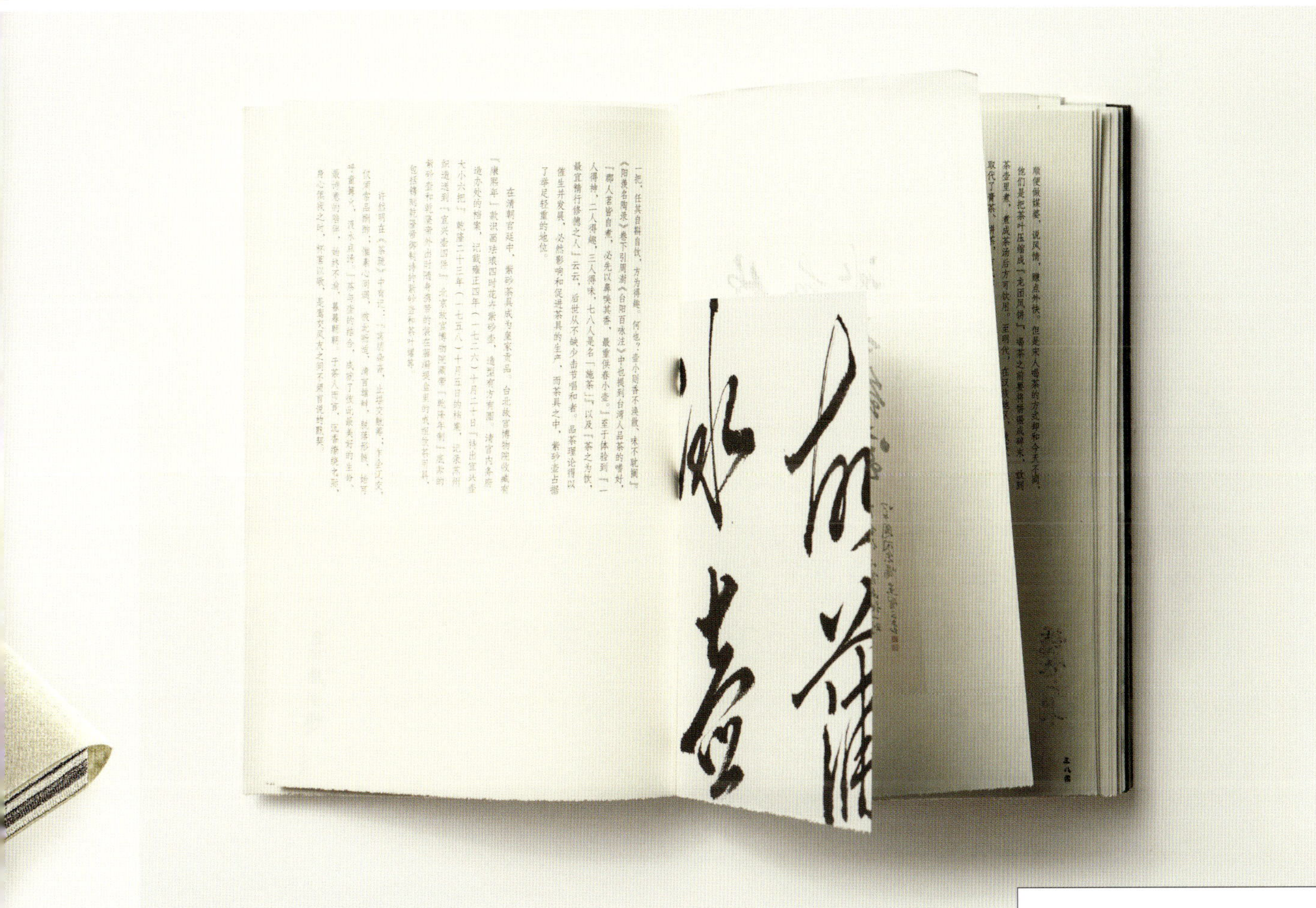

SPECIFICATION
130 mm × 250 mm, 408pp

BINDING & FINISHING
Bare spine

PAPER
Felt, Xuan paper

TYPEFACE
Fang Song by FounderType

Sixty Years of Taohuawu New Year Prints

DESIGN
Pan Yanrong

PUBLISHER
Jiangsu Phoenix
Fine Arts
Publishing House

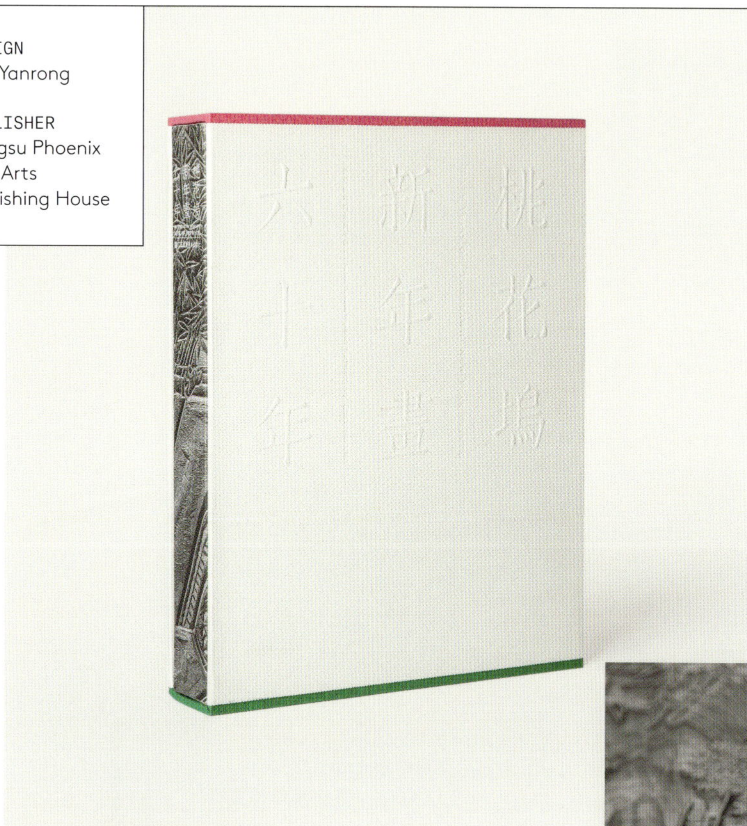

SPECIFICATION
220 mm × 280 mm, 560pp

BINDING & FINISHING
Butterfly binding, debossing

PAPER
Fang Xuan paper, Bible paper,
Ya Zhi paper, poster paper

TYPEFACE
Da Biaosong, Shu Song, Fang Song
by FounderType

Sixty Years of Taohuawu New Year Prints is a collection of paintings and New Year's prints in the 60 years after the founding of the People's Republic of China.

These are superbly painted and beautifully engraved works. The butterfly-bound book is printed on Xuan paper and the hot-stamped cover is exquisite. The interior pages alternate between red and green papers, creating a colourful world of red peach blossoms and green willows and the atmosphere of the New Year.

Talk about Kunqu

DESIGN
Qu Minmin & Jiang Qian

PUBLISHER
Jiangsu Phoenix Fine Arts Publishing House

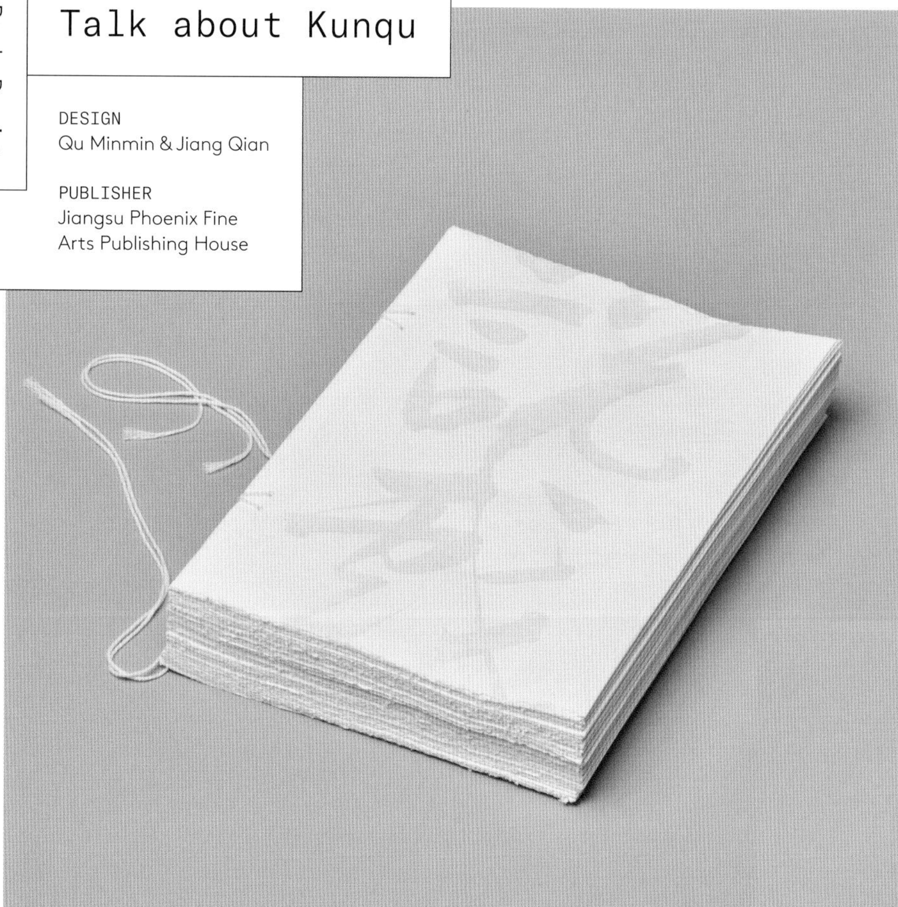

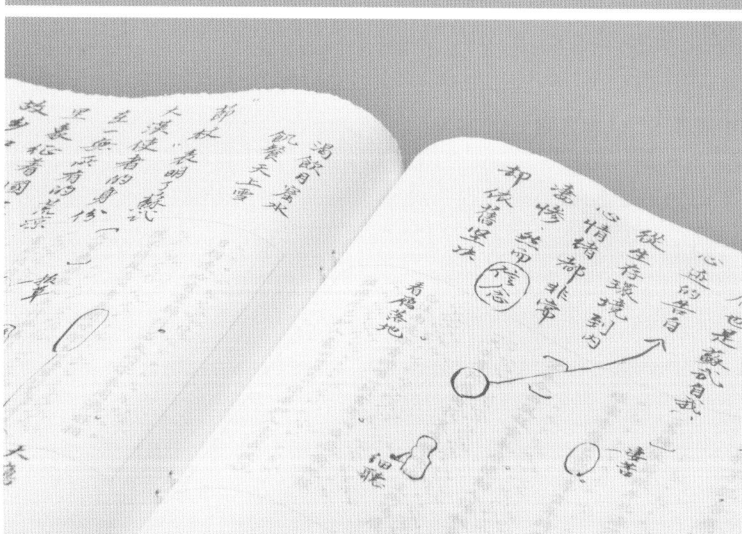

SPECIFICATION
184 mm × 260 mm, 588pp

BINDING & FINISHING
Sewn binding

PAPER
Bible paper

TYPEFACE
Fang Song by FounderType

The book discusses Kunqu opera. The designers re-edited the text when they designed this book. As Kunqu is intangible cultural heritage, they believe Kunqu opera should not only be treated as a part of traditional culture, but also a new contemporary spirit.

The whole book revolves around a Kunqu opera artist and an obsessed autistic audience. There are a total of 11 plays. Each play is a unit, similar to a scenario. Originating from traditional elements, a new contemporary Kunqu opera is shown to the readers through the stories of the artist and the autistic audience.

In design language, they tried to use paper and binding without any eastern characteristics. Culture knows no borders, and the eastern temperament comes from the internal.

Mountain Ocean Poetry

DESIGN
Pan Yanrong

PUBLISHER
Kinakaal Forlag

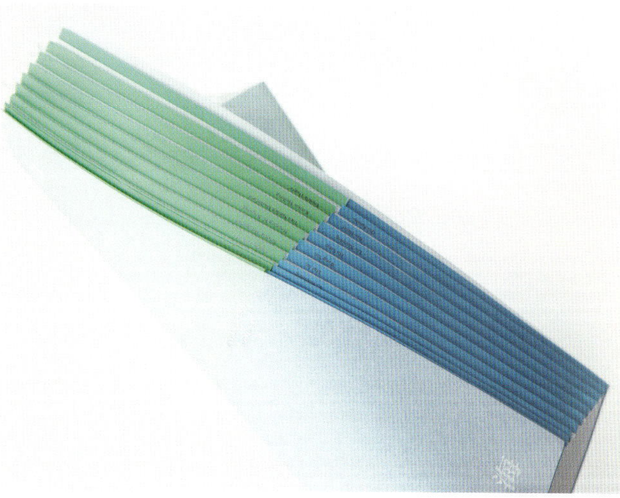

Mountain Ocean Poetry (*Fjell Hav Poesi*) is a collection of poems for the cultural exchange between Shanghai and Bergen. The 'mountain' represents Bergen and the 'ocean' represents Shanghai. The green top half of the book symbolises the mountain, while the blue bottom half symbolises the ocean. And the border connecting these two parts is similar to the horizon. The text is printed in spot colours. The edge of the upper margin is made rough, which creates a poetic expression, light texture and beauty.

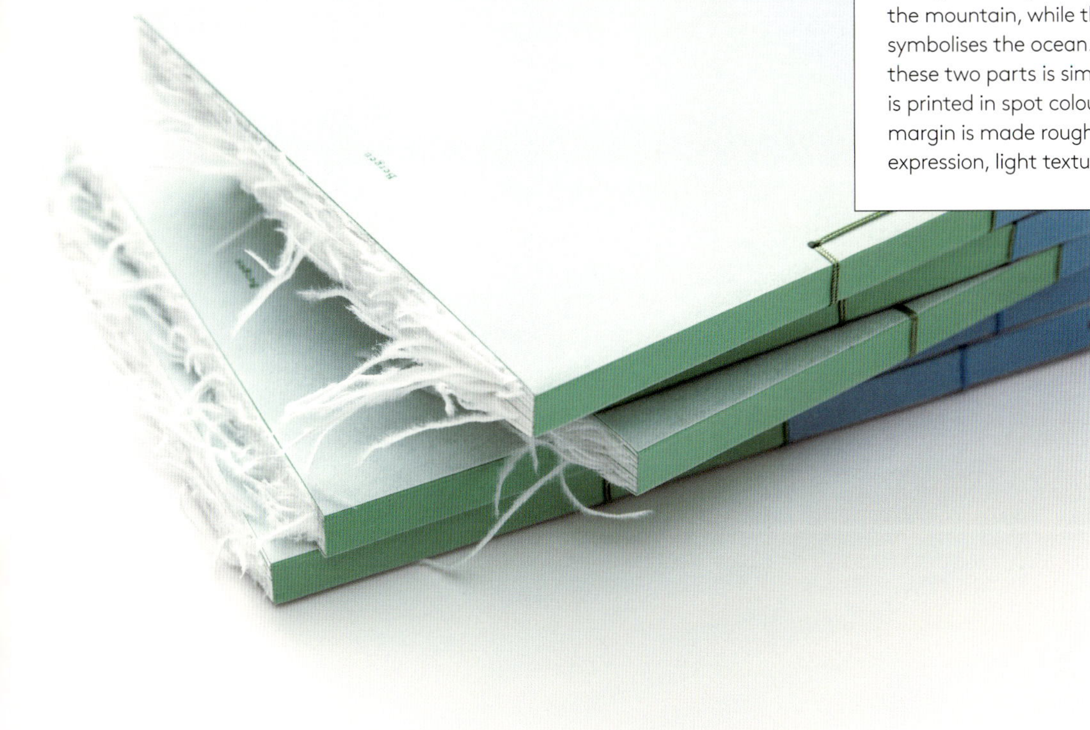

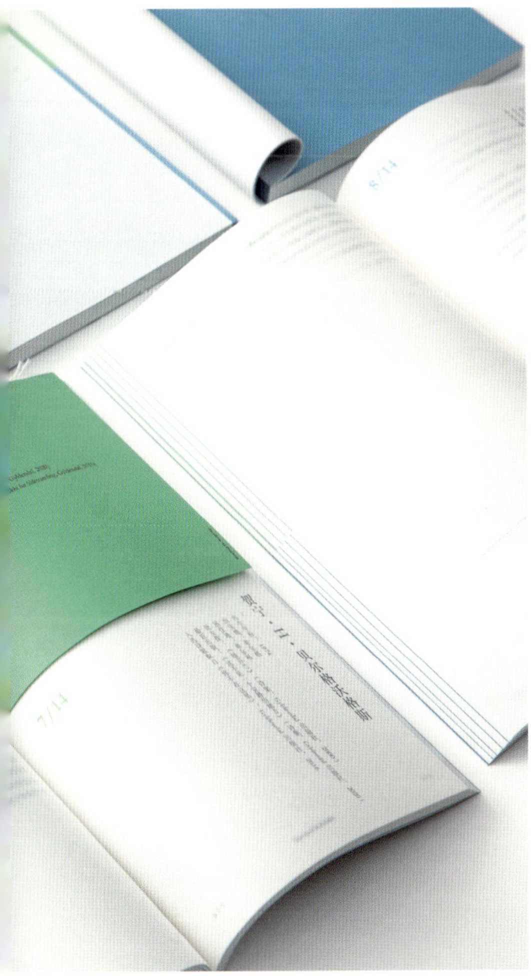

SPECIFICATION
170 mm X 260 mm, 170pp

BINDING & FINISHING
Sewn binding, hot stamping

PAPER
TAKEO MBS 100gsm, Bomull Xuan 70gsm, coloured paper

TYPEFACE
Shu Song, Zhun Yasong by FounderType; Garamond

INDEX

A Black Cover Design

www.ablackcover.com

A Black Cover Design (ABCD) is a global branding agency established in 2015 by Guang Yu and Nod Young, based in Beijing and San Francisco. ABCD provides branding, visual identity, product package, user interface, printed matter and design strategy services. Their design concept is systematic and targeted, which won their client's recognition and numerous international and domestic awards.

P192-193

Adrienn Császár

www.behance.net/adrienn_csaszar

Adrienn Császár is a Budapest-based freelance graphic designer, aspiring to create experimental designs with clear features.

P182-183

Ákos Polgárdi

submachine.co

Ákos Polgárdi is a Budapest-based graphic designer specialising in editorial design, visual identities and wayfinding. Apart from working on solo project, he is the founding member of SUBMACHINE and a guest lecturer in book design at Metropolitan University, Budapest.

P168-169, 170-171

Alessia Oertel

www.alessiaoertel.com

Alessia has a Master's degree in Communication Design from Muthesius University of Fine Arts and Design in Kiel, Germany. Since 2020, she has been working as a freelance designer. Her goal is to make luxury brands more accessible to the public. Working with these premium brands, she creates unique visual languages that help differentiate the client and get the message across without words.

P130-131

Alien Wu

www.behance.net/wuhaolun

Alien Wu is a graphic designer and an expert in translating his aesthetic experience into a unique visual language. He established Absence Lab in 2017, working on brand identity planning, event visual design, product packaging and book design. His work was included in the *Asia Pacific Design Yearbook* and won the Golden Pin Design Award.

P196-197

Ana Resende

www.ana-resende.com

Ana Resende studied architecture and editorial design in Porto. She was the coordinator of the publications of the 2016 Lisbon Architecture Triennale. Since 2016, she has been running her practice on books, architecture and films in collaboration with several authors, and academic and cultural institutions.

P204-205

Anna Bárdy

www.annabardy.com

Anna Bárdy is a Budapest-based independent graphic designer and art director from Hungary. Her primary fields of design are branding, editorial and book design. Anna looks on her field as a playground that gives her space to do technical experimentation. Her conceptual approach stands out with straightforward visual answers.

P126-127

Atelier d'alves

www.atelierdalves.com

Located in the heart of Porto in Portugal, the studio develops identities, strategies, campaigns, websites, and editorial projects for companies and institutions that want to have an impact in their sector. The studio's grand philosophy is the intersection of methodologies and concepts, resulting in innovative approaches to each new proposal.

P128-129, 132-133

Baillat Studio

Baillat.ca

Baillat Studio is a design studio based in Montreal. Their work is carried out in all formats - print, digital, motion and artistic installation, creating striking identities that reach far beyond the limits of traditional advertising. Their creative sensibility is driven by an emphasis on play, where every detail is carefully considered. Passion, people and determination are at the core of their practice.

P156-157

Bureau Hardy Seiler

www.hardyseiler.de

The Bureau creates a straightforward and compelling communication design. It specialises in corporate, editorial, graphic and web design, often joining forces with other experts to solve more complex challenges.

P174-175

Carla Cabras

carlacabrasdesign.wixsite.com/home

Carla Cabras is a graphic designer from Sardinia, Italy. She studied new art technologies at the Academy of Fine arts of Sassari. She is currently working as a freelance graphic designer.

P184-185

CarnokyType

carnokytype.com

As the founder of CarnokyType, Samuel Čarnoký (1981) focuses on type design, typography and editorial design. He is the author and co-author of the publications about typography in Slovakia. He participated in many creative workshops and art symposia as well as individual and collective exhibitions and presentations in Slovakia and abroad. He was awarded Slovak Design Award for communication design in 2016 and 2018.

P152-153

Daniel Zenker

zenkerdaniel.de

Daniel Zenker is a Hamburg-based designer. He focuses on analogues, digital identities and publications. In his design, visual identities and stories are brought to the point and into the world with a concept-based and typography-driven design. Passionate and with an eye for small details and the bigger picture, the design process is carried out through material advice and production handling.

P146-147

David Pearson

www.typeasimage.com

David Pearson is a UK-based graphic designer specialising in print design where typography is the principal form of expression.

P040-051

Desislava Danova, Susana Xavier

www.behance.net/desislavadanova
susanaxc.com

Susana and Desislava have different cultural backgrounds and have different understandings of design. They were in the same group for their book class in their Master's study. Surprisingly, they complemented each other perfectly. Their aesthetics and needs for an intricate storytelling narrative and emotional responses from the readers were the main approaches that helped them produce the book.

P122-123

Erik Bovio, Mauro Murano, Lorenzo Ritorto, Francesco Zivoli

www.behance.net/erikbovio
www.behance.net/mauromurano
www.behance.net/ritortolorenzo
www.behance.net/francescozivoli

During the degree course in Design and Visual Communication at the Politecnico di Torino, they decided to complete the course of study with a thesis project together for their affinity and their common design vision. Their four points of view brought them a broader vision of the whole book, allowing them to complete a project with a strong identity.

P180-181

Flowing Design

flowingdesign.co

Flowing Design is a design studio that pursues positive social impact by its design. They believe in the rule of 'Form Follows Function.' They believe every single element engaged in the work is not only a decoration but a modification and design responding to functional requirements.

P198-199

Genis Carreras

www.studiocarreras.com

Genís Carreras (aka Studio Carreras) is an award-winning designer and illustrator who specialises in creating ingenious, minimal and bold pieces of visual communication for brands, events and publications. His work uses geometry and abstraction to convey complex ideas in accessible and attractive ways.

P154-155

Hanqingtang Design

weibo.com/hanqingtangdesign

Hanqingtang Design is a design company founded by Zhao Qing. Zhao Qing is the twentieth Chinese member of the Alliance Graphique Internationale (AGI). Since 2000, the company creates commercial brand identities and cultural media following marketing strategies and its corporate spirit, providing tailor-made visual communication solutions for clients.

P078-091

Huang Wan-eng

behance.net/WE_STUDIO

Huang Wan-eng is a graphic designer and she graduated from the Department of Visual Communication Design at Chaoyang University of Science and Technology. Her graduation design work was included in the collection of *DESIGN 100 COOL*. In 2014, WE STUDIO design house was established. The design agency is currently focusing on visual design planning for existing and new brands.

P190-191

Kenneth Kuh

kennethkuh.info

Kenneth Kuh is an award-winning designer based in Portland, LA, and Shanghai. He graduated from ArtCenter College of Design in 2020 and is now a designer at Nike. His work covers a wide range of disciplines from branding, editorial design, typography, to motion graphics and transmedia installations.

P136-137

Luca Longobardi, Alessandro Latela

www.longobardiluca.com
www.behance.net/alessandrolatela

Luca Longobardi is a graphic designer based in Italy. His works focus on communication, editorial design and typography. Alessandro Latela is a student of Master's degree in Communication and Design and Publishing at ISIA Urbino.

P138-139

Lundgren+Lindqvist

lundgrenlindqvist.se

Lundgren+Lindqvist is a Sweden-based design studio founded in 2007. It is led by Andreas Friberg Lundgren and Carl-Johan Lindqvist. Their services cover visual identity design, art direction, design for print and digital applications, packaging design, signage and web development.

P120-121, 158-159

Mak Kai-hang

makkaihang.com

Mak Kai-hang (b.1993) is a Hong Kong graphic designer who mainly focuses on an in-depth exploration of typography and printed matter. He established his design studio in 2018. His work has received several awards including One Show, D&AD, Art Directors Club (ADC), Type Directors Club (TDC), Tokyo TDC Annual Awards and so on.

P212-215

Marc Villalba

www.behance.net/marcvillalba

Marc Villalba is a Barcelona-based graphic designer. He is passionate about editorial design and photography. And he has completed projects from large runs to small editions and experimental zines. He studied graphic design at the School of Art and Design, Llotja and had his postgraduate study majoring Photography and Editorial Design at EINA, University Center of Design and Art of Barcelona.

P188-189

Matúš Hnát

www.behance.net/MatusHnat

Matúš Hnát is a freelance graphic designer with a background in cultural studies. He was shortlisted in Slovak Design Award many times. His domains are mainly editorial design, posters and campaigns.

P194-195

Melville Brand Design

melvilledesign.de

Melville Brand Design is a Munich-based creative agency that specialises in 360-degree branding and communication. They work across all areas including visual and editorial, print and digital design, experimental and virtual design.

P160-161

Mistroom

www.behance.net/mistroomart

Founded in 2010 by Peng Yu-jui and Huang Jui-i, Mistroom provides services in performing arts, book design, vinyl design and packaging.

P106-117

Moby Digg

mobydigg.com

Moby Digg is an award-winning digital design studio engaging in versatile conceptual and visual projects. Its commissions range from brand strategy, branding and visual identities to in-house web development – always focusing on connecting the best of design with technology.

P172-173

Oscar Maia

www.oscarmaia.com

Oscar Maia is a communication designer based in the city of Porto, Portugal. Specialised in developing creative strategies in print, editorial, branding, and web design projects, he is currently working with a wide range of clients. His work is recognised as aesthetically simple and bold, with a steady balance between great attention to details, typography, and composition.

P150-151

Pan Yanrong

weibo.com/u/1391870422

Pan Yanrong is a member of AGI and a member of the Book Design and Art Work Committee in the Publishers Association of China. He is also the creative director of T-change design studio.

P216-217, 220-223, 226-227, 230-231

Péter Morvai

morvaipeter.com

Péter Morvai is a European graphic designer and artist. He has a keen interest in experimenting with light and typography, and he is open to making special visual solutions.

P186-187

Qu Minmin & Jiang Qian

qqqqdesign.com

The studio was established by Qu Minmin and Jiang Qian in 2013, focusing on book design, branding, packaging, publishing and exhibition design. Seeking the balance between experimentality and publicity in design performance is the design pursuit of the studio.

P218-219, 224-225, 228-229

Rebeka Arce Studio

byarce.com

Rebeka Arce is a multidisciplinary designer and art director based in Madrid. Her distinct sense of rhythm and balance and passion for observation, synthesis and approach of future scenarios has led her to move through a variety of design fields, especially on the brand identity, narrative visual strategy and image creation for audiovisual media. She aims to elevate business and brand offerings by translating their core values into a significant visual form.

P176-177

Renata Motyka

www.renatamotyka.com

Renata Motyka is a graphic designer from Warsaw, Poland. She is involved in print design, installations and painting.

P148-149

Riccardo Savioli

www.behance.net/RiccardoSavioli

Riccardo Savioli (1996, Portomaggiore, Italy) is a graphic designer and had his Bachelor'degree in New Technologies for Arts at the Academy of Fine Arts in Venice, he is now a student of Master's degree in Communication and Design and Publishing at ISIA Urbino.

P124-125

Sarah Schrauwen

www.sarahschrauwen.com

Sarah Schrauwen is a graphic designer who specialises in books and editing. Her work is clean, functional and content-driven. She loves projects that she can approach holistically by providing overarching guidance from the conceptual and research phase, over-content curation and editing, to design and production. Sustainability is an important aspect of her life, both professionally and personally.

P166-167

Sebastian Schubmehl

smehl.com

Typographer and graphic designer Sebastian Schubmehl designs books, visual identities, custom typefaces and communication concepts for brands, companies and events. Target-oriented, with pragmatism, passion and precision, he takes good design seriously. He is based in Trier, Rhineland-Palatinate, Germany.

P134-135

Studio de Ronners

www.deronners.nl

Studio de Ronners is a creative agency founded by the two brothers Arwen and Matthijs Ronner. They develop visual identities for renowned museums, cultural institutions and clients from the business and non-profit sectors. Their goal is to reach the audience in a convincing, purposeful way.

P164-165

Studio Joost Grootens

www.joostgrootens.nl

In addition to designing digital information environments, maps, typefaces and spatial installations, SJG works primarily in the field of book design. They are constantly challenged to develop appropriate formats that justify the production of printed materials, acknowledging the growing need for the visual representation of data.

P066-077

Tim Bisschop

www.timbisschop.be

Tim Bisschop studied typography and graphic design at the Luca School of Arts in Ghent (Belgium) and works as an independent graphic designer since 2011. His main work contains books, covers, posters, brochures, magazines and branding projects.

P162-163

Toby Ng Design

www.toby-ng.com

Toby Ng Design is an independent branding and design studio formed by creative communicators. Their work begins with the search for essence and simplicity. They believe distilling a core idea builds the best foundation for any compelling design solution. Together with clients, they bring their philosophy to life by shaping voices of value and significance.

P178-179

Todojunto

todojunto.net

Todojunto is a design and communication studio based in Barcelona and founded in 2007. It mainly focuses on cultural projects and the dissemination of knowledge. Their work aims for a transversal, transmedia study of the communication fields, with projects that go from research with vintage printing techniques to web or exhibition design, passing through music-related or editorial design.

P140-141

Tsai Chia-hao

www.behance.net/tsaichiahao

Tsai Chia-hao is a graphic designer. He was nominated for Golden Bee Global Biennale, GDC, Golden Butterfly Award, and *Asia-Pacific Design*. Now he is mainly engaged in the business of graphic design, such as book design, movie posters, visual identities for events and exhibitions, branding and packaging design, etc.

P142-145

Wu Chia-lin

www.behance.net/ChiaLinWu

Wu Chia-lin, born in 1991, is a graphic designer. She is engaged in book design, key visual or identity design of exhibitions and cultural performances, etc. She is good at expressing emotion, words, and individual style through printing and paper. She looks forward to developing more reading experience with varied designs of books and creating unlimited designs with limited sources.

P200-203

XXL Studio

www.xxlstudio.design

Founded by AGI member Liu Xiaoxiang, XXL studio provides services in all areas of graphic design.

P052-065

Zhang Zhiqi

weibo.com/u/1959938610

Zhang Zhiqi is a graphic designer dedicated to book design. His works were awarded The Beauty of Books in China and Best Book Design from All Over the World.

P092-105

Zhu Yingchun

www.zhuyingchun.com

Zhu Yingchun is a book designer and artist based in Nanjing, China. His clever concepts and playful designs have attracted wide attention in China and abroad, particularly his two major works: *Bugs' Book* and *Cacaform Birds*. Zhu Yingchun credits nature as his sole source of inspiration and is at his happiest while studying the patterns and rituals of bugs and flowers around his studio. His creations express an inquisitive approach to the world and his belief that every part of nature has a distinctive beauty.

P206-211

CREDITS

P025
Picture C
Old Textbooks Postcards
Design: Lau Chi-chung
Printer: Ink'chacha

P027
Picture A
Tea Canon
Design: Pan Yanrong

P042-043
Keep the Aspidistra Flying
Illustration: Petra Börner
Down and Out in Paris and London
Illustration: Paul Catherall

P044-045
Some Thoughts on the Common Toad
Illustration: Joe McLaren

P050
The Virgin and the Gipsy
Illustration: Victoria Sawdon
A Russian Affair
Illustration: Victoria Sawdon

P052, 054-055
Breeze Blows to the Page, You Read
Design: Liu Xiaoxiang, Miao Qian, Peng Yixuan

P056-057
Design Changes Our Reading
Design: Liu Xiaoxiang, Fan Meiling

P058-059
Traditional Clothes of Beijing and Western Regions
Design: Liu Xiaoxiang, Zhang Yu

P062
In All the Voices, I Only Listen to You
Design: Liu Xiaoxiang, Fan Meiling

P066, 068-069
Formafantasma Cambio
Design: Joost Grootens, Dimitri Jeannottat, Clémence Guillemot

P070-071
The Academy of the Sublime
Design: Joost Grootens, Dimitri Jeannottat

P072-073
Blind Maps and Blue Dots
Design: Joost Grootens, Dimitri Jeannottat

P074
Parliaments of the European Union
Design and Data Visualisation: Joost Grootens, Dimitri Jeannottat, Carina Schwake
Lithography (back cover image): Marjeta Morinc

P076
The Grand Projet
Design and Map Editing: Joost Grootens, Carina Schwake, Julie da Silva, Megan Adé

P078, 080-081
Infinite Blooming
Design: Zhao Qing, Jiang Jiajia

P082-083
Facing the Ocean, Flowers Blossom in Warm Spring
Design: Zhao Qing, Jiang Jiajia

P084-085
The Choice of Leipzig 2019-2004
Design: Zhao Qing, Zhu Tao

P086-087
Browse Leipzig 1991-2003
Design: Zhao Qing, Zhu Tao

P120-121
Lukas/Markus
Author: Kalle Sanner
Essay: Karl Palmås
Design: Andreas Friberg Lundgren, Julius Åsling

P124-125
Identità oltre il tempo
Author: Cecilia Rabeschi, Silvia Palmi

P128-129
Traços de Gente
Art Direction: Sergio Alves
Design: Sergio Alves, Cátia Lima, Gilberto Ribeiro

P132-133
A Garden at Night
Art Direction: Sergio Alves
Design: Sérgio Alves, Cátia Lima

P134-135
Kyiv Type: Graphic Design & Typography Visual Treasures from Kyiv
Creative Supervision: Prof. Andreas Hogan

P136-137
God Does Not Play Dice
Art Direction: Brad Bartlett

P152-153
Fonts SK - Digitised Type Design in Slovakia
Text, Art Direction and Design: Samuel Čarnoký

P156-157
Age of Union
Creative Direction: Jean-Sébastien Baillat
Art Direction: Jean-Sébastien Baillat, Louis Dollé
Design: Louis Dollé, Sara Thion, Capucine Labarthe, Matthieu Jeanson
Illustration: Stéphane Poirier

P158-159
The Bird Project 2006-2017
Author: Erik Berglin
Design: Andreas Friberg Lundgren, Julius Åsling

P160-161
Makers Bible - Human Space (Black Edition)
Creative Direction: Lars Harmsen
Art Direction: Hannah Pohlmann
Design: Mara Schneider, Johannes König

P162-163
Carcasse: The Butcher's Kitchen
Art Direction: Tim Bisschop, Natacha Hofman

P164-165
Wish/Wonen in Stadshart
Art Direction and Design: Arwen Ronner, Matthijs Ronner

P166-167
Wanderspace/Zwerfruimte
Visual Essay: Poolhert Productions, Jee Kast

P172-173
Made in Fukushima
Creative Direction: Maximilian Heitsch
Art Direction: Gabriela Baka, Sebastian Haiss
Design: Ricardo Abbaszadeh, Gabriela Baka, Sebastian Haiss

P176-177
Pasatiempos Modernos
Illustration: Rebeka Arce

P178-179
Inside Muses
Creative Direction: Toby Ng
Design: Toby Ng, Banana Chan, Ken Li
Illustration: Wong Chi-lui

P180-181
Slash: Between Identity and Differences
Creative Direction: F. Guida

P186-187
Cuenca Debajo de la Segunda Farola - Erasmus Book
Photography: Bence Boldogh

P190-191
Insight Independent Bookshop
Creative Direction: Kuo Tzu-lin
Art Direction: Huang Wan-eng
Box Structure Planning: Kuo Tzu-lin

P192-193
Cheers Book Covers
Art Direction: Guang Yu, Nod Young

P198-199
Thing-ology
Creative Direction: Flowing Design
Art Direction: Adam Chen
Inner Page Design: Zeng Song-hong

P204-205
Possible Anatomies
Creative Direction: Corpo Atelier

P212-213
A Study on Hong Kong Beiwei Calligraphy & Type Design
Typeface Design: Adonian Chan

P214-215
Asia-Pacific Design No. 16
Art Direction: Mak Kai-hang
Design: Yeung Yan-shek

ACK-NOWL-EDGE-MENTS

We would like to express our gratitude to all of the designers and agencies for their generous contribution of images, ideas and concepts. We are also very grateful to many other people whose names do not appear in the credits, but who have made specific contributions and provided support. Without them, the successful compilation of this book would not have been possible. Special thanks to all of the contributors for sharing their innovation and creativity with all of our readers around the world.